# LOST POWERS

# LOST POWERS

## RECLAIMING OUR INNER CONNECTION

The search to reestablish our innate ability
to tap into the Universal Fountain of Understanding

edited by
## J. DOUGLAS KENYON

FROM THE ATLANTIS RISING® MAGAZINE LIBRARY

Published in 2016 by Atlantis Rising®
Distributed to the trade by Red Wheel/Weiser, LLC
65 Parker St., Unit 7 • Newburyport, MA 01950-4600
*www.redwheelweiser.com*

ISBN 978-0-9906904-3-6

Library of Congress Cataloging Data available on request

Cover and text design by Kathryn Sky-Peck
Photos and Illustrations © *Atlantis Rising Magazine*

PRINTED IN CANADA
10 9 8 7 6 5 4 3 2 1

# CONTENTS

# RECLAIMING OUR INNER CONNECTION

Have we lost our way? Lost our inner "sense of smell"? The conventional notion of the human psyche is that it is a product of our mass culture, and we are conditioned to see and understand only the stimulus that is provided to it. In other words, we are merely regurgitating the knowledge we have been conditioned to experience and to believe is true. This collection of 32 articles by world-class philosophers and theoreticians is a guide for those who wish to find their way back to what we can call a "subconscious truth detector": this is key in determining whether we buy into the premises of the many mainstream "truths" presented to us in popular culture and popular science.

There is some truth to the story in the latest Indiana Jones epic (*Indiana Jones and the Kingdom of the Crystal Skull*), even if the producers did get somewhat carried away. The same can be said for many Hollywood productions, including some that are even more outrageous. The producers in Tinseltown like to grab a fact or two as their starting point and then venture into the imaginary. Mutant powers, as in the *X-Men* franchise, are based on actual medical anomalies, robots of the future (such as represented in the film *Ironman*) are taken from current lab experiments, extraterrestrial agendas (*Roswell*) are extrapolated from abduction case histories, and so forth. All of the facts gathered in support of such fiction are intended to serve the purposes of entertainment, thus making the essential willing suspension of disbelief easier to achieve—or that, at least, is the theory.

Could, in fact, something else be going on?

There is, we suspect, a deeper process at work, something coming from an innate ability to discern greater truth—something that plays a fundamental role in determining whether we accept the underlying bases of the many yarns presented to us in popular entertainment. For one thing, we all are connected to the same world of dreams that has been with us since time immemorial and investigated in our time by such luminaries as Carl Jung and Joseph Campbell. Contact with the dream world—also known as the universal unconscious—gives us an ability to appreciate the presence of universal themes and archetypes. George Lucas has made it clear that he consciously employed such elements in his *Star Wars* stories, and the same can be said for many of the classics of cinema, from *Casablanca* to *Citizen Kane*. Like storytellers for millennia, the best in the business today still try to tap the same universal fountain of understanding that inspired Homer. Whether or not they succeed is a measure of their own atunement with the process, and that gets us to our point.

In a world that accepts the conventional notion of the human psyche as a product of the mass culture, our human psyche is reduced to merely an echo of the stimulus that is spoon-fed to it. We are, in other words, merely expressing the tastes that we have been conditioned to experience. In such a world, it really doesn't matter what images are shown to us, we will learn to react to them in the way we are trained. Like Pavlov's dogs, we will learn to salivate when the bell signaling meal time is rung. Suppose though, that within us all, there is some deeper truth detection mechanism at work—some connection with the absolute, which the current fad makers cannot touch. Could, in fact, there be within every soul an unconscious knowledge of the ultimate truth of things—a kind of crystalline geometry, which, though ordinarily inactive and perhaps somewhat damaged, will, when a particular note is sounded, suddenly begin to sing?

That such a thing is true has long been taught by the great spiritual teachers of all ages East and West, and is regularly experienced by many who try to follow the spiritual path. The reality of such a faculty, is, of course, denied by those whose own internal tuning fork has long since ceased to vibrate. Nevertheless, they, for purposes of controlling others, struggle to recreate the lost effect. Such counterfeit displays may fill the media, but for those who have glimpsed the real thing, the illusions offer little charm.

For those with ears to hear and eyes to see, the distinction between fact and fiction remains strictly personal.

# PART ONE

# RESTORING THE BODY

"An alchemist in search of the philosopher's stone discovers Phosphorus" (painting by Joseph Wright)

# 1

# SECRETS OF THE ALCHEMISTS

*Is Modern Science Simply Rediscovering*
*Lost Ancient Knowledge?*

## BY JOSEPH ROBERT JOCHMANS, LIT.D.

Without a doubt the best known claim of the alchemists was the transmutation of lead into gold. Modern physicists up until the end of the 19th century dismissed such a notion as ridiculous, for it violated all known laws of the stability and constancy of the elements. But then came Madame Joliot-Curie, radium, and the discovery of radioactive substances that can be transformed by isotope decay from higher atomic number elements to lower number elements.

So far, physicists have been able to synthesize elements up to element 116, which is stable for only a few milliseconds before it deteriorates. Scientists now theorize that elements of even higher atomic numbers may be possible to synthesize, which might even exhibit a higher degree of stability.

One such synthetic element that proved more stable is element 114, known as also as "eka-lead" because it belongs to the lead family, and displays many of the same properties as lead. In fact, there are definite indications that eka-lead may exist in natural forms, and in minute quantities along with normal lead.

What is very significant is that, if eka-lead were induced to decay, the material would break down into several elements of lower atomic number, and the major end-product left would be gold.

Thus there may be truth in the old claim after all—the alchemists knew of some way of precipitating eka-lead from normal lead, and then induced decay in order to obtain the much sought-after yellow element.

Much of ancient alchemical experimentation dealt with water, and changing its properties in both chemical and biological functions. They spoke, for example, of producing from water at room temperature a solid, plastic-like substance that had unusual properties.

In 1967, Russian chemists N. Fedakin and Boris Deryagin of the Moscow Academy of Sciences successfully produced what they called "polywater"—a polymerized form of water with a mass density of 40, a boiling point of 650 degrees Celsius, and a freezing point of minus 40 degrees Celsius. It has the appearance of clear plastic.

It is now believed that polywater occurs naturally, in certain types of clay, in plants, and it is now thought to have a function in the cohesion of living cells.

It would be interesting to know just how much the early alchemists knew about polywater, for they appear to have drawn upon knowledge based on experimentation over many centuries, while modern chemists have known about it for barely half a century.

The ancient alchemists had not only an understanding of electricity, but how it could be used to separate water into its two component parts—hydrogen and oxygen. In the Princes' Library at Ujjain in India, there is preserved a document called the *Agastya Samhita*, which dates to the first millennium BC. In it is this description:

"Place a well-cleaned plate of copper in an earthenware vessel. Cover it with copper sulfate and then with moist sawdust. The contact of all these elements in this manner will produce an energy called Mitra-Varuna. By it water can be split into Pranavayu and Udanavayu. A chain of one hundred jars will give a very active and effective force."

We have here not only instructions for making a battery, but a description of the electrolysis of water into oxygen and hydrogen. It appears, too, that the Hindus were equally knowledgeable of the reverse process, of creating water out of the elements in the air. Both the Rig Veda and the Brihat Devatas mention that when "Mitra Varuna" is placed in a water-jar and exposed to the heavens, the "god" born is named Khumba-Sambhava, the Indian equivalent to Aquarius, the Zodiacal god who carries on his shoulder a water jug that never empties.

Alchemists from ancient China once employed unknown techniques for manufacturing a metal that did not find its full potentials until our modern age. In 1956, twenty metal belt-fasteners with open-work ornamentation were discovered in the burial site of the notable Chinese general of the Tsin era, Chou Chu, who died in AD 297.

The fastener was examined by the Institute of Applied Physics of the Chinese Academy of Sciences and the Dunbai Polytechnic. Their analysis showed that the fasteners were composed of metal that was an alloy of 5 percent manganese, 10 percent copper, and 85 percent aluminum.

Now, aluminum was supposedly not discovered until 1807, and not produced successfully in industrial form until 1857. Today the process of extracting aluminum from bauxite mineral is very complicated and involves the use of a Reverbier oven, refraction chamber, and regenerator, and utilizes temperatures exceeding 1,000 degrees Celsius. What is more, electrolysis plays a key role.

The question is, where did the Chinese acquire these elements of present-era technology in the 3rd century? Or is it possible that they may have possessed methods of producing aluminum that are unknown today, employing a simpler long-lost forgotten technique not yet rediscovered by modern science?

Joseph Needham, the leading historian of Chinese science, has voiced his opinion that the anomalous 3rd century aluminum was the product of an unknown alchemist, someone who had access to a lost science. What else could the ancient alchemists have produced using the same methods? Many age-old sources identified the element mercury as having mysterious powers that have been lost to us today.

"L'alchimiste," by David Teniers the Younger

Chapter 31 in the classic Sanskrit work, the Samarangana Sutradhara, contains 230 stanzas that describe the workings of a mysterious mercury engine used for powering flying craft called vimanas: Here are the relevant texts:

"In the flying craft four strong containers of mercury must be built into the interior. When these are heated by controlled fire from the iron containers, the craft possesses thunder-power through the mercury. The iron engines must have properly welded joints to be filled with mercury and when fire is conducted to the upper part it develops power with the roar of a lion.

"By means of the energy latent in mercury, the driving whirlwind is set in motion and the traveler sitting inside the vehicle may travel in the air to such a distance as to look like a pearl in the sky."

Very curiously, British nuclear physicist Edward Neville da Costa Andrade, in a speech delivered at Cambridge in July, 1946, noted that the famed discoverer of the laws of gravity, Sir Isaac Newton, knew something about the secret of mercury. Quoting Lord Atterbury, a contemporary of Newton, Andrade remarked:

"Modesty teaches us to speak of the ancients with respect, especially when we are not very familiar with their works. Newton, who knew them practically by heart, had the greatest respect for them, and considered them to be men of genius and superior intelligence who had carried their discoveries in every field much further than we today suspect, judging from what remains of their writings. More ancient writings have been lost than have been preserved, and perhaps our new discoveries are of less value than those that we have lost."

Andrade continued, quoting Newton:

"Because of the way by which mercury may be impregnated, it has been thought fit to be concealed by others that have known it, and therefore may possibly be an inlet to something more noble, not to be communicated without immense danger to the world."

What it is about mercury that could be of "immense danger" we do not know. Yet it seems apparent that the ancient alchemists were well aware of the practical application of mercury.

In the 1970s, Soviet explorers excavating a cave near Tashkent, Uzbekistan, discovered a number of conical ceramic pots, each carefully sealed and each containing a single drop of mercury. A description and illustrations were published in several Russian scientific periodicals. There is no clue what these mercury containers were used for, but they must have been highly treasured and used for something that is beyond our present understanding and technology. It was a secret that was found, used, and preserved by a select few—only to be lost again to this day.

Ancient legends from the early days of the Silk Road speak of unknown alchemists from Central Asia who developed a thread of material which, when sown into a garment, made its wearer invincible: it could deflect arrows and spears, as well as be impervious to fire. It is said that Emperor

Yu of China paid a small fortune in royal gold and jade in order to obtain just one such garment, a vest that was lightweight yet could not be penetrated by any known weapon or consumed by any flame.

In 2006, Yu's descendants from the University of Beijing announced their success in creating threads of fullerene carbon (chemically designated as C-60) in the form of microscopic nanotubes, which when "sown" together formed material that will one day prove to be much more resilient than present bullet-proof vests and fire-resistant clothing. We today know that fullerene carbon exists in very minute quantities in nature along with regular carbon-12 and carbon-14 molecules. Did the ancient alchemists once understand a method of how to "distill" natural C-60 and collect it, then develop it into a thread in the same manner as silk was harvested in our modern age?

Another Chinese legend spoke of alchemists producing a second suit of armor that provided its wearer with perfect camouflage. It did not cause invisibility, but rather made a body "obscure" and difficult to see because it was "blacker than black." Researchers at the Rensselaer Polytechnic Institute and Rice University have recently created the darkest material known, which reflects back less than one tenth of one percent of light falling on it. The material is composed of carbon nanotubes grown on iron nanodots on top of a silicon wafer, and then meshed together, forming an irregular surface that minimizes reflection and maximizes light absorption.

What little light is reflected is scattered and diffused to such an extent that, when observed against most partially illuminated backgrounds, the outline of the material is hard to see. Against a dark background, it blends in and remains unseen. Like its ancient Chinese counterpart, the "extreme black" material makes a good "stealth" covering, and thus minimizes detection.

Another modern form of carbon that may have been anticipated by alchemists is called graphene, and consists of a single layer, one atom thick, of graphite—an element found in common everyday soot. What today's industrialists are discovering is that graphene, and its by-product graphene oxide, might be utilized as ideal reinforcements in composite materials, combinations of two substances that possess the desirable properties of both. Several alchemical references were made to the "magical" fusion of otherwise incompatible materials bonded together through a "secret" process using "black powder."

Graphene is also the only known substance at room temperature through which electrons flow at the same relativistic speed as neutrinos, giving it very unique and unusual electromagnetic properties. Arranged in specific chemically-induced patterns, graphene could serve as ultra-high speed transistor circuitry and be used to store a tremendous amount of information in a very small space. Were some alchemical manuscripts, in fact, made from graphene oxide "pages" that contained knowledge not only written on their surfaces, but also preserved within the sheets themselves?

Arabic alchemical manuscripts make several references to "a bendable glass that is stronger than Damascus steel" and was also non-magnetic. In 2007, physicists at the Chinese Academy of Sciences announced after two years of research the creation of a metallic glass that can be bent at right angles without breaking. Liquid metal is first supercooled, which makes it three times stronger than its natural crystalline state. During this process, minute quantities of zirconium, copper, nickel, and aluminum are interjected, much in the same manner that alchemists of old added tinctures to their metallurgical solutions.

The result is an amorphous glassy steel that holds no electrical charge. The overall final composition contains hard areas of high density surrounded by soft regions of low density. With small manipulations made to its new molecular structure, the end product develops plasticity and helps prevent internal cracks from forming and spreading.

As yet we cannot say with certainty that this was the same method used by ancient alchemists to produce their own version of "bendable glass," but the fact that it has now been accomplished by modern processes, and its characteristics are identical to the ancient alchemists' descriptions point for point, gives credibility to our forebears having been able to do the same, perhaps in ways simpler and less complicated than today's methods.

Going a step further, our modern research into the secrets of biochemistry only dates to the last century, but for other civilizations now lost in our past, the research may have extended over millennia. Many alchemical treatises are filled with formulas for perfumes, incense, and aromatic therapeutic mixtures that were meant to enhance memory and intelligence. Recently, researchers at the University of Lubeck in Germany performed a number of computerized memory tests using some subjects under normal or control conditions, while others were tested in a room filled with the smell of roses. In addition, a group of the control subjects were also kept in a room with rose scent during sleep.

Not only did the added rose odor significantly enhance initial test performance, but those who slept with the rose stimulus also dramatically improved their scores when the same memory test was given the following day. Brain scans taken during sleep showed that while slow-wave activity was occurring, the scent cue heightened output of the hippocampus, pointing to a direct correlation between olfactory stimulation and brain performance. We can only wonder, what else did the alchemists of old know about the use of specific aromas and their effects on the mind?

For thousands of years a resin extracted from the boswellia tree, which grows in southern Arabia, was burned as incense in major temples and sanctuaries throughout the ancient world. It was said to have the unusual effects of bringing peace of mind, relaxation, and a heightened sense of spiritual experience. Today we know this resin as frankincense; it was a highly prized ingredient that appeared in several alchemical treatises linked with other curative substances and methods of rejuvenation.

In early 2008, Arieh Moussayeff, a pharmacologist from the Hebrew University in Jerusalem, led a team of American and Israeli scientists in successfully isolating from boswellia tree resin a compound they named incensole acetate. By injecting mice with this substance, they discovered the subjects had significantly reduced levels of stress and anxiety. The new

Boswellia Tree, Oman
(Photo by
Eckhard Pecher)

chemical helps to regulate the flow of ions in and out of neurons in a similar way that modern antidepressant drugs work today. The experimenters concluded that their findings will one day aid not only in developing a new class of chemicals that will shed light on the molecular workings of the brain, but will also facilitate in creating a general calming effect to promote a healing mental state.

The question is, what other hidden properties of frankincense did the ancient alchemists explore that present-day researchers have yet to even suspect?

Louis Pauwels and Jacques Bergier, French authorities on the history and development of alchemy, reported in their landmark book *Morning of the Magicians*, that studies have been made of powders, perfumes, and scents preserved in prescription form in ancient and medieval literature, and some of the results of tests run on these were very unexpected. Many of the powders were so complex that modern scientists are still unable to completely break down their molecular structure. Some perfumes, such as certain musk concoctions, on the other hand, have formulas almost identical to DNA, the basic genetic building blocks of life.

What had these perfumes been used for? Were they information carriers that generated illusions and hallucinations for gaining power over crowds? Or were they some form of "instant knowledge," whereby students inhaled the appropriate scent to learn secrets imparted to them on the cellular level? Here is an aspect of ancient wisdom we can only guess at, but which certainly needs further investigation. As Pauwels noted, "Such an investigation would prove that the magicians of antiquity knew more about the psychological effect of perfumes than the best specialists of our own times."

There is a growing realization that portions of the alchemical treatises left from unknown ages contain knowledge we are only now rediscovering; so, too, such realization makes us pause to wonder about what other texts and treatises might exist that have not yet been discovered or deciphered.

Into this category must be placed the lost wisdom of the most mysterious substance of all, the Philosopher's Stone, that alchemical elixir of life so often spoken of in medieval circles, yet the secret of which still lies hidden away in crumbling manuscripts. Perhaps someday modern chemists will provide the answer—if some enterprising scholar of long lost books does not find it first.

Physicist Frederick Soddy made this significant statement in 1920:

"The philosopher's stone was accredited the power not only of transmuting metals, but of acting as the elixir of life. Now, whatever the origins of this apparently meaningless jumble of ideas may have been, it is really a perfect but very slightly allegorical expression of the actual present views of physics we hold today. Can we not read in these legends some justification for the belief that some former forgotten race of men attained not only to the knowledge we have so recently won, but also to the power that is not yet ours?"

What was the real source of the alchemists' wisdom? To have held the knowledge they had, they must surely have been the heirs to a body of lore that was the final product of many ages of forgotten experimentation and observation. Yet from where did such a science reach our era today?

Pauwels and Bergier considered every possibility of where the medieval "magicians" acquired their learning, and came to this conclusion:

"Only one source would answer the question: lost cultures that had attained a higher level of technological advance than we have, and of which a few traces have been preserved in the rites and alchemical recipes."

This conclusion was echoed by the eminent German philosopher Friedrich Nietzche, who remarked, "Do you believe that the modern sciences would ever have arisen and been great if there had not beforehand been in a previous age magicians, alchemists and wizards who thirsted and hungered after forbidden powers?"

# 2

## PLANT WISDOM

*Author Stephen Buhner Seeks Restoration of a Forgotten
Understanding of the Intelligence of Nature*

### BY CYNTHIA LOGAN

With an IQ reportedly off the charts, Stephen Harrod Buhner might rightly claim to be one of the most intelligent people on the planet. Nevertheless, for this member of MENSA, Intertel, and Colloquy—all societies formed for the mentally gifted—the most important thing is the balance of head and heart, knowledge and wisdom. After graduating from high school with a GED at 16, he has gone on to obtain degrees in mathematics and transcultural epistemology, but the intelligence which has held the most fascination for Buhner is that found in nature and the earth—inspiring him to author ten award-winning books on nature, indigenous cultures, the environment, and herbal medicine. *The Lost Language of Plants*, *The Secret Teachings of Plants* (not to be confused with 1960s classic *The Secret Life of Plants* by Peter Tompkins and Christopher Bird) and *Sacred Plant Medicine* comprise a trilogy he hopes will reinvigorate the "acuity of perception."

Buhner believes our senses developed from long-standing communicative contact with earth: "The sensory capacities of human ears were shaped by sounds of the world, our smell formed through long association with the delicate chemistries of plants, our touch by the nonlinear, multidimensional surfaces of earth, our sight by the images that constantly flow into our eyes." A voracious reader ("I read at least 300–400 books and 1,000 articles every year"), Buhner was a rare books and manuscripts dealer from 1990–2000 and is listed in *International Authors and Writers Who's Who*. He lectures on the history of the book, nature writing, and the roots of American environmentalism, as well as on the art of both fiction and nonfiction. Children's author Toni Knapp claims, "Stephen Buhner does for nonfiction what John Gardner did for the art of fiction." A soft-spoken guy whose voice is similar to that of National Public Radio's movie critic Bob Mondello, Buhner speaks about "writers and the earth." His work has appeared in such publications as *Common Boundary*, *Apotheosis*, *Shaman's Drum*, and *The New York Times*, and has been featured on CNN and *Good Morning, America*. Recognizing that academia wasn't his path, Buhner took a wilderness survival training course in the Colorado mountains, rebuilt a turn-of-the-century cabin and learned forgotten crafts after leaving Berkeley in the 1970s, then pursued training in psychological and bodywork therapies such as Transactional Analysis, Neuro-Linguistic Programming, Biofeedback, and Hellerwork Movement Re-education. He and his wife, Trishuwa (currently the editor of the *Journal for the Foundation for Gaian Studies*) established a full-time psychotherapy practice, were active as clinical herbalists, and now facilitate nationwide workshops on such varied topics as indigenous and folk herbalism, nonlinear dynamics of organ systems, fractal physiology, molecular self-organization, and plant dynamics in ecosystems. They recently held a "one-time only" apprenticeship program.

Buhner, now Senior Researcher for the Foundation for Gaian Studies, grew up in Kentucky along the Ohio River. He comes from a long line of healers, including Leroy Burney, Surgeon General of the United States under Eisenhower and Kennedy, and Elizabeth Lusterheide, a midwife and herbalist who practiced in rural Indiana in the early 19th century. But it was his great-grandfather C. G. Harrod who deeply inspired him. As a physician in rural Indiana in the early 20th century, Harrod used botanical medicines almost exclusively, and taught his grandson the magic and mystery of plant medicine. Describing himself as an "Earth Poet," the younger Harrod's *A Taste of Wild Water* is a tribute to his progenitor, and describes their walks in the woods together. "There is a special kind of shadow that happens in deep woods that are old and have been left undisturbed," he writes. "Underneath the canopy of ancient hardwood trees the

greens are deeper, the soil blacker, the smells richer. I remember the particular way my great-grandfather walked through those woods...that way of walking has a particular smell, a particular gait, a particular rhythm, a particular integration with earth and plant and water." Buhner noticed that his great-grandfather's feet seemed to interact with the tension of the soil; the soles of his feet seemed to speak to it as they walked in silence to a favorite pond. "Sometimes we would drop a word into the silence like a stone into the water and the word's meaning would send ripples through us until they ebbed, slowed, and stopped," he recalls. "Still, even then I knew those words were unnecessary. For in our time together, we were doing something without words that humans have done for millennia. As we lay with the smells, the sounds, and the feeling of that place, deep inside something would leave his body and enter mine. I would breathe it into me as slowly as I breathed in his smell; something in my soul found purchase in it. It was a food without which I could not become human." Buhner says this mysterious transfer is always passed in silence between the man and the boy, between the woman and the girl. "It is handed down from one interior world to the next. Its essence penetrates the muscles of the body, the oxygen of the blood, the substance of the spirit. And this was the time in which I first tasted wild water."

It is this experience, the transfer of soul essence, that Buhner feels is the crux of true knowingness. It's something he says can't be captured with words, nor even in the systems of mathematics. While many people see mathematics as a universal, unbiased language that can explain everything around us, Buhner finds it limiting. "Its just a language, another interpretation of experience," he explains. The real deal is that inexplicable transfer of energy/emotion that occurs when we connect with someone we know in a crowd, or encounter a puppy, or a plant. "The Greeks had a word for this: *aisthesis*. It means to breathe in, and comes closest to expressing soul essence. It is the heart's ability to perceive meaning from the world." Buhner further explains the phenomenon as eliciting a gasp and a touch, as when we react in awe to a sight like the Grand Canyon, when we recognize our friend and move to greet or embrace them, or when the puppy runs toward us for that rollicking, unbounded frolic. "Aisthesis denotes the moment in which a flow of life force, imbued with communications, moves from one living organism to another," he states. "It is a taking in of the world, a taking in of soulful communications. When we experience this sharing of soul essence, we have a direct experience that we are not alone in the world." It's a matter, he says, of using the heart as an organ of perception, a skill we've ceded to the head for far too long. Throughout the world there is a tradition of direct perception of nature through the intelligence of the heart.

Buhner also mentions that "plant teachings" are the foundation of modern discoveries in both medicine and plant foods. This capacity to learn directly from the world and from plants was demonstrated by the German poet Goethe when he discovered the metamorphosis of plants. It was also employed by Luther Burbank, George Washington Carver, the Japanese farmer Masanobu Fukuoka (whose methods consistently exceed yields of farmers using more scientific approaches). And it was used by Nobel prize-winner Barbara McClintock and by Henry David Thoreau (who, says Buhner, was "a great deal more than a naturalist"). This gathering of knowledge directly from the wildness of the world is known as biognosis—meaning "knowledge from life." Buhner asserts that this is an aspect of our humanness inherent in our physical bodies and is therefore something that each of us has the capacity to develop.

Stephen Buhner

*The Secret Teachings of Plants* is arranged in two parts: "Systole" and "Diastole," after the functional phases of the heart. Buhner likens the systolic contraction to "analytical explanations of why and how," the diastolic relaxation to "poetry and doing" (learning to communicate with and harvest plants, for example). As he notes, all indigenous people insist their knowledge of plant medicines comes from the plants themselves and not through trial-and-error experimentation. "The first step in learning to talk to plants is cultivating politeness, realizing that the pine trees that have been here for 700 million years must have been doing something before we came on the scene a mere million years ago—the first step is to respect our elders." In his prologue to "Diastole, Gathering Knowledge from the Heart of the World," Buhner describes digging for skunk cabbage. "We're going to get dirty on this one...as you look at the roots you feel something odd happen to your brain. Some older part, some ancient, reptilian part, is being stirred into life....You take the powdered root and put it in some alcohol and water, making a tincture. You visit it each day, talking to it, sending your caring into it, shaking the bottle to mix it well. When the process is complete, you label the bottle, writing skunk cabbage. You know this captures none of the living reality of the plant. But, inside you, the name of the plant resides, and you can call it up in memory, say it any-time...though not in words."

Buhner's first experience with plant medicine came when a friend directed him to an herb to relieve bouts of acute stomach pain ("pain so intense I would pray to die," he remembers). He took the herb, and the next time he had an attack, it was about half as bad; the next time half yet again, and so on, until he was free of the pain. "I felt the essence of the substance very clearly," relates Buhner. "It was as if what I ingested had companioned me." That plants may possess such a healing presence was perceived by the great Indian botanist and researcher J. C. Bose, who stated that "the characteristics of conduction in the plant nerve are in every way similar to those in animal nerve." Now in his fifties, the once politi-cally nervy Buhner says he'll leave lobbying to others. Nevertheless, his voice is still heard through books, articles, and workshops. Though he feels strongly that words don't do justice to the concepts he describes, he is careful in using them, and is quite perturbed about errata in his writ-ings. His website explains a number of errors, expresses his apologies, and contains detailed corrections. His concerns for planetary and envi-ronmental health are eloquently recorded in an elegy to what he calls "the green nations." He cites the Geneva 1997 International Union for the Con-servation of Nature (IUCN) Species Survival Commission's "Red List of Threatened Plants" (a six-pound, 862-page book three inches thick) as the inspiration for the poem "Herbelegy." "Once we found them wherever we walked. Their songs, heard by deeper ears than the physical, filled the for-ests. Their smell uplifted us, their medicine healed us, their colors shaped our senses. Where do they go once they are gone? What holes within us will remain unfilled once they are no more?" he asks. Interspersed between stanzas are the names and countries of origin of once plentiful herbs now disappearing. "Two-thirds of the evolutionary ancestors of our food crops are endangered," Buhner warns. "Viruses and transposons intermixed the wild and domesticated genes throughout the past ten thousand years so that our food plants remained strong. But the genes are going now, they are going now." As he continues the elegy, the lines become more personal. "There is only emptiness in the forest where I used to find you. I used to come to you when I was ill in prayer. I would dig you and make you into medicine. On a long couch at home I lie, my coughing worse....In long cabinets your remains lie, pressed, flattened a map accompanying them shows where you used to grow. A scientist says he can make you live again when 'we' learn more. What about your only pollinator—the tiny bee with the long antennae that I used to see? Will we make him again as well? Who are 'we', anyway?"

# 3

# THE AGE OF A SAGE

*The Relationship Between Spirituality and Longevity*

**BY JOHN WHITE**

Arecent talk show on a major network said that some scientists studying longevity believe humans can, through medical science, live to 125 years. The critical factors, the show host said, were diet, exercise, and replacement of worn-out parts with new ones grown in the laboratory.

Apparently, they'd never heard of yogis and other spiritual masters living to 200 and beyond.

That is not to say all yogis and sages are long-lived; they clearly aren't. Nor is it to say they have the longest average lifespan; there is no census of yogis and sages from which to draw such data. Nevertheless, as a class of people, certain individual yogis and sages have demonstrated extreme longevity, which is directly attributable to their spiritual practices—and which is far beyond what conventional science recognizes as possible. (However, there are a few scientific researchers who speculate that medical science and technology may be able to extend the normal lifespan to 150 years or even to several hundred.)

Confirmed documentation is not available for the following cases, but taken as a group, they are highly suggestive of the possibility claimed in some sacred traditions; namely, that a person can attain a greatly extended lifespan with good health.

## CASES OF EXTREME LONGEVITY

An Indian yogi named Sri Govindananda Bharati lived to 137 years, dying in 1963; also known as the Shivapuri Baba, his life's story is told by the British writer J. G. Bennett in *The Long Pilgrimage*. Another yogi named Shriman Tapasviji, who died in 1955, lived to 185 by rejuvenating his aged body three times through a little-known yogic regenerative process called kaya kalpa, an aspect of Ayurvedic medicine; that, too, is described (without great detail, however) in a book, *Maharaj,* by T. S. Anantha

A Hindu sadhu (holy man)

Murthy. Author Daniel Goleman, formerly the social science writer for *The New York Times*, told me in the 1970s of a yogi in Brindaban, India, said to be at least 200 years old. His name was Devara Baba; I've heard that he died recently. In **Kumbha Mela: The World's Largest Act of Faith** by Jack Hebner and David Osborn, Devara Baba is shown in two photographs and described as "a 250-year-old sage." Rishi Singh Grewal, in *Lives and Teachings of the Yogis of India*, tells of his 1937 meeting at Kedarnath, India, with the Captain Yogi, whose age was over 360. He was a captain in the army under the Moghul rule of India, as documented by historical records, Grewal states.

Interestingly, western medicine is discovering what yoga has known for millennia about health and diet. Among the latest "revolutionary" health regimes prescribed by physicians is *Dr. Atkins' Age-Defying Diet Revolution* by Robert C. Atkins, M.D. In an interview with *The Walden Book Report* (January 2000), Dr. Atkins said, "The age-defying diet is a lifestyle, not a regimen. The typical adult on the program would eat plenty of low-carbohydrate fresh vegetables…and plenty of high-quality protein…with some fresh berries or melon for dessert. He or she would also have a cup or two of green tea a day. You don't count calories on the age-defying diet—you avoid carbohydrates and look for nutrient-rich vegetables and fruits." Welcome to the yogic lifestyle!

Beyond the Atkins diet is the CRON approach to diet. It seems to take the yogic approach and put it on a scientific basis. CRON stands for Calorie Restriction/Optimal Nutrition. The calorie restriction approach was pioneered by Dr. Roy Wolford in the 1980s and is one of the factors pointed to in the recent television program about longevity. It requires a person to eat 20 to 30 percent fewer calories per day than his or her average daily caloric intake, and to supplement the near-starvation diet with an array of nutritional supplements such as resveratrol, a derivative of grapes. Scientific studies of animals indicate that near-starvation levels of food intake cause survival mechanisms that are normally dormant to kick in. (For more information, see *The Longevity Meme Newsletter* [*www.fightaging.org*], a free weekly email containing "news, opinions, and happenings for people interested in healthy life extension: making use of diet, lifestyle choices, technology, and proven medical advances to live healthy, longer lives.")

## Quality, Not Quantity, of Years Is Primary

In spiritual traditions, however, mere accumulation of years is not the point of extraordinary life extension. Yoga and other sacred traditions aim at enlightenment and stepping off "the wheel of death and rebirth," so additional years in the body are regarded as an opportunity for further spiritual practice and service to the world. Quality, not quantity, of years is primary.

Nevertheless, in the course of seeking total self-mastery, yogis and practitioners of esoteric disciplines in other sacred traditions have, over millennia, gained astounding knowledge about the operation of the body and how to prolong life. In fact, nearly all our knowledge about higher human development comes from sacred traditions and hermetic schools that have developed disciplines and psychotechnologies for what is now in the West called transpersonal psychology. Transpersonal psychology scientifically studies growth beyond ego to enlightenment, but its emphasis is on the mental or noetic aspects of the process. Paralleling that are changes in the body, including the brain and nervous system, which reflect mental changes; this aspect of higher human development of the body-mind is little known to Western science, even less studied, and does not have a name, so I propose the term "transpersonal physiology."

Transpersonal physiological changes in the human body may occur spontaneously or be deliberately induced. They are said to involve subtle energies that are presently unknown to mainstream science but which have been described by esoteric science. The energy or energies are known by many names: chi or qi (Taoism and Confucianism), ki (Japanese), prana (Hindu), mana (Hawaiian/Polynesian), baraka (Sufism), yesod (Kabbalism), orenda (Iroquois), megbe (Ituri pygmies). In Christianity, it is called the Holy Spirit (see "The Paranormal in Judeo-Christianity" in my 1998 book *The Meeting of Science and Spirit*). More than 100 names for this mysterious energy have been identified from various sources around the world. (See Appendix 1, "The X Energy: A Universal Phenomenon" of my 1977 Anchor/ Doubleday anthology *Future Science: Life Energies and the Physics of Paranormal Phenomena*.) These traditions claim to recognize and, in some cases, control a vital cosmic energy underlying paranormal phenomena, and mental and bodily functions. Broadly speaking, all these traditions refer to it as the "life energy." This process of self-directed consciousness unfoldment is becoming known in the West as "the awakening of kundalini," a phenomenon associated with higher stages of spiritual development.

## LONGEVITY IN OTHER SACRED TRADITIONS

In studying self-directed bodily changes and longevity, science should look not only at yoga, but also at Tibetan Buddhism and Taoism. In Tibetan Buddhism, for example, there is a wide variety of means and methods for extending life, and reports of great success with them. There are, for example, "longevity pills" reported by Dr. Glenn Mullin in *Death and Dying: The Tibetan Tradition* (1988). Mullin, a Canadian-born Tibetan Buddhist, spent 12 years in the company of the Dalai Lama; during that time he observed a lama at Dharamsala, India, live on nothing but water and longevity pills (herbal-mineral compounds) for two years. At first the lama lost a slight amount of weight, but then his weight stabilized; at the end of his two-year fast, he had actually gained some weight, Mullin reports. The American-born Lama Surya Das, author of a collection of Tibetan wisdom tales entitled *The Snow Lion's Turquoise Mane* (1992), also includes some information on longevity. He told me privately that he has access to information on mineral substance fasts (longevity pills), breathing exercises, visualizations, mantras, prayers, and longevity empowerments.

In Taoism, there is the concept of the diamond body for which Taoists strive; it is the final stage of enlightenment. The diamond body is a deathless vehicle for consciousness to operate in, freed of the limitations of mortal flesh. (It is the counterpart of the resurrection body or glorified body in Judeo-Christianity, the solar body of mystery schools, the adamantine body of yoga, the light body of Tibetan Buddhism, the vajra body of tantrism, the radiant body of Gnosticism and Neoplatonism, the Winged Disk or Flying Disk of pharaonic Egypt, and the fravashi or fravarti of Persia.) Taoists have a variety of means for life extension, and there are reports of some "immortals," as they are called in Taoism, who live for hundreds of years. It is a fact attested to by an obituary in *The New York Times* for May 6, 1933, that a Chinese herbalist, Li-Ching Yun, lived to at least 197. He was probably 256 but the historical records didn't exist to support the claim, so the more conservative age was reported. Li-Ching Yun claimed his longevity was the result of certain dietetic and herbal practices, as well as the daily practice of pa kua chang, a martial art and healing system.

A landmark book by Michael Murphy, *The Future of the Body* (1992) examines the potential we humans have for what he calls metanormal development. It can also be called self-directed evolution. Such is the aim and effect of spiritual disciplines and sacred traditions. Murphy describes the evidence for human transformative capacity, including bodily changes, which in their totality, he argues, offer insight into the next stage of human evolution.

Murphy in his early years was a student of Sri Aurobindo, the Indian yogi whose teaching, called Integral Yoga, pointed to the final stage of yoga as one in which, after attaining union with the Supermind, the yogi begins a structural reorganization of his body on the molecular level. He alters his cellular construction and transmutes his physiological functioning. This alchemical transmutation of the body leads to an immortal body.

Do some yogis and sages actually know how to do this? Are tales about yogis living hundreds of years in the Himalayas mere fantasy or—as I speculated in *The Meeting of Science and Spirit*—have they learned how to regenerate their organs, as some lower orders of the biological kingdom do, and how to obtain "food" (i.e., energy) directly from the sun via photosynthesis? There are intriguing hints of this as an intermediate stage of higher human development, prior to attaining the light body itself. Transpersonal physiology is a field of study deserving scientific attention.

# 4

# MYSTERIES OF BODY WISDOM

*Does Muscle Testing Really Work or*
*Is It Just New Age Mumbo Jumbo?*

## BY PATRICK MARSOLEK

Does your body know what is right or wrong for you? Can you use your body to discover the roots of an illness, find out what foods are good for you, look into your future, or even find truth? There are many practitioners of alternative therapies who believe you can. Have you been to a chiropractor, experienced Touch For Health or Body Talk, or had your naturopath test you to determine what allergies you have or which vitamins you should be taking? All of these therapies use a variation of a modality called "muscle testing" as part of the therapy they offer.

This tool is used in many different ways; it is strongly supported by practitioners and equally strongly ridiculed by skeptics. So what is it exactly? The most common form of muscle testing requires one person to act as the practitioner and one as the patient. The patient extends his arm out to the side of his body and holds it firmly in place. The practitioner pulls or pushes down on his arm while holding an intention or asking a question. If there is a strong response (that is, if the patient's arm resists), this is taken to be a "Yes" response. If there is a weak response (little or no resistance), it means "No." Depending on the therapy that is being used, the strength of particular muscles may also relate to particular physical organs or energetic systems in the person's body.

This basic tool is called by many names—energy testing, manual muscle testing, applied kinesiology, and neuromuscular biofeedback—just to name a few. Even dowsing uses the muscle response, which is amplified by the movement of a pendulum or dowsing rods. The information obtained from the muscle testing is then applied in many different ways, depending on the treatment modality. For example, in Touch for Health, the anterior deltoid muscle is correlated to the gallbladder meridian. A weakness in that muscle suggests that a certain treatment of that energy system is needed.

Applied Kinesiology (AK) is an established chiropractic diagnostic system that evaluates structural, chemical, and mental aspects of health using manual muscle testing alongside more conventional diagnostic methods. AK is different from kinesiology, which is the scientific study of human movement. The essential premise of AK is that every organ dysfunction is accompanied by a weakness in a specific corresponding muscle, a viscerosomatic relationship. Applied Kinesiology has thoroughly mapped out correlations that are not based on traditional anatomy but are understood in terms of meridians similar to those used in Chinese medicine. Proper positioning of the muscle that is being tested is paramount to ensure that the muscle in question is the prime mover, minimizing interference from adjacent muscle groups.

Therapy localization is another diagnostic aspect of AK. The patient places the hand which is not being tested on the skin over an area suspected to be in need of therapeutic attention. This fingertip contact focuses the mind on the relevant area leading to a change in muscle response from strong to weak or vice versa when therapeutic intervention is indicated. If the area touched does not need intervention, the muscle response is unaffected.

In 2003, AK was the tenth most frequently used chiropractic technique in the United States, with 43.2 percent of chiropractors using it in their practice. It is also being used by naturopaths, medical doctors, dentists, nutritionists, physical therapists, massage therapists, and nurse practitioners. In Germany the use of AK is commonly used by dentists to determine the patient's intolerance for certain dental materials.

These correspondences between muscles and organs in AK are not shared by mainstream medical theory. There is no scientific understanding of the proposed underlying theory of a viscerosomatic relationship. Skeptics have called AK "quackery," "pseudoscience," "magical thinking," and a misinterpretation of the ideomotor effect, of which I'll say a bit more about later.

There have been some studies of AK showing clinical efficacy. For example, one study showed a high degree of correlation between AK muscle testing for food allergies and antibodies for those foods. The AK procedure in this study involved stimulation of taste receptors followed by muscle testing for change in strength. The patient was determined to be allergic to foods that disrupted muscle function. Blood drawn subsequently showed the presence of antibodies to the foods that were found to be allergenic through AK assessment.

On the critical side, some recent peer-reviewed studies looking at all of the AK research that has been done have concluded that the evidence does not support the use of AK for the diagnosis of physical diseases. In 1998, the Danish Chiropractic Association, following public complaints from patients receiving AK instead of standard chiropractic care, determined that applied kinesiology is not a form of chiropractic care, must not be presented to the public as such, and should not be performed in a chiropractic clinic. One of the difficulties for the skeptics and for mainstream science is that there is no scientific understanding or detailed theory to explain how muscle testing works. Still, there are many practitioners who believe the effectiveness of AK and use it frequently, and their patients are pleased with the outcomes.

Some alternative therapies that use muscle testing don't require the correlation of one muscle to one system or organ, but believe, instead, that whatever muscle is being tested is giving feedback for the whole energetic system of the person. Thus, no matter which muscle is being tested, its strength or weakness will relate to the question being asked by the practitioner. If a naturopath is testing a patient for a particular supplement, she will have the patient hold the supplement in her hand. The patient's entire mind/body system will get stronger or weaker in response and be revealed in the muscle test of the arm or another muscle in the body.

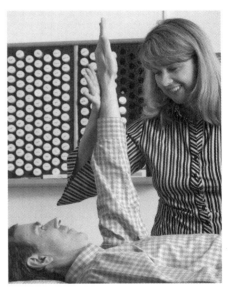

Health practitioner tests a patient's arm strength

Amazingly, this same response can also show up in a surrogate. Another person can stand in for a patient when the patient cannot be present or for some reason can't be tested. The practitioner can test this surrogate as if she were the patient and achieve similar results. Some therapists will even use their own bodies to ascertain the effectiveness of a therapy for their patients.

One common technique for self muscle testing is to touch the index finger and thumb of each hand together so that they are interlocked like a chain. Then the practitioner asks a question of herself and pulls her hands apart while noticing how much resistance she feels before the hands separate. If she feels a strong resistance, this is a "Yes" response. Another variation is to just rub the thumb and forefinger of one hand together and notice how much resistance or stickiness there is. A smoother response, indicates a "Yes."

The sense of stickiness or resistance is another hybrid of muscle testing that was used in the past by the chiropractic profession in tools such as the Toftness Device or Sensometer. A Toftness Device is essentially a hollow tube with a plate or membrane on top of it. The practitioner places this device on the body of a patient while rubbing the membrane with a finger. The practitioner would then "read" the stickiness perceived. It is believed that these kinds of devices are able to sense subtle energies in the body, similar to radionics devices, which have been around since the early 1900s. The medical establishment rallied against the use of these kinds of devices, labeling them pseudoscience and quackery as early as 1920. Although the Toftness Device and similar devices were banned by the United States District Court in Wisconsin in January 1982, they are still being used and are available today.

Critics claim that all the forms of muscle testing are tapping into the ideomotor response. The ideomotor concept has been around for over 150 years and refers to the process whereby a thought or mental image (ideo) brings about a seemingly automatic reaction in the muscle (motor). This mind-body response can be outside the conscious awareness of the individual.

Ray Hyman, Professor Emeritus of Psychology at the University of Oregon, has argued that muscle testing is heavily influenced by the ideomotor and ideodynamic responses in individuals, and has no validity as a medical practice. In 1992 he was hired by the State of Oregon as an expert witness in a trial of four chiropractors using a Toftness-like device. He argued very convincingly that a muscular response could be influenced by the subconscious expectations of the practitioner. He produced a video for the court showing how easily a group of students experienced effects with a pendulum and with a sticky plate in accordance with implanted expectations.

You can try it for yourself in a simple exercise. Find something that will act as a pendulum. It could be a necklace, a washer tied to a string, or some similar weighted object. Then let the pendulum dangle from your fingers. Hold your hand still and imagine watching a turning wheel like a potter's wheel or a record turntable. Without doing anything consciously, your pendulum may start to rotate in a similar direction. If you have a strong response, you may even have the sense that something else is controlling the movement of your pendulum.

Dr. Hyman's argument, and that of most skeptics, is that all muscle testing and dowsing responses can easily be explained by the ideomotor response. He also argues that elaborate and grandiose theories are devised to explain the observed effects, usually involving some form of energy, some kind of external force, or an energy new to science or as yet undetected.

I agree with Dr. Hyman that often grandiose theories are proposed. Yet, as I mentioned earlier, I have experienced some of the uses of muscle testing quite successfully. I've even seen a dowser use a pendulum to locate water. There are hundreds of thousands of people around the world who are using variations of muscle testing and are quite happy with the results. What is going on?

Dean Radin and other parapsychological researchers have conducted replicable studies on gut feelings, showing that a person's gut responds to someone else's distance intention or influence. These seemingly intuitive responses are physically measurable in the body, though they are often not consciously recognizable. He proposes that there is an entanglement of minds and bodies related to the entanglement of quantum particles, which might account for these responses and a wide range of other phenomena. (I discussed this entanglement in more depth in chapter 31 of this book.)

What these studies and others like them might suggest is that even if muscle testing is an ideomotor response, the source of that movement could be coming from outside the conscious mind and even outside the physical body. It has been shown how this response is connected to intention or awareness. If this is the case, no elaborate theories of physical energies or obscure forces are necessary to explain how we can receive information through the body.

When people attempt to explain how muscle testing works through physical cause and effect means, their theories fall short and can't stand up to critical scrutiny, as is the case with radionics, Toftness-like devices, and even some dowsers. There may not be a causal explanation. This lack of causal explanation may be why the chiropractic profession as a whole is struggling with the use of AK. When a practitioner tries to explain it or teach it as a physical, mechanical process, he will run into error. Those who rely only on their logical understanding of the physical connections, without having the intuitive sensibilities, won't be as successful. The non-materialistic implications of muscle testing might also explain why the medical establishment so strongly resists its use.

Another challenge when using this tool is how to determine if a conscious or unconscious expectation is driving the ideomotor response or if it is coming from another source. As with the pendulum experiment, it is easy to influence the effects. I do believe that people with an intuitive gift or those who have learned to use the technique accurately can use the muscular response very effectively. In teaching people how to experience intuition, I've seen that some people have more talent than others, in the same way people have a talent in music or mathematics. Without lots of natural talent, someone can learn to play the piano or receive an accurate muscle testing response.

There are energy healers, chiropractors, and physicians who do enjoy very good results. There are dowsers who can find water and are regularly employed all over the world by ranchers and farmers. There are people who live healthy lives choosing for themselves what foods to eat or what supplements to take, while utilizing their own "Yes" or "No" response with their sticky fingers.

Yet there is always a chance that your muscular response—be it the strength of your arm or the feeling in your gut—might be influenced by your own unconscious beliefs and expectations. Be suspicious of a person or a group who claims to have 100 percent accuracy with any modality that uses muscle testing. Your doctor or your dowser may not always be correct. David Hawkins, the author of *Power vs. Force* (2014), claims to have developed a system using muscle testing that differentiates truth from falsehood and is always accurate. Moreover, he claims to be able to evaluate the evolution and level of people, thoughts, ideas, even his own writings, which, of course, rate extremely high. Dr. Hawkins also claims that anyone getting different results isn't evolved enough to perceive reality accurately. It is not unusual that an intuitive source of information like this is taken as the absolute truth. I doubt his claims.

Even if you don't use muscle testing to boost yourself up and create impenetrable, self-supporting theories, the results from muscle testing can be hard to duplicate. The expression of this intuitive form has uniqueness and individuality. Many intuitives have a gift and they develop a system that works. Yet they find it hard to teach. One example I've experienced is the ColorPrint system developed by Jamie Champion. He has developed a typology whereby different colors have different energetic, emotional, and physical qualities. He proposes that each person has five basic colors that reveal different aspects of his nature. Champion muscle tests you to determine what your colors are. Then you can explore the colors for yourself as you would the personal significance of your astrological sign. The colors Jamie "read" as my ColorPrint really fit me and brought insight into my life as I engaged with them. I feel that he is a gifted intuitive, and he uses muscle testing to channel his talent. He shared with me that he was having difficulty finding someone who can duplicate his "reading" ability.

If you are seeing a chiropractor, a doctor, or a gifted intuitive, you may receive the benefits of muscle testing. If they are skilled and have learned to use their intuitive ability, you can save yourself lots of time, money, and resources and quickly move toward better health. Regardless of who they are however, I recommend that you also trust your own felt senses. As with any intuitive reading, take the information you receive and weigh it against what you know within yourself. If you are curious about how muscle testing works, you may want to learn to do it. You can always weigh the intuitive information you receive from your doctor or your own intuition against what you know through more logical means. Healthy skepticism can help you make an effective choice. You can listen to your gut when it's telling you something.

# 5

# SURGEON SEARCHES FOR THE SOUL

*Neurosurgeon Dr. John L. Turner Looks*
*Where Others Dare Not*

**BY MICHAEL E. TYMN**

There is one short question that sums up mankind's greatest concern: Are brain and mind one and the same? If, as mainstream science chooses to believe, they *are* the same, we live in a purely mechanistic world without any real meaning, and we are all marching toward an abyss of nothingness. The materialist who waves the banner of humanism will argue that meaning is found in building a better world for future generations, but that begs the question of what future generations will strive for once they have achieved that "better world"—apparently a world of peace and harmony offering unsurpassed comforts, conveniences, and pleasures, but still a world in which the prospect of total extinction is no different than now. Will those future generations find themselves like the Romans of Nero's time—eating, drinking, and being merry with no real goals in life beyond their hedonistic pursuits? Aren't we already well into that state?

If, however, the brain is not the same as mind, the inference is that consciousness is a product of the mind and rests outside the physical organ called the brain. This suggests that we are more than our physical shells—that we are, as most religions have taught, spiritual beings of some kind or other. In that case, the mind might be synonymous with soul. The question then turns to whether that soul survives physical death and continues on in other realms of existence.

As a long-time neurosurgeon, Dr. John L. Turner is very familiar with brain matter. He has studied it, examined it, dissected it, and repaired it many times in his 18 years of surgical practice, followed by 11 years of consulting practice, most of which have been served in Hilo, Hawaii, where he now lives and practices on a limited basis. In his recently-published book,

*Medicine, Miracles, and Manifestations* (2009), which discusses his experiences with energy medicine, Turner states that he had often wondered if we are merely "brief candles strutting and fretting on the stage of life, only to be extinguished when the play ends." Various experiences during his practice led him to believe that such is not the case, but it was not until recently, after cutting back his practice to occasional consultations, that he has been able to pull it all together and begin to view it systematically.

Turner now devotes several hours a day to exploring matters that seemingly fall outside the mainstream medical paradigm. He has studied the Brazilian healer known as John of God, and Turner is also heavily interested in the study of near-death experiences, remote viewing, electronic voice phenomena (EVP), orbs, and the language of Alzheimer's patients.

"But what interests me the most these days is the connection between true forgiveness and unconditional love," Turner offers. "I believe the evidence coming to us through hypnotic regressions, near-death experiences, out-of-body experiences, and mediums is clear that we live a multitude of lives, perhaps some simultaneously and others in keeping with reincarnation; and that when a life reaches its end, one is given a period of time to review the lessons learned (and perhaps not fully learned) during that life time, and then a period to reflect and refine the lessons for the next incarnation, much as the Buddhist belief that is akin to passing the flame from one candle to another. Many of the 'teachings' that patients report at the end of life involve lessons of love."

As Turner thinks back on it, energy medicine started to become part of his practice around 1995. "Before that, I didn't employ energy healing methods, even though I became increasingly aware of them," he recalls, adding that his interest in such matters began while pursuing a Ph.D. in physics at Ohio State University. "I was given the book, *The Sleeping Prophet*, about Edgar Cayce. That completely changed the course of my life, pulled me into a search for other dimensions and the spiritual world, and it was the primary factor in my changing from physics to medicine."

Still, it wasn't until reading the books *Into the Light,* by Dr. William Campbell Douglass and *The Secret Life of Plants,* by Tompkins and Bird, during 1995 that things began to fall into place. "It was during a period of forced rustication resulting from a marital separation that I took the books on light therapy and experiments with plants, both of which were gifts from patients, to read in the country," he relates. "I was astounded to learn

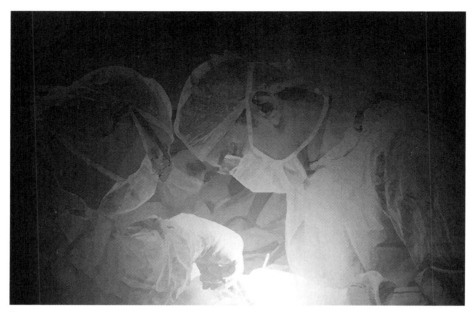

Surgical operation

something never taught in medical school—the fact that all cells of the body emit light in the ultraviolet range and in the visible light range. And I became aware of the fact that not only do plants emit similar light, but they are able to tune into human emotions and perhaps even human thought."

Turner next read about the life of Mokichi Okada and his practice of Jorei, which Okada called The Medical Art of Japan. "Okada's work centered around three crucial themes," Turner explains. "First, the proven fact that natural foods—fruits and vegetables—grown without the use of pesticides and fertilizers were important in the diet to help eliminate and prevent disease. Second, the appreciation of art and beauty, such as flower arranging and the tea ceremony, which can literally lift one's spirit. In fact, the Japanese word *Jorei* means uplifting of the spirit.

"The third and equally important component was the channeling of the physical-spiritual light from the palm of the hand for healing purposes."

While the Jorei channeler appears to be working like the Reiki practitioner, there is definitely a distinction, Turner points out. Reiki involves directing a "universal energy" to the patient, while Jorei is channeling of a specific spiritual energy, that of Mokichi Okada, who currently resides in the spiritual world.

LOST POWERS

Turner spent 10 days in Japan studying Jorei and returned to Hilo on Christmas Day, 1995. At the hospital the following day, he was approached by Dr. Sam De Silva, whose patient was suffering from Xmas Disease (a type of hemophilia) and was in a comatose condition. After studying the patient's scans, Turner suggested to De Silva that he attempt to treat the patient with a blend of Eastern and Western medicine. De Silva confessed ignorance but gave Turner permission to talk to his patient's family about what he had in mind.

After explaining his Western medicine approach, which involved clotting factor replacement, vitamin K infusion, and transfusions of fresh frozen plasma in advance of surgery to remove a hematoma, Turner told them of the Okada method, which called for channeling Okada's light to the patient. He showed them his o-hikari amulet and gave them a rundown on the spiritual cords that link to Okada and also recommended a fresh flower arrangement at bedside. Dr. De Silva apparently looked on with a very perplexed expression.

After the family gave consent, fresh flowers were brought to the bedside, and a Jorei channeler came in daily for three days prior to surgery. Following the surgery, Turner gave the patient 20 minutes of intraoperative Jorei, "letting Okada's light flow through a spiritual cord to me, and then to my patient."

According to Turner, the recovery was spectacular. Shortly after the patient's discharge, the patient's oldest son, a pump technician for cardiac surgery in Honolulu, approached Turner to thank him and also tell him that prior to the surgery, he and another brother watched the Jorei channeler administering to their father, and they were certain that they saw traces of light extending from the channeler's hands to their father.

In another case, Turner was called in on a gunshot victim. The 26-year-old man had been pronounced brain dead and his mother was asked to consider donating his organs. However, when she heard that Turner, who had treated her son some years before, was in the hospital, she asked that he take a look at her son—she was hopeful because her son had squeezed her hand a short time before. By the time Turner got to him, the respirator had been discontinued and only occasional agonized breaths were detected. Although Turner determined that the young man was not "brain dead," but his condition was so bad that there were concerns as to whether attempts should be made to put him back together again.

The young man, who prefers to remain anonymous (but whom we'll call Daniel), was contacted by phone for this article. "I don't know how to explain it, but while I was supposedly dead, I saw Dr. Turner driving down the road in his Ferrari and into the parking lot; and then when he was examining me and asking me to squeeze his hand, I was standing right there next to him," Daniel recalled. "It was very strange. And the other thing is that my grandmother, who passed away in 1988, was there at the foot of the bed telling me that everything would be okay and not to worry."

Daniel also recalled that eight years before the injury, he was on an automobile trip and was discussing organ donations with his traveling companion. He clearly remembered being concerned that he might be in some kind of accident, end up in a coma, and have his organs removed when he was not actually dead. Over the next several years he had recurring thoughts about this and of being near death while having his kidneys removed. As a result, he decided then not to sign an organ donation card.

In the operating room, Turner applied Jorei for 30 minutes immediately after removing the necrotic tissue and bullet fragments as the head operating nurse and the scrub nurse looked on, no doubt with some amazement. "I explained to them that it was not my energy being transmitted, but that of Mokichi Okada, who currently resides in the spirit world," Turner says.

Although Daniel has no recollection of the surgery, he does recall receiving Jorei treatments after the surgery and feeling heat coming from the hands of the Jorei channeler. He further recalls one of the channelers sensing something wrong in the abdomen area, a problem he was not aware of at the time but which, seven months later, showed up as gallstones.

The Okada Jorei is "spiritual light" Turner explains when asked whether the surgical gloves he is shown wearing in a photo in his book obstruct the healing rays. "It does not matter any more than clothing, which is not removed for treatment."

Turner also recalls a case in which a malignant brain tumor disappeared after seven Buddhists monks intervened; and still another case—one involving brain surgery—in which he seemed to have exhausted all options to control severe and massive bleeding before asking for assistance by means of prayer. It apparently worked, since the surgery was successful.

But even when unsuccessful in saving a patient, Turner came to see spiritual implications. He studied reports of near-death experiences and "began to realize that we have a spirit that does not extinguish at death but lives on to begin a new journey."

Of course, Turner realizes that skeptics will ask how anyone can possibly know whether Jorei and prayer were factors in the healing of these patients. Who is to say that they would not have recovered with the Western treatment alone? "It is a difficult pill for science to swallow," he says, "but there is a research institute in Japan where Okada's Jorei is studied scientifically. I have been there twice. There is evidence available for anyone who wants to really study it."

While his blending of Western and Eastern medicine would no doubt raise eyebrows in many parts of mainland United States, Turner says he has never been criticized or ridiculed, at least to his face, in Hilo. He mentions that he had recently talked with a mainland surgeon who had her staff privileges removed after using remote viewing during surgery. "I remember a doctor in Ashville, North Carolina, saying that some lawyers, at the behest of drug companies, were threatening to pull physicians' medical licenses if they practiced non-traditional medicine, as it was not in keeping with 'the standard of care' in the area," he nods. "So here, on this island, where no neurosurgeon ventured before, due to lack of equipment and income limitations, I had no opposition at all, but rather, encouragement to do what I felt best for the patient."

A planned project with Dr. Eldon Taylor and Dr. Ingrid Irwin, along with Ernie Morgan, a general systems theorist, involves an analysis of patients with Alzheimer's disease that had advanced to the stage of incoherent speech. "We believe that there is some meaning in the babble and that we can find out what it is by a careful investigation of this speech using specialized techniques," he explains.

Turner has also been involved with two films—*Spirit!* (2009) produced by Vivienne Somers and Anna Reeves, and *Quantum Wisdom* (2015), directed by Nick Mendoza. "Each deals with presenting evidence for the afterlife that will leave viewers to decide if this proof substantiates the case for the afterlife beyond a reasonable doubt," he adds.

Turner's interest in Electronic Voice Phenomena (EVP) and Instrumental TransCommunication (ITC) is fairly recent and was encouraged by Martin Simmonds, a resident of England. After they talked about EVP and ITC, Simmonds complained of abdominal pain and died from cancer shortly thereafter. In some recent experiments, Turner seems to have made EVP contact with his old friend.

Does Turner see any hope for energy medicine being accepted by Western physicians? "Unfortunately," he shrugs, "many physicians stand fast to their allopathic (conventional) training and refuse to budge even in the face of verifiable evidence of the efficacy of incorporating universal energy techniques into their bag of tools." However, he believes that in time, when selfishness takes a back seat to love, they will "see the light."

As an afterthought, Turner suggests that physicians who try to add non-conventional techniques should keep in mind the Bulgarian proverb, "The wolf who acts alone must have a thick neck."

# 6

# THE HUMAN AURA: REAL OR IMAGINARY?

*Research Casts New Light on Some*
*Very Old Emanations*

## BY PATRICK MARSOLEK

Japanese researchers have recently proven that the body emanates light. A man sits in a darkened room in front of a highly sensitive camera. In the next room, an image projecting on a screen shows visible light emitting from the man's body, especially from the face and neck. The light being recorded is definitely not infrared radiation but is visible light. The researchers noted the light intensity is at its lowest in the morning and seems to peak in the afternoon. It may be linked to the metabolic rhythms of the body.

This research has created quite a buzz in the media. It has been taken by some to prove that there is such a thing as the human aura—a field of energy or light that is purported to exist around living beings. Skeptics are being careful to say that the intensity of light the body emits is approximately 1,000 times less than what the human eye is capable of perceiving.

Does this new research prove that auras exist? I think a person has to be very clear about what this question is asking. The dictionary defines an aura three ways: 1) as an invisible breath, emanation, or radiation; 2) as an intangible quality that seems to surround a person or thing, an atmosphere; or 3) as sensation, as of a cold breeze or a bright light, that precedes the onset of certain disorders, such as an epileptic seizure or an attack of migraine. In New Age metaphysics, the aura relates to the first two definitions but also represents a perceivable manifestation of universal energy. It can be "read" (or decoded) and can even be healed or "cleaned" if dirty. It is this popular perception of what the aura represents, and that it can even be perceived, that irks skeptics.

This current Japanese research would seem to confirm the first two definitions; an invisible or intangible radiation and an intangible quality that is, in this case, around a person. Skeptics are quick to point out how it doesn't confirm the existence of the metaphysical aura, especially since the light is far too subtle to be perceived by the human eye.

As American psychologist and parapsychologist Charles Tart pointed out many years ago, there are so many different variables involved in what we call the aura that it might be hard to determine if it is real. Is the aura physical? or something projected in the psychological sense? Is it real if it is perceivable by scientific instruments, people, or animals? Is it real if it informs you in some way?

Speaking to the physical aura, it has been shown by scientific means that there are many different kinds of emanations coming from the human body. Along with the light we now can measure, our bodies also generate infrared radiation, creating a heat gradient around us. With sweat and other body chemical reactions, we also create a field of electrical ions. Any living being also generates some sound waves that pulse outward from the body. All of these energies create a mixture of perceivable auras around a living body.

But there is also the whole realm of electrical and magnetic radiation. The energy field of the heart was the first to be well documented with the electrocardiogram. Then it was also discovered that the brain emitted its own electrical fields. These fields have been shown to travel throughout the body and even extend beyond. These bioelectric fields also produce biomagnetic fields, which also travel outside the body. These more subtle energies are detectable by modern, and sometimes quite expensive, equipment.

It has also been discovered that all tissues and organs produce specific magnetic pulsations, or biomagnetic fields. The traditional electrical recordings, such as the electrocardiogram (ECG) and electroencephalogram (EEG), are now being complemented by biomagnetic recordings, called magneto-cardiograms and magneto-encephalograms. Proponents of energy healing believe that mapping the magnetic fields in the space around the body can provide a more accurate indication of physiology and pathology than traditional electrical measurements. The Japanese researchers proposed that they could monitor a person's health by tracking the light they're emanating. This is beginning to sound more like the

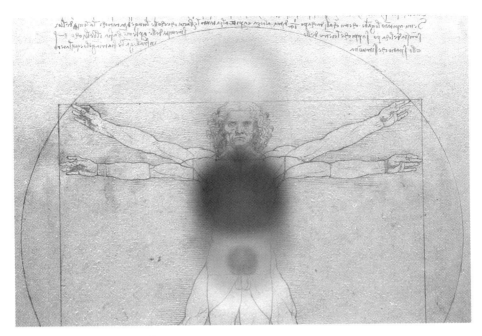

Da Vinci's Vitruvian Man with aura

aura of New Age thinking. But are these kinds of energies actually perceivable by humans *without the aid of instruments*, in the sense of being able to "read" someone's aura?

The Heartmath Institute has done quite a bit of research on the energies of the heart (see *www.heartmath.org/research*). They have shown how the frequencies of a person's heart and brain can be monitored three or four feet away from a person. This tracking is only limited by the sensitivity of the instruments. Scientists know that these kinds of energy fields may not have limits, but only become more subtle the farther they travel. The human body, it seems, is much more sensitive and has the ability to sense these energies and respond. Researchers have been able to measure how the coherency of one person's heart can affect another's at much greater distances by monitoring their EEGs and ECGs. This may physically explain how one person's energy can have a calming or irritating affect on another.

If, as modern physics tells us, all matter and living organisms are made up of energetic and vibrational structures, then matter is not as solid and separate as previously believed. Thus it would make sense that there is always a flow of information or energy between everything living, and perhaps even non-living, objects. It might be as if we are living in a great vibrational soup. We have sensory organs for detecting a very small percentage of these energies, the narrow ranges of sound, sight, feeling, smell, and touch. Yet there are many other spectrums of energy that we don't perceive consciously, which are practically bathing us in other kinds of information. The research from Heartmath clearly shows we do perceive some other frequencies, perhaps only at a subconscious level.

In one example of how responsive our bodies are, it has been shown that the human eye is sensitive to the polarization of light and may even be a magnetic receptor as well as a light receptor. Researchers have found specific nerves in the eye that send signals when a magnet is brought close to the eye. So when considering the perceivable aura, it's conceivable that the body can at some level perceive changes in the electromagnetic field around another body through the eyes, although these energies and interactions exist at far below the threshold of conscious perception.

In terms of perception, we also don't perceive what we have not learned to recognize or what we believe does not exist. This is a well proven phenomenon of perception. A tribe of jungle pygmies were taken to the plains. They thought the distant buffalo were ants because, in the jungle, they had never seen depth on that scale. Qi Gong masters, Reiki practitioners, and other healers have been sensitized to perceive the energies of the body that most people cannot sense. Perhaps if we practiced sensing and were told subtle energy fields were perceivable, that ability of perception would be part of our lives.

One of the common techniques to learn to see auras is quite simple to practice. Gaze at your hand or another person in front of a gray or white surface. As you focus on the person, soften your gaze and attend to your peripheral vision and the boundary around the person or hand you're looking at. As you relax your gaze, your vision may become unfocused. You may start to notice distortions in your vision, waves, or even shifting of the brightness or color of the light around your object. Paying attention to these changes is a beginning to perceiving more subtle visual information.

Another way to practice using feeling rather than vision is to use your hands. Rub them together briefly to warm them up and energize them. Then separate them and hold them a short distance apart from each other,

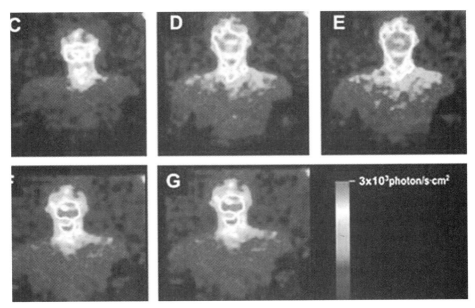

Aura photos taken by Japanese researchers

palm facing palm. Then relax, or even close your eyes, and focus on the sensation in your hands. Slowly move one hand away and then toward the other hand. Notice the subtle sensations you perceive in your hands as you do this. Many people feel a pressure, a lightness, or perhaps a warmth or coolness that shifts with the movement. You may be able to perceive changes in the non-moving hand also.

If you attend to these kinds of sensations, you will become more aware when they occur. If you don't value them at all, you won't notice them. For me, I am surprised from time to time when I see a clear glow around a person who's giving a lecture. I perceive it as a lightness, like a soft cloud all around the person. It may be closer or farther out at different times. If I focus on it sharply, it goes away. I've also seen this glow around the outline of trees when I am lying on my back on a lazy afternoon, looking up at the sky. Skeptics and scientists propose that this kind of perception may be a result of fatigue in the eyes, or an optic effect of receptors in the eyes that have fired, or even a visual illusion similar to the way you can see colors between black and white lines in certain visual images. Also, it's well known that our vision is not a perfect, all encompassing "recording" of the outside world. Our brain fills in much of our perception. If you see

An ancient depiction of Persian priests in flames referenced the human aura

a glow around someone, it may not be evidence that you are seeing an actual energy field, but it may be something happening in your eyes or in your awareness.

This brings us back to Tart's proposal that there are multiple distinctions of what we call an aura. The light you see or energy you feel in the above exercises may be what he calls the projected aura, or the aura that you see on someone else, but is a result of your own mind and perceptions. What makes this confusing is that you may see this aura exactly where science has confirmed there are energy fields. It still may not be the field that you are perceiving. It is your projected experience. Skeptics claim that this invalidates the claims of aura readers since it's not real. But what makes this all the more interesting is that you may perceive valid information in that aura that you have picked up unconsciously at some other level in the body.

For example, if I am an energy healer and I am working with a patient, I may be softly gazing at my client while I'm holding my hands near her body. As I'm doing this, I might "see" a darker color in the soft glow I see around her torso. At the same time, I may "feel" a heaviness around her stomach. As I perceive these things, I may feel some sadness and ask her what she is holding in her stomach. She might then look at me with surprise and describe an experience she had that she feels in her stomach. The information I perceive in this instance may have come from many unconscious or even intuitive channels. I may have subconsciously sensed a holding in her stomach when she walked in, through very subtle observations of her body. The cells and nerves in my body may also have perceived less light or a lower magnetic field in that part of her body. I may have felt a change in the resonance of my heart. All of this reached my consciousness in the form of the darkness and the heaviness I perceived and led to my conscious awareness.

Tart proposes calling this kind of aura an information display system. It is a way our unconscious mind brings very subtle information into our conscious awareness. I believe this "projected aura" is what is most commonly described in the New Age Metaphysics, and this is the one that troubles the skeptics the most. Since everything I perceive is filtered through my beliefs, past experiences, fears, expectations, and even the limitations of my own abilities, there is much room for error. There is also a lot of variety. I may see blue where another person may see red. Also, I may be sensing things in that aura that are practically impossible to perceive consciously. Yet my unconscious *does* sense it, just as some part of me does sense the coherence of a heart beating close to me as well as the brain waves carried in that field.

Another way of describing this phenomenon is through the phenomenon of *synesthesia*, which means "senses together." You hear about this with musicians who can literally see colors and shapes corresponding to the sounds they are hearing. Jeffrey Mishlove and others have proposed that it is basically a more subtle form of synesthesia that is at play with the aura. We see in the visual field information we've received through other unconscious channels. From my experience researching intuition, I believe this blending of the senses can happen with any of our senses. For example, have you ever heard a voice in your mind telling you something important? That may be a similar form of auditory synesthesia, your unconscious telling you something you need to hear. Have you ever had a gut feeling about something? Is your gut really able to sense right and wrong?

A beautiful example of this kind of visual aura is presented in Jim Nollman's book, *Dolphin Dreamtime* (1987). He describes a time when he was trying to use his flute to communicate with a herd of buffalo in

Yellowstone Park. He walked toward the herd as he was playing his flute and was able to come close to the herd, about 25 feet away. At this point, he perceived a yellow glow around the animals. He stepped into the glow. At that instant, the lead buffalo snorted and turned toward him. Nollman pulled his foot back and the buffalo stopped snorting and soon seemed to ignore him. He continued playing his flute as he watched the yellow glow move slowly back toward the herd. He followed the herd as he played his music, staying outside the glow.

Over the next several hours, playing his flute the whole time, he ended up in the middle of the herd, a place that would normally have been quite dangerous. There was no yellow glow recorded by the film crew. Yet Nollman was clearly able to perceive the boundary of his danger zone. What he saw may have been the personal space of the buffalo, which relaxed the longer he played. That is a very subtle perception, perceived in other, more subtle ways.

There are physical vibrations or energies in which we live our whole lives. This latest Japanese research adds to our knowledge of our vibrational bodies. Can we sense these energies? I believe so, though perhaps not the way, or as directly, as we think. If we want to sense auras or energy fields, we can practice. If you see something in someone's aura, you might wonder at the beautiful interconnectivity of the vibrational universe we live in and the awesome complexity of your mind/body system.

# PART TWO

# Beyond the Senses

Traditional Buddhist depiction of the kundalini structure

# 7

# KUNDALINI

## *Universal Ladder of Awakening*

### BY JOHN WHITE

Sexuality and spiritual experience have traditionally been linked in the literature of mysticism. Religious ecstasy seems strikingly similar to erotic excitement in the accounts of saints and holy people who have spoken of enlightenment—knowing ultimate reality or, in their usual term, God—in language that evokes sexual imagery. Such images, they said, were the best they could find for describing an otherwise indescribable experience. Such terms as "rapture," "passion," "union," and "ravish" occur frequently. St. Theresa recorded that she felt "stabbed through and through" by Christ's spear. Madame Guyon wrote that "the soul...expires at last in the arms of love." Likewise, the poetry of Sufi and Hindu mystics is highly erotic.

Orthodox psychology tends to smugly dismiss such language as the products of disturbed minds grappling with repressed sex, causing a regression to infantile behavior. But conventional psychological interpretations could be wrong. Why? Because in an ironic turn of events, evidence of a physical linkage between sexual and spiritual experience is emerging and it promises a major upheaval in Western psychology. According to this emerging view, sexuality is really unexpressed or unfulfilled religious experience.

Notice that term "religious experience." The common element between it and sexual experience is consciousness. The states of consciousness experienced by lovers in union and mystics in God-intoxication are states in which the usual sense of self as a separate, isolated, lonely individual is dissolved. The individuals are no longer locked in the prison of ego, no longer in conflict with the world because of a socially-conditioned image of who they are. Lovers sometimes attain this momentarily during orgasm and, afterward, universally regard it as one of their most cherished experiences. It has a sacred quality to it, as if they had contacted something greater than themselves, something at the wellspring of life itself, something that transcends the merely human and takes them into a higher state of existence.

Mystics, of course, experience this state with greater frequency, intensity, and duration. Some of the greatest mystics declared they were constantly in that state of mind, although to outward appearances they were simply performing their daily activities.

That state would be foreign to our range of experience—even to our whole culture—and we lack the language to describe it well. But we have hints and glimpses of it handed down to us in the sacred writings of various religious traditions and revered spiritual teachers. Moreover, they tell us there are techniques and disciplines that can be systematically employed to alter consciousness toward that state. Meditation is an example of such a discipline. Yoga is another.

In view of these facts, orthodox psychology ought to drop its illusion of knowing more than those poor, mixed-up mystics—whom it labels as cases of infantile regression—and recognize that there are realms of experience of which it is pathetically ignorant.

This, in fact, is happening. Because of rapidly increasing interest in consciousness research, psychology is being challenged in many directions. What transpersonal psychologist Abraham Maslow called "the farther ranges of human nature" is being considered more thoughtfully. Psychic phenomena, meditation, altered states of consciousness—the data from the study of these are causing psychology to seriously reexamine mainstream concepts and traditions in light of what Robert Ornstein, in *The Psychology of Consciousness* (1995), calls "the esoteric psychologies."

The essence of the esoteric psychologies, which so challenges Western psychology, is precisely what lovers and mystics have discovered to varying degrees for millennia: humans have a potential for expanded awareness that can radically change their lives and transform them to the roots of their being. We may taste a small measure of that in moments of sexual ecstasy, but there is so much beyond the experience that compared to it, orgasm is just a pale show.

So we find ourselves in the fascinating position of discovering new dimensions to the psyche—dimensions that could bring a tremendous evolutionary advance to humanity. If the nature of higher consciousness can be widely understood and experienced, there would undoubtedly follow a societal transformation around the globe.

That is why research in this area is so important. And the person who has commented most on it is the now-deceased Indian yogi-philosopher-scientist Gopi Krishna, who maintains that the language of sexual mysticism is to be understood literally and that it holds fundamental significance for psychology. There is, Gopi Krishna maintains, a direct physical linkage between sexual and spiritual experience.

This ancient yogic concept, recorded in literature and oral tradition, is becoming widely known in the West as people such as Ram Dass and Shirley MacLaine speak and write about it. But, perhaps, the most important voice among them is Pandit Gopi Krishna, who died in 1984 at the age of 81. He brought a marked degree of good sense and insight to the field of esoteric/New Age studies. I knew him personally, having interviewed him in Zurich for four days in 1976 and on several later occasions when he came to America from his home in Srinagar, India. I also read with deepest interest his dozen-plus books on the subject of kundalini, beginning with his first book, an autobiography entitled *Kundalini, the Evolutionary Energy in Man* (1970). I was deeply impressed by the man, not only for his obvious

Gopi Krishna

erudition and clear thinking about this most profound human experience, but also by his character—his honesty, kindness, and humility. All that marked him, in my judgment, as a sage.

*Pandit* is an honorific term meaning "learned man," so Gopi Krishna should not be thought of as a guru. He said clearly that he sought no followers, accepted no disciples, and made no demands for asceticism. Rather, his mission was to arouse interest in the nature of evolution and enlightenment, and to do that he wanted *colleagues* in scientific and scholarly research, not devotees. Most important, he said that the truth of his observations about a potent biological link between sex and higher consciousness—which he claims is the motivational force behind evolution and all spiritual and supernormal phenomena—should be tested, using the principles, methodology, and (insofar as possible) technology of science.

The essence of his claims is threefold: first, he has discovered that the reproductive system is also the mechanism by which evolution proceeds; second, religion is based on inherent evolutionary impulses in the psyche; and, third, there is a predetermined target for human evolution toward which the entire race is being irresistibly drawn. Whether humanity will arrive there or extinguish itself is another matter—one which Gopi Krishna says is the fundamental motive behind his efforts to demonstrate our "divine destiny."

## A NEW SPECIES OF HUMANITY

*Kundalini* is the key term in Gopi Krishna's theory of evolution. Coming from ancient Sanskrit, it means "coiled up," like a snake or spring, and implies latent energy or potential to expand. Gopi Krishna often translates it as "latest power-reservoir of energy" or "psychosomatic power center." Kundalini, he claims, is the fundamental bioenergy of life, stored primarily in the sex organs but present throughout the entire body. This potent psychic radiation is normally associated with the genitals for simple continuance of the species by providing a sex drive. This is what Freud called libido (although the Freudian conception is strictly psychological and lacks the energy tie-in to physics and biology, which Gopi Krishna is pointing out).

However, Gopi Krishna says, kundalini is also the basis for the attainment of a higher state of consciousness. The kundalini energy can be concentrated in the brain to produce enlightenment and genius—higher mental perception. Its potency is our potential. Such a state, if widely attained, could mean a new species of humanity, a higher human race. Thus, kundalini, the bridge between mind and matter, can be the evolutionary cause of creation as well as procreation. It is, Gopi Krishna says, the evolutionary energy and mechanism operating in the human race.

Kundalini is traditionally symbolized in Hindu, Vedic, and Tantric texts as a sleeping serpent coiled around the base of the human spine to indicate its close relationship with the sex organs. The concept is not limited to Indian literature, however. It has been described in the ancient records of Tibet, Egypt, Sumer, China, Greece, and other cultures and traditions, including early Judaism and Christianity. The Pharaoh's headdress, the feathered serpent of Mexico and South America, the dragon of oriental mythology, the serpent in the Garden of Eden—all are indicative of kundalini, Gopi Krishna maintains.

The source of the "serpent power" is prana, a primal cosmic energy outside the electromagnetic spectrum and other forces known to official Western science. However, many prescientific and unorthodox scientific traditions have identified a life force from which other energies and paranormal phenomena are derived. Acupuncture calls it chi, the Greeks wrote of ether, Christianity terms it the Holy Spirit, Wilhelm Reich named it "orgone" and Soviet psychic researchers have their "bioplasma." Carl Jung said there are more than 50 synonyms for prana or *prima materia* in alchemical literature.

In a *New York Times* article, Gopi Krishna pointed out that sublimation—raising up—of sex energy is the basic lever of all spiritual disciplines. But, he said, "the all-inclusive nature of sex energy has not yet been correctly understood by psychologists. In fact, the very term reproductive, or sex, energy is a misnomer. Reproduction is but one of the aspects of the life energy, of which the other theater of activity is the brain."

Surrounding and permeating the gross tissues of the body, Gopi Krishna writes in *The Dawn of a New Science* (1999), "a living electricity, acting intelligently and purposefully, controls the activity of every molecule of living matter. It carries the life principle from one place to the other, energizes, overhauls, and purifies the neurons and maintains the life-giving subtle area of the body much in the same way as the blood plasma maintains the grosser part."

That vital essence is extracted by the nervous system from surrounding tissue in the form of an extremely fine biochemical essence of a highly delicate and volatile nature. In humans, this essence, existing at the molecular or sub-molecular level, especially focuses itself in the sexual organs, where the kundalini process begins.

## FROM SEXUALITY TO SPIRITUALITY

There is a subtle but direct connection between the brain and the organs of generation via the spine, Gopi Krishna maintains. The spinal cord and canal through which it runs serve as the avenue for transforming sexuality to spirituality. Through certain techniques known and practiced since ancient times, the kundalini energy can be aroused and guided up the center of the spinal cord (*sushumna*, in yogic terminology) to a dormant center, called the Cave of Brahma (Brahmarandhra), in the brain's ventricular cavity, the site of the entryway to the seventh chakra. (I'll explain that term in a moment.)

This "living electricity," or "superintelligent energy," as Gopi Krishna sometimes calls it, is an ultrapotent, high-grade form of bioplasma—concentrated prana. But the techniques for controlling it are extremely dangerous. They are equivalent, figuratively speaking, to letting a child play with a nuclear reactor and should be undertaken only under the guidance of a proven master of that tradition.

The nature of the chakras in yogic physiology is not clearly agreed upon by modern interpreters—so be careful of accepting dogmatic pronouncements by spiritual teachers and New Age commentators. For example, author Sam Keen and psychologist Robert Ornstein feel that the chakras are strictly metaphoric, lacking in any physical reality. Scholar Joseph Campbell likewise regards them as psychological teaching devices—merely concepts. Others, such as M. P. Pandit, an exponent of Sri Aurobindo, and William Tiller, Professor of Materials Science at Stanford University, maintain that chakras exist in the "subtle body" of man, sometimes called the astral or etheric body, and influence the physical body through the endocrine system, with which they correlate at a nonphysical level of existence. Gopi Krishna says that chakras are nerve plexus—major ganglia along the spine—observed directly in the body through clairvoyance by ancient yogis.

There are said to be six major chakras along the cerebrospinal column, but the location of the seventh chakra (termed *sahasrara*) is disputed. It has been identified by various authorities as the pineal gland, the pituitary gland, and the anterior fontanelle. Gopi Krishna, however, says it is the entire brain itself.

From its repository in the reproductive organs, a fine stream of living energy filters into the brain as fuel for the evolutionary process. As the energy moves upward, it passes through various chakras along the central channel of the spinal cord into the topmost, the brain. This does not happen in every case. In fact, it is quite rare for the kundalini process to be carried to completion. But the genetically-ripe person to whom it happens experiences a golden-white light within his head. Apparently this is the same light that is visibly seen by people as the aura or halo around saints and highly-evolved sages.

The flow of kundalini into the brain has been described by mystics as "ambrosia" and "nectar," giving rise to exquisite sensations similar to those of orgasm but surpassing them by many orders of magnitude. The sensations are felt most intensely above the palate in the midbrain, and in the hindbrain in a descending arc parallel to the curve of the palate. This is known in yoga physiology as the *sankini*, the curved duct through which the bioplasma passes into the brain.

Jacob's Ladder (WilliamBlake)

Kundalini is at work all the time in everyone, and is present from birth in mystics and seers; however in most people there is only a "dripping" rather than a "streaming." This upward streaming, which is a biological restatement of what Freud apparently meant by the term "sublimation of the libido," explains the source of an artist's or an intellectual's mental creativity. Beyond that are those rare people whom Gopi Krishna calls "finished specimens of the perfect man of the future," such as Buddha, Jesus, and Vyasa. In them we see "an incredible combination of factors, both favorable heredity and cultural readiness, which produced those who, endowed with a superior type of consciousness and in possession of paranormal gifts, amazed their contemporaries with their extraordinary psychical and intellectual talents which [ordinary people] ignorant of the Law [of evolution] ascribed to special prerogative from God" (Gopi Krishna, *Dawn of a New Science*).

Variations in the size of the energy stream determine the intellectual and aesthetic development of an individual, geniuses having a comparatively larger volume of bioplasma streaming into the brain. The wide variation in types of genius depends on the particular region of the brain that is irrigated and developed. Thus, through certain occult techniques and spiritual disciplines, an individual of normal intelligence can accelerate the evolutionary process to attain the stature of an intellectual prodigy and beyond, to genius. This concept directly challenges current notions that intelligence is basically determined at birth by one's genes.

## THE SECRET BEHIND YOGA

Prana, the fine biological essence, is not in itself consciousness. It is only the means of nourishing our consciousness receiving equipment, that is, the nervous system—the body's link with universal consciousness. During the kundalini process, the entire nervous system undergoes a microbiological change and is transformed, especially the brain. The result of a fully awakened and developed kundalini is both perceptible changes in the organism and a new state of consciousness, the cosmic consciousness of mystics and enlightened seers. This vital awareness of unity with God, Gopi Krishna says, is the core experience behind all the world's major religions and is the goal of all true spiritual and occult practices. Humanity has an innate hunger for this state of paranormal perception. Moreover, bountiful nature has provided the means of achieving it: kundalini, the biological basis of religion and genius.

This is the "secret" behind yoga and all other spiritual disciplines, esoteric psychologies, hermetic philosophies, and genuine occult mysteries. It is also the key to genius, psychic power, artistic talents, scientific and intellectual creativity, and extreme longevity with good health. (An age of 120 with unimpaired mental faculties was commonly achieved among the ancient illuminati, Gopi Krishna says, and an age of 150 is quite probable in the kundalini-altered future.) But if improperly aroused, without right guidance and preparation, kundalini can be horribly painful and destructive, even fatal. Unsustained by a sensible, healthy manner of living—meaning regulated and balanced, not ascetic or orgiastic—kundalini can turn malignant and become the source of deteriorating health, terrible physical heat and pain, many forms of mental illness, and even sudden death. In physiological terms, the pranic stream has gone astray into one of the two side channels of the spinal cord (the left side being called *ida* and the right side *pingala* in yogic physiology).

The pranic stream, Gopi Krishna says, is affected by "every shade of passion and emotion, by food and drink, by environment and mode of life." It is altered by desire and ambition, by conduct and behavior and, in fact, by all the thousands of influences, from the most powerful to the slightest, which act on and shape life from birth to death.

Thus the need for balanced, moral living is based on a biological imperative.

There is another condition, too, even worse for humanity. Kundalini-gone-astray has been the cause of evil geniuses in history, such as Hitler. However, in such cases the kundalini energy has been active since birth. Their lives are usually so filled with difficulties that the kundalini energy can become malignant if the finer qualities necessary for psychological stability have not been made a part of their upbringing. Lack of these finer traits constitutes a built-in safeguard of nature which bars the unstable individual from access to higher levels of consciousness. This moral dimension is what distinguishes seers and sages from psychics and gifted intellectuals who are otherwise quite ordinary.

Knowledge of kundalini, Gopi Krishna says, is the only real means of preventing further Hitlers. It is also the best means of preventing history from ending in either the bang of nuclear holocaust or the whimpering slow death of an overpopulated, starving, resourceless planet. "The only way to safety and survival lies in determining the evolutionary needs and in erecting our social and political systems in conformity with those needs," he maintains. His writings envisage a new structure of human society, a new social and political order to enable the entire race to devote itself to the development of the powers and possibilities latent within.

All reality is governed by one mighty law which is simultaneously biological and spiritual: Thou shalt evolve to a higher state of consciousness via the kundalini process. This law of evolution, Gopi Krishna says, can be objectively demonstrated in people with unquestionable proof using the techniques and technology of science. "The awakening of kundalini is the greatest enterprise and most wonderful achievement in front of man."

The above is excerpted from *The Meeting of Science and Spirit* by John White. Copyright ©1990. Published by Paragon House, St. Paul, MN, and reprinted by permission.

# 8

# CRIMES, CLAIRVOYANCE & A. CONAN DOYLE

*Why Was the Creator of Sherlock Holmes
so Interested in the Invisible World?*

**BY SUSAN MARTINEZ, PH.D.**

"Gradually, the mists will clear and we will chart the shadowy coast."

SIR ARTHUR CONAN DOYLE

It was in 1919 that London's semi-secret Crimes Club enjoyed a talk by Sir Arthur Conan Doyle on the subject of "Crime and Clairvoyance." The twelve distinguished members of the all-male and highly exclusive club were connoisseurs of crime, a dozen Sherlocks who, over cigars and port, shared their insights on real-life mysteries and villainies. Sir Arthur—as agreeable as his Dr. Watson and as perspicacious as his Holmes—cited cases in which a trance-vision, a dream, or perhaps an instance of traveling clairvoyance, held the key to an unsolved murder, or to a mysterious disappearance. He went so far as to suggest that "every great police centre" could and should avail themselves of "the best medium that can be got," thus demonstrating to the world one of the many "practical benefits given by psychic science to humanity."

Although forced (by fans) to resuscitate the fictional detective, Sherlock Holmes, from his fatal plunge into the Reichenbach Falls in the Swiss Alps ("The Final Problem"), Conan Doyle had better things to do than tell tall tales of a reclusive and eccentric sleuth's adventures in crime-solving. The real world, problem-ridden and hungry for answers, was calling; and Doyle, a good-natured man, outspoken, approachable, and immensely popular, was not unaware of his personal charisma. Even his detractors would admit that "he was an influential figure in many fields outside literature."

On friendly terms with the likes of Rudyard Kipling, Robert Louis Stevenson, H. G. Wells, Lord Kitchener, Lloyd George, Winston Churchill,

Bram Stoker, as well as the era's finest mediums and literati, Sir Arthur Conan Doyle was knighted in 1902 for his patriotism in the Boer War. Over the same decades that the canny and controversial writer slowly but surely became a convinced spiritualist—and indeed its heartiest propagandist in modern times—the Edinburgh-born Irishman had been a ship's doctor (on voyages to the Arctic—"a jolly time"—and South Africa), a physician at Southsea, England, as well as in the Boer War; Deputy-Lieutenant of Surrey (1902) and a nominee to Parliament; a great sportsman and aficionado of billiards, cycling, boxing, golf, football, rugby, soccer, bowling, and cricket (credited also as helping to introduce skiing into Switzerland); official historian of the Great War's campaigns on the Western Front; researcher in organic chemistry, criminologist (with an impressive library covering the crime histories of many lands); poet, journalist, social reformer, pamphleteer, and champion of the underdog, defending both the wrongly accused and politically oppressed— see, for example, his biting attack on Belgian rule in Africa, *The Crime of the Congo* (1909)—for which he refused to accept payment ("It's every man's business to see justice done," says Holmes).

Holmes/Doyle composite
[*Atlantis Rising* artwork]

Born in May of 1859, Doyle became a freethinker and lapsed Catholic even in his school days: "the foundations of the whole Christian faith…were so weak that my mind could not build upon them…" At the Jesuit school to which he was sent, Doyle commented that Father Murphy, "a great fierce Irish priest, declare[d] that there was sure damnation for everyone outside the Church, I looked upon him with horror." Early on, the future author and evangelist of the spirit world distanced himself from the world's "wooden creeds and petrified religions." And to prove, if only to himself, that he was no hypocrite, he would not allow his influential relatives to recommend his medical practice to their church connections. (His practice did suffer, but in his spare time he began writing adventure, gothic horror, and detective stories.) Warm-hearted and conscientious, Doyle was nonetheless (according to a recent biographer) "more of a Christian, not being one, than many who professed to the faith."

Organized religion would prove no less daunting an opponent of Doyle's than the science stronghold; the churches, as he saw it, were "to the last degree formal and worldly and material. They have lost all contact with the living facts of the spirit." Railing at the Church of England's "narrow and bitter" attacks against mediums, he chronicled affairs such as the "high clergy's" interference with press coverage of the 1872 St. Petersburg séances.

Yet even among the spiritualists themselves, Doyle stood apart, observing the silly and petty inquiries of sitters "entirely preoccupied [with] their grandmother's second name or the number of their uncles"; none showing the least realization that with revelations from the Other Side, "a firm foundation for religious belief could at last be laid." Indeed, it was Sir Arthur's vision that the new spiritualism was "the grand religion of the future," one which could usher in global harmony—whereas "the old religions...have all been tried and all have failed." At least, the movement—cosmic and universal—might "throw down some of the barriers which stand between great sections of the human race."

But, he argued, "A religion to be true must include everything from the amoeba to the Milky Way." To Doyle, both medical man and creative genius, there was no such thing as a conflict between religion and science. They were mirror images of the same thing. There were no "miracles," only laws of action which had not yet been understood.

Sherlock Holmes' "passion for definite and exact knowledge" (*A Study in Scarlet*, 1887) is easily traced to his creator. The general view that paranormal phenomena fly in the face of science or rationalism made no sense to Doyle, whose son Adrian regarded his father as a man unequaled in powers of "deductive observation." Even those who thought that Sherlock's painstaking logic was the very antithesis of Doyle's belief in the Unseen, may have missed the point where these "opposites" meet ("There is nothing in which deduction is so necessary as in religion. It can be built up as an exact science by the reasoner," Holmes, *The Naval Treaty*).

Was Holme's legendary tour de force of analytical reasoning really abandoned by his creator when he turned his wits to unraveling the mystery of Afterdeath? Was Doyle's new faith a "monstrous deal of slop," "a load of rubbish"? Was he "deluded," "buncoed," or "fooled over and over again"—as his various critics made out? In answer to the many who publicly scorned his credulity, Doyle would calmly aver, "A man who is credulous does not take twenty years of reading and experiment before he comes to his fixed conclusions."

Sir Arthur did indeed take his sweet time before arriving at any conclusions, and this he did in stages, beginning simply with experiments in hypnosis and telepathy, after joining the Portsmouth Literary and Scientific Society. Then, starting in 1885, while still a young doctor at Southsea, he began "sitting" at the phenomenal séances held by (the still controversial) General Alfred Wilks Drayson (whose erudition helped form the character Prof. Moriarty). But at the Drayson Circle, Doyle frankly did not know what to make of the "table turning" and strange apports that he witnessed. But by 1887, when he was 28, his experience at mediumistic circles convinced him "at last that ... intelligence could exist apart from the body" (*Light*, 1887). And two years later, sharing the vice-presidency of the Hampshire Psychical Society with Prof. William Barrett, Dr. Doyle, the crime-writing spiritualist, was asked by newsmen to solve the Jack the Ripper case (1888) by calling upon the spirits of his victims!

Somewhere along the way Doyle, the rising celebrity, also joined the London Ghost Club, a private circle of eighty men whose pantheon included such stellar lights as Bligh Bond, William Butler Yeats, Sir William Crookes, and Harry Price. And in 1893, three weeks after the death of his father, Doyle joined the British Society for Psychical Research (SPR), festooned with such names as the future Prime Minister Arthur Balfour, philosopher William James, and naturalist Alfred Russel Wallace. Doyle, from that time on, would study everything from self-moving coffins to posthumous writings and messages from such masters as Oscar Wilde, Jack London, and Charles Dickens. Organizing expeditions to haunted houses, he took all precautions against fraudulent ghosts, such as placing "worsted thread across the stairs." It is of enduring interest that Doyle was able to trace a number of ghostly appearances and poltergeist outbreaks to a sudden or premature death. Sent to investigate the mysterious sounds (tortured moaning, chains dragging) at a home in Dorset in 1894, Doyle and two other SPR members spent several evenings until, one night, all peace was disturbed by a "fearsome uproar." Yet no cause could be found, Doyle even wondering if it was a hoax. But when the body of a small child was later discovered secretly buried in the garden, Conan Doyle became convinced that the phenomenon had been caused by the troubled spirit of the dead child. Out of a "bundle of records" sent to him from a circle sitting in Uruguay in 1928, he once again found that a number of communicants had died by violence—two murdered, one executed, one drowned, one expired in a motor crash… "Quite a large proportion…came to their end in an untimely way." Yet eighty years later, we have yet to incorporate this crucial observation into our understanding of psychic phenomena and earthbound spirits. Even more essential was Doyle's no-nonsense explanation of apparitions and phantoms.

"No ghost was ever self-supporting," he once said. Meaning: No external intelligence can possibly operate in this world of matter without a proper medium to supply the energy. It is give-and-take; but the medium is mostly "give" and the spirit mostly "take." "The disembodied," declared Sir Arthur, "have no power of their own, but…it is always derived from the emanations of the living…the effluvia of the human organism which furnish the basis of physical manifestations from the unseen."

It was more than abstract theory. Visited one night by a contrite phantom asking for Doyle's forgiveness, the author, during the short span of the manifestation, was "utterly unable to move." Discomfited by the sudden albeit brief paralysis, he commented later that "it is the one occasion upon which I have been used as a physical medium, and I am content that it should be the last."

On another occasion he said, "We are ourselves spirits here and now." It is true that Doyle's fervor for spiritual enlightenment became a mission, his *raison d'etre* during the closing decades of his life. Harnessing his life-long enormous energy and restlessness, he (along with his family) toured the world, filling lecture halls from Australia to Scandinavia in hundreds of speaking engagements on discarnate life and "soul wanderings," thus earning the honorific— "The St. Paul of Spiritualism." And it is also true that both his reputation and substantial wealth suffered in proportion to his unremitting crusade for the world's least popular "ism." For close to a century, his critics have haphazardly attributed his "conversion" to the bereavement he suffered on losing a son (Kingsley) and a brother (Innes) as a result of the Great War, even though those losses post-dated his public espousal of the "sacred cause"! World War I did change him, though. Disillusioned with selfish, bitter and violent politics (including Ireland's bid for Home Rule), he turned his all to the truths beyond the veil. The war, if nothing else, had proven to him that the "school of materialism...holds the world in its grip...and is the root cause of all our misfortunes." The enemies of spiritualism, moreover, "have done more harm in the world than the smallpox!" Indeed, "Every materialist, as I can now clearly see, is a case of arrested development."

Advancing from pulp fiction to prophetic jeremiad, daring any other philosophy to match the "dignity and brainpower" of spiritualism—is it any wonder that Sir Arthur invited the rancor of the establishment, reigning on the very throne of materialism? Even his biographers tend to regard Sir Arthur's spiritualism as unfortunate, embarrassing. And what a feast has been had upon his one big mistake—supporting the Cottingley fairies (1920), photos of little winged woodland creatures, promoted through the Theosophical Society in Bradford, which turned out to be fakes. His Celtic soul notwithstanding, Doyle also faced the hoax-hunters' firing squad when he aligned with the Crewe spirit photographer William Hope, the scandal (1922)—as Nandor Fodor saw it—"largely built on surmise and suspicion." Even Doyle's ill-fated friendship with the great magician and ferocious quack-buster Harry Houdini has been used as ammo by doubt-

ers and debunkers. Doyle, who was not above confessing the occasional blunder ("Only last year I had the experience of backing the dream of a friend for the Derby, and being five pounds poorer as a consequence")—would conclude that less than 10 percent of mediums were actually "hyenas," in other words, frauds. "If we desire the truth," he warned, "we should not only be critical of all psychic asser-

The Cottingley fairies

tions, but equally so of all so-called exposures in this subject," some of them being "downright fraud" themselves.

Less than four months before his death in 1930, Sir Arthur, exasperated with the "obtuse negation" of the SPR itself, resigned his membership after 36 years, deeply antagonized and entirely disgusted with the "reactionaries…hindering and belittling…real psychical research." It was times like this—(the society had cavalierly dumped on the Italian séances at Millesimo Castle)—that Doyle sighed at the "thankless quest" of spiritual exploration, wondering "if the sacrifice was worth it." Yet, wasn't it Sir Arthur himself who had once remarked—"Fate is never in a hurry"? Indeed, the fate of spiritualism still hangs in the balance.

The good fight was with him to the end. Not one week before his death, he led a delegation in London which called on the Home Secretary to end the persecutions (against genuine mediums) permitted by the Fortune Telling Act. And shortly before his departure from this life, he wrote that, against the backdrop of his many earthly adventures, "the greatest and most glorious of all awaits me now." And in the world he left behind, while adherents all but deified the nonexistent sage of Baker Street (dubbing the Holmes stories the "Sacred Canon"), its creator's "search for the Holy Grail," as he phrased his spiritual quest, is all but forgotten. Fellow spookists, though, have on many occasions called back the shade of Sir Arthur who, speaking to Harry Price through the mediumship of Eileen Garrett three months after his "death," communicated his difficulty in "getting through the wall of density that stands between us." It was and is a tough divide; and Price—who made his name more by exposing "hyenas" than by explaining genuine phenomena—reckoned the big Irishman far too uncritical, though completely honest: "Poor, dear, lovable, credulous Doyle! He was a giant in stature with the heart of a child."

# 9

# TELEPATHY: A SYMPATHY OF SOULS

*What Can 21st-Century Science Learn from the
Pioneers of Psi Research?*

## BY ROBERT M. SCHOCH, PH. D.

W hile on a mission to meet with the French King Henry IV, the cleric and poet John Donne (1572–1631) had a vision. He saw his wife carrying a dead child in her arms. At the time his wife was pregnant, and Donne was so taken by the incident that a messenger was dispatched to England to check on his wife. Unfortunately, it was learned, Donne's wife had gone into labor and delivered a stillborn, and this occurred on the same day and, as far as could be determined, around the same hour that Donne saw the apparition.

Somewhat apologetically this story is related by Donne's biographer Izaak Walton (1593–1683):

"This is a relation that will beget some wonder, and it well may; for most of our world are at present possessed with an opinion, that visions and miracles are ceased. And, though it is most certain, that two lutes being both strung and tuned to an equal pitch, and then one played upon, the other, that is not touched, being laid upon a table at a fit distance, will— like an echo to a trumpet—warble a faint audible harmony in answer to the same tune; yet many will not believe there is any such thing as a sympathy of souls; and I am well pleased, that every Reader do enjoy his own opinion" (Walton, 1640).

Indeed, although such a story may to this day "beget some wonder," similar incidents have been recorded over and over again. Such cases are encountered throughout the annals of history and are found among all cultures and societies, savage and civilized, Eastern and Western. But, do they have any significance and meaning? Or are they simply to be dismissed as chance coincidences or faulty reporting, combined with perhaps overly vivid imaginations?

In order to address these types of questions systematically and scientifically, the Society for Psychical Research (SPR) was founded in London in the year 1882. One of the first tasks of the SPR was to collect cases similar to the one recorded by John Donne. But the SPR did not simply scour the literature for cases; it actively sought out more recent cases (primarily from the 1870s and 1880s) that could be well documented. They interviewed witnesses and checked and crosschecked facts and data to ensure, to the best of their ability, that they were not being duped by fabricated stories (whether purposefully or simply due to faulty memories). In 1886 the fruits of their labors up to that point were published as a massive two-volume work titled *Phantasms of the Living* (by E. Gurney, F. Myers, and F. Podmore).

The title of this work bears some explanation. The core of *Phantasms* is a collection of "crisis apparitions" or "crisis hallucinations" (sometimes referred to as cases of "crisis telepathy") that occur to a "receiver" or "percipient" in conjunction with a crisis situation, often death, near death, or some other very traumatic incident such as the stillborn child in John Donne's case, on the part of the "agent" or "sender." The authors of *Phantasms* interpreted such apparitions to be "veridical" (carrying true information) hallucinations formed in the mind of the percipient based on information telepathically communicated from the agent, often at the approximate moment of death (although the telepathic message might be received in the subconscious of the agent, and remain dormant or latent for a period of time, before being brought to the conscious realm). The word phantasm, etymologically related to phantom, refers to any such apparitions or hallucinations. As used in *Phantasms*, the term "hallucination" could refer to a visual hallucination, an auditory hallucination, an olfactory hallucination, a tactile hallucination (such as the feeling of being punched or brushed against), or even what might be called emotional or ideational hallucinations and impressions (suddenly feeling sad, or a sudden awareness, such as when an idea enters one's head that a friend or family member is in trouble or just died). The title of the work, *Phantasms of the Living*, stresses the notion that living persons transmitted the telepathic messages cataloged in the work.

*Phantasms* includes 702 cases with analyses of the common characteristics and patterns found among them. Perhaps most importantly, *Phantasms* includes a statistical analysis that strongly supports the argument

"Glory to the Hero," by Nicholas Roerich

that all of these cases cannot be the result of "chance coincidence." Based on surveys of thousands of people, the primary author, Edmund Gurney, takes into account such factors as how often people simply "hallucinate" an apparition; how often a relative, friend, or acquaintance will die; what the chances are that the death and hallucination will coincide; and so forth. In the end, he develops a very powerful argument that the vast majority of the cases meticulously recorded in the two volumes must have meaningful significance.

To this day *Phantasms* sets a standard, and stands as a valuable collection of raw data for the study of this aspect of the paranormal—apparent mind-to-mind communication between individuals; that is, telepathy. Subsequent studies have served to support and complement the findings published in *Phantasms*, including a "Census of Hallucinations," based on surveying 17,000 people, published by the SPR in 1894. It is important to note that arguably the data on crisis apparitions collected in the 19th century could never be duplicated today. Much of this data was compiled before the widespread use of quick communication, such as telephones and telegraphs. So when a soldier stationed in India hallucinated one night that his grandmother, who was in England, was standing at the foot of his bed, he had plenty of opportunity to mention this hallucination to friends (who could then independently verify his story) before receiving a letter, perhaps a week or two or a month later, announcing that his grandmother had died that night. In our day of virtually instantaneous communication, we are immediately skeptical of anyone who claims to have had a hallucination prior to learning of a loved one's death. Even if such a story is given in good faith, it can easily be argued that the "percipient" is "confused" as to the timing of the hallucination and the time when the news of the death was received.

Crisis apparitions, as collected in *Phantasms*, are examples of a class of "spontaneous psi." Psi is a general term that encompasses two aspects of the paranormal as typically studied by psychical researchers and parapsychologists: 1) Mental phenomena, such as telepathy, clairvoyance, and precognition; and 2) Physical phenomena, such as psychokinesis (the moving of objects without any known intervention or physical connection) and levitation.

The significance of crisis apparitions and similar cases of apparently spontaneous telepathy lies not just in statistical arguments that, on the whole, they must be more than chance coincidence. In particular, two other lines of evidence are also extremely impressive as support for the reality of such spontaneous psi. The French astronomer and psychical researcher Camille Flammarion (1842–1925) and the parapsychologist Louisa Rhine (1891–1983) collected thousands of cases of spontaneous psi along telepathic lines (indeed, the number of cases Louisa Rhine had on file numbered in the tens of thousands; admittedly, however, Flammarion and Rhine did not apply the same rigorous standards for determining authenticity as was used for *Phantasms*). Like the authors of *Phantasms* and the "Census of Hallucinations," Flammarion and Rhine found that there are elements and patterns common to most of the cases (and, when viewed cross-culturally, such commonalities persist), and these do not fit the standard preconceived cultural notions of "ghost stories," suggesting the veracity of most reported incidents.

Perhaps even more compelling is the work of various modern researchers that has demonstrated a weak but persistent correlation between low levels of geomagnetic activity on Earth and cases of apparent spontane-ous telepathy (based on cases going back to the latter half of the 19th century). This, in my opinion, is a very strong argument supporting the contention that there is something genuine to the concept of "crisis appari-tions." It suggests that spontaneous telepathic psi is real and natural and, as might be expected of a natural phenomenon, its manifestation is influ-enced by other natural parameters. Alternatively, are we to hypothesize that hundreds of hoaxers over nearly a century and a half have conspired to fake crisis apparitions in identical correlation with geomagnetic activity? This latter hypothesis strikes me as rather far-fetched, if not downright ludicrous.

Note that a correlation between geomagnetic activity and spontaneous telepathy does not necessarily imply that the "telepathic signal" is mag-netic or electrical in nature. The human brain is influenced by magnetic and electric fields, and whatever may be the carrier of the telepathic signal, the transmission, reception, and manifestation of the message by the brain could be hampered or enhanced by differences in the magnetic and elec-tric fields that the brain is subjected to.

For many people a phenomenon is not "real" unless it can be dupli-cated in a laboratory setting under controlled conditions. Being a natural scientist and field geologist, I have never agreed with this contention. After all, can we create a genuine volcanic eruption in the laboratory or even on command in the field? Until about two centuries ago the scientific commu-nity routinely rejected the concept of rocks falling from the sky (meteor-ites). Nevertheless, attempting to induce, capture, observe, and experiment with apparent telepathy under controlled conditions is a worthy endeavor. Unfortunately, however, to this day it is fraught with problems and, though numerous experiments have tested positive for apparent telepathy, others have had negative results and replication is a persistent problem. The bot-tom line is that we really do not know exactly what parameters make for good telepathic transfer, much less how to control for them.

In the late 19th century, accompanying the work on spontaneous cases of telepathy, members of the SPR were undertaking experiments in "thought-transference." Experiments included a percipient (receiver) guessing words or playing cards that an agent (sender) was concentrat-ing on. Statistical analyses applied to such experiments clearly indicated that more information than would be expected by chance was being transferred between the individuals involved. However, in hindsight (as even admitted in some cases by the experimenters not many years afterward), many of the experiments did not impose rigorous enough controls and it now appears clear that cheating and fraud were involved in at least some instances (indeed, some of the subjects subsequently admitted to cheating). Personally, while I feel that many of the cases of spontaneous telepathy collected by the SPR stand up to careful scrutiny, to be on the safe side, I would not accept any of their earliest experiments as carrying evidential value for telepathy.

A new era in the application of experimental methods to the problem of telepathy opened in the early 1930s with the work of Joseph Banks Rhine (1895–1980; husband and scientific partner of Louisa Rhine mentioned above) at Duke University. Although he tried other methods first, the mainstay of Rhine's early work was the use of specially designed cards that came in packs of 25, with five each bearing the following symbols: circle, square [or rectangle], plus sign, star, and wavy lines (often referred to as either ESP cards or Zener cards, after Rhine's colleague Dr. K. E. Zener who designed them). In a typical experiment, an agent (hidden from the percipient) would focus on each card in turn drawn from the top of a randomly shuffled Zener deck. The percipient would guess the card. Working through a complete deck in this manner, it was expected that

one would on average call on the order of five cards correctly by chance, and indeed this was the case for most subjects. But Rhine found some individuals who could consistently call six, seven, or more cards correctly in a deck. Rhine also ran experiments in which the percipient called the cards down through a deck, from top to bottom, without the deck being touched by anyone.

Zener Cards

Afterward the calls were checked against the deck, and in these cases, too, certain individuals could consistently rise above chance expectation.

In his card calling experiments, Rhine initially distinguished between telepathy (where apparently the percipient received the thoughts of the agent) and clairvoyance (where the percipient appeared to somehow be aware of the symbols on the cards directly). But it was quickly realized that in practice it was virtually impossible to distinguish between telepathy and clairvoyance. In the so-called telepathic experiments, the percipient could be "reading" the cards directly. If we accept the concepts of precognition and receiving information telepathically from the future (and there is evidence for such, but that is beyond the scope of this essay), then the percipient in a so-called clairvoyance experiment might actually be receiving information telepathically from the future when the cards are checked by a human mind. As a general term to encompass both telepathy and clairvoyance, Rhine popularized the term "extrasensory perception" (originally written as extra-sensory perception, and commonly abbreviated as ESP).

Over the years numerous researchers in different labs duplicated Rhine-type experiments, many getting statistically positive results. Sets of Zener cards were also sold to the general public, and in the late 1930s and 1940s testing for ESP was a popular sport. Masses of data were collected, and it seems clear that at least in some cases information was "leaking through" by paranormal means (that is, outside of the known means of acquiring information by the recognized senses). Not only have Zener cards been used, but pictures, videos, images, and emotions have been sent "telepathically" with statistical significance to percipients while fully awake and aware, while in a relaxed state with mild sensory deprivation, or while asleep. However, decades of such experiments have done little more than establish that there is "something" there. How to consistently invoke and control mental psi phenomena remains elusive. Likewise, though various theories to account for psi have been proposed, including theories based on quantum physics, none have generally been accepted, even among parapsychologists (those who professionally study psi phenomena).

In my opinion it might be fruitful to focus more serious attention again on spontaneous cases of psi. Additionally, I believe it is important to explore further the physical parameters that may enhance or impede psi experiences. As already mentioned above, spontaneous psi correlates with geomagnetic activity. It has also been found that incidents of psi correlate with Local Sidereal Time (which relates to the position of the horizon at any particular point on earth relative to the center of our galaxy).

In my studies of ancient temples, shrines, and other sacred sites, I have come to the conclusion that often they were purposefully designed and situated to enhance psi experiences. There is suggestive evidence that at many ancient temples, such as the Temple of Hathor at Dendera, Egypt, signs and messages (interpreted as coming from the deity) would appear in dreams of sleeping supplicants, imparting veridical, but otherwise unknowable, knowledge. That is to say, I believe in at least some cases psi experiences were being purposefully induced. Psi experiences, religious ecstasy, and mystical revelation appear to be intimately entangled (a topic for another essay). By studying the factors common to genuine time-honored sacred sites, I believe we may be able to more closely circumscribe the principles involved in eliciting strong psi experiences. When it came to psi, I suspect that various ancient and so-called primitive cultures had a much better grasp of the subject than society at large does today.

# 10

# HARRIET BEECHER STOWE AND THE SUPERNATURAL

*With Help from Her Husband, the Author of* Uncle Tom's Cabin *Was Buoyed Up by Spiritualism*

## BY JOHN CHAMBERS

"My childish steps were surrounded by a species of vision or apparition so clear and distinct that I often found great difficulty in discriminating between the forms of real life and these shifting shapes, that had every appearance of reality, except that they dissolved at the touch. . . . Particularly at night, after I had gone to bed and the candle was removed from my room, the whole atmosphere around my bed seemed like a palpitating crowd of faces and forms."

These are the words of Horace Holyoke, the narrator of *Oldtown Folks* (1869), the fifth novel of the great American author Harriet Beecher Stowe, whose first novel, *Uncle Tom's Cabin* (or, *Life Among the Lowly*, 1851–1852), probably did what few individual persons or books have ever done: changed the course of history.

Stowe drew details of the childhood paranormal experiences of Horace Holyoke from the lifelong encounters with the supernatural of her own husband, the eminent professor of theology Calvin Stowe. Professor Stowe was never quite able to dismiss these experiences as fantasy or delusion because, as he wrote in later years: "I cannot discover that I possess either taste or talent for fiction or poetry. I have barely imagination enough to enjoy . . . the works of others in this department of literature, but have never felt able or

Harriet Beecher Stowe

disposed to engage in that sort of writing myself . . . my style has always been remarkable for its dry, matter-of-fact plainness."

Imagination or not, on almost every night, between the ages of 3 and 5, as Calvin lay in bed trying to fall asleep, strange apparitions swam before him: fairies, demons, solicitous mortals—figures so bizarre there were no words to describe them. They came tumbling out of the closet or wardrobe; they marched or wafted in through the window; they emerged from pulsing holes that opened before Calvin's eyes. A small Indian-looking man in black, and a much larger Indian woman similarly dressed, wandered in with a huge bass-viol between them; they fought crossly for use of the bass-viol, the Indian man managing to pluck a few chords on the instrument (which, amazingly, Calvin could feel all through his body) before the two disappeared into the kitchen where they seemed to chat with Calvin's mother, then vanished into a pile of straw outside the door. A boy named Harvey often appeared; Calvin thought this was his soul mate and communed with him telepathically. Five demons appeared from hell and dragged a neighborhood bully named Brown down to eternal damnation; the demons didn't look like devils but well-dressed 19th century gentlemen. Calvin woke up one bright moonlit night to find an ashy-blue

Calvin Ellis Stowe

human skeleton lying in bed beside him; he fled screaming to the bedroom of his parents, who didn't believe him. Calvin Stowe's lifelong visions were so pervasive that, one day much later in his life, when his wife Harriet returned home unexpectedly from having missed a train, Calvin twice wandered into her study but completely ignored her. When she asked him why, he replied: "Oh! I thought you were one of my visions!"

Calvin Stowe often told these stories to his wife and children. They became part of the atmosphere the author of *Uncle Tom's Cabin* lived and breathed every day. They nourished in her a lifelong belief in spiritualism, the doctrine whose central tenet is that we can communicate with the dead. They encouraged her to argue passionately on behalf of spiritualism in brilliant correspondence with authors such as novelist

George Eliot (*The Mill on the Floss*, *Middlemarch*) and the poet Elizabeth Barrett Browning (*Sonnets from the Portuguese*). Her husband's true tales of encounters with other realities, spun at the Stowe family fireside over many years, inspired Harriet to seek help from the spirit world when, in 1857, the couple's son Henry drowned at the age of 19; the results of these searches were as beguiling as they were equivocal.

Harriet had been surrounded by powerful influences ever since the day—on June 14, 1811—when she was born into the Litchfield, Connecticut, household of the celebrated fire-and-brimstone preacher Lyman Beecher. A man of uncommon eloquence and power, Beecher was a Calvinist, believing that most of us are damned at birth and all of us remain so if we don't unremittingly do good works. Lyman preached this dark doctrine, albeit with warmth and love, to both his parishioners and his children. Seven of his sons and four of his daughters survived to adulthood; Harriet was the seventh of thirteen children, two having died soon after birth. With gentle but powerful insistence, Lyman maneuvered all seven of his sons into the ministry; one, Henry Ward Beecher, became the outstanding American preacher of his day. Almost all of Beecher's preacher-sons, and all his daughters, became involved with spiritualism. For them, this was a first, essential, and abiding step away from the balefulness of Calvinism toward a more sun-filled version of Christianity.

When Harriet Beecher was growing up, women almost never became preachers, and almost never went to college. Lyman's eldest daughter Catharine founded one of the first girls' schools in Hartford, Connecticut; the precocious Harriet, after attending as a pupil, became, while still in her teens, one of its teachers.

In 1832, Lyman Beecher decided to fight Roman Catholicism in the West and moved the family to Cincinnati, Ohio. Here Harriet cofounded a new girls' school with her sister Catharine, began to have articles published, and, in 1836, married Calvin Stowe.

In the 1830s, Cincinnati was an uneasy free zone between the slavery abolition groups of the North and the slave owners of the South. Harriet saw fleeing slaves rounded up by their masters and taken back South. She witnessed the Underground Railway transporting escaped slaves to Canada. She was appalled to learn of black children torn away from their parents, sent South, and auctioned off, never to be heard of again. She was fiercely indignant that black husbands and wives often suffered the same fate.

In 1850, Lyman Beecher, having utterly failed to vanquish Catholicism, took his family back East. Over the decade of the 1840s, race riots, minor slave rebellions, and growing animosity between North and South had set America's teeth on edge. Harriet had become increasingly outraged. In 1851, at the age of 40, with two previous books to her credit and several children underfoot, she sat down to write an anti-slavery novel.

*Uncle Tom's Cabin (or, Life Among the Lowly)* appeared in installments in the antislavery journal *National Era* in 1851–1852. As a book, it was published on March 20, 1852, in an edition of 5,000 sets of two volumes each. The first printing sold out in two days and 50,000 sets followed in the next eight weeks. By the end of the year, 300,000 copies had been sold in the U.S. and a million-and-a-half copies in Great Britain and its colonies. No book of any kind, including the Bible, had ever sold so well.

"Uncle Tom" is a black slave of gravity, compassion, strength, and Christian faith. He is torn away from his wife and children and sent South to be auctioned off in New Orleans. His first owner is a kindly man, who soon dies. Tom is auctioned off to a cruel owner, Simon Legree. Legree torments him and finally has him beaten to death by two black overseers. Through all this Tom has refused to betray the whereabouts of a runaway slave, and dies forgiving his murderers. Other plot lines, including Eliza's famous escape across the ice-floes of the Ohio River with her baby in her arms, radiate out from the central core of Tom's story.

It's easy today to speak disparagingly of *Uncle Tom's Cabin*. In fact, the black novelist James Baldwin said of it in 1949 that its emotions were "spurious and that of the three most admirable slaves, Eliza and George [Eliza's husband] were simply disguised whites and Tom was esteemed only because he was robed in the white garment of salvation. In its use of 'theological error,' Baldwin asserted, the book breathed the spirit of witch-burners and lynch mobs."

But, even today, over 150 years later, the reader who approaches *Uncle Tom's Cabin* with fresh eyes is stunned by the novel's emotional impact. Stowe said the book came to her in pictures; her vivid portraits of the black slaves make us see and feel their suffering. Their humiliation when treated as pets; the agony they go through when separated instantly and permanently from loved ones—Stowe turns all of this into living reality. Her words had the power to make men and women act in the name of good. The great Russian novelist Leo Tolstoy praised *Uncle Tom's Cabin* as a masterpiece "flowing from love of God and man."

The novel brought howls of execration from the South. Imitation pro-slavery novels were rushed out, painting lyrical pictures of joyful blacks singing choruses in the fields. Perhaps the Civil War was inevitable; but *Uncle Tom's Cabin* may have tilted the scales in that direction. When Stowe visited Abraham Lincoln in 1862, the great president called her—the story may be apocryphal—"the little woman who made the great war."

All through the 1850s, as she continued to write both fiction and non-fiction, *Uncle Tom's Cabin* opened doors for Harriet Beecher Stowe. She traveled to Europe three times and was acclaimed in England and France; and she became close friends with Queen Victoria, George Eliot, Elizabeth Barrett Browning, and John Ruskin, among many others.

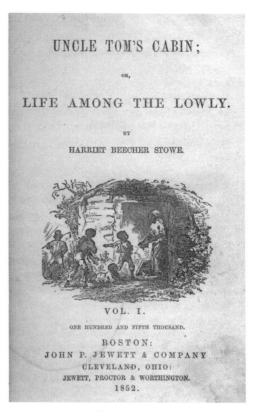

*Uncle Tom's Cabin*, first edition

Spiritualism was an urgent subject of discussion between her and her new friends. Calvin Stowe joined in the debate with George Eliot, writing her that, "[the famous psychic Daniel Dunglas] Hume spent his boyhood in my father's native town [Currie, near Edinburgh, in Scotland], among my relatives and acquaintances, and he was a disagreeable, nasty boy. But he certainly has qualities which science has not yet explained, and some of his doings are as real as they are strange. My interest in the subject of spiritualism arises from the fact of my own experience, more than sixty years ago, in my early childhood. I then never thought of questioning the objective reality of all I saw and supposed that everybody else had the same experience . . . I have noticed that people who have remarkable and minute answers to prayer, such as Stilling, Franke, Lavater, are, for the most part, of this peculiar temperament. Is it absurd to suppose that some peculiarity in the nervous system, in the connecting link between soul and body, may bring some, more than others, into an almost abnormal contact with the spirit-world (for example, Jacob Boehme and Swedenborg), and that, too, without correcting their faults, or making them morally better than others?"

But Eliot was highly equivocal about spiritualism. She asserted, "I would not willingly place any barriers between my mind and any possible channel of truth affecting the human lot." But it soon emerged that she doubted mankind's ability to make mature use of any religion. She told the Stowes: "A religion more perfect than any yet prevalent must express less care of personal consolation, and the more deeply awing sense of responsibility to man springing from sympathy with that which of all things is most certainly known to us—the difficulty of the human lot."

Harriet encountered no such resistance to spiritualism in her correspondence with Elizabeth Barrett Browning. In fact, the wife of the poet Robert Browning was an avid believer, who had attended many productive séances with Daniel Dunglas Hume and even (to the dismay of her non-believing husband) been smitten romantically with Hume. She wrote to Harriet: "I don't know how people can keep up their prejudices against spiritualism with tears in their eyes, how they are not at least thrown on the wish that it might be true. . . . My tendency is to break up against it like a crying child." She told Stowe that only serious appreciation of spiritualism could "keep it from the desecration of charlatans and fanatics." In reply, Harriet told Elizabeth she had been in contact with the spirit of Charlotte Brontë—though no details of this encounter survive in her letters and journals.

On January 1, 1857, Harriet and Calvin's son Henry drowned swimming in the Connecticut River while a freshman at Andover College. The devastated couple tried to contact his spirit at séances. In January, 1860, when Harriet was in Florence, Italy, Calvin wrote her that he thought he might have received a communication from Henry in the form of a guitar, hanging on the wall in the room in which they sometimes conducted séances, that suddenly, briefly, played chords.

In reply, Harriet told Calvin she had "become acquainted with a friend through whom I receive consoling impressions of these things—a Mrs. E., of Boston, a very pious, accomplished, and interesting woman, who has had a history much like yours in relation to spiritual manifestations. Without doubt she is what the spiritualists would regard as a very powerful medium, but being a very earnest Christian, and afraid of getting led astray, she has kept carefully aloof from all circles and things of that nature."

Harriet's advice to Mrs. E., she told Calvin, was to "keep close to the Bible and prayer" when contacting the spirit world, and then "accept whatever came." Harriet told Calvin that, "when I am with her I receive very strong impressions from the spiritual world, so that I feel often sustained and comforted, as if I had been near to my Henry and other departed friends. . . . Today I went down to sit with Mrs. E. in her quiet parlor. We read in Revelation together, and talked of the saints and spirits of the just made perfect, till it seemed, as it always does when with her, as if Henry were close by me. Then a curious thing happened. She has a little Florentine guitar which hangs in her parlor, quite out of reach. She and I were talking, and her sister, a very matter-of-fact, practical body, who attends to temporals [practical concerns] for her, was arranging a little lunch for us, when suddenly the bass string of the guitar was struck loudly and distinctly. 'Who struck that guitar?' said the sister. We both looked up and saw that no body or thing was on that side of the room. After the sister had gone out, Mrs. E. said, 'Now, that is strange! I asked last night that if any spirit was present with us after you came today, that it would try to touch that guitar.' A little while after her husband came in, and as we were talking, we were all stopped by a peculiar sound, as if somebody had drawn a hand across all the strings at once. We marveled, and I remembered the guitar at home."

Harriet Beecher Stowe died in Hartford, Connecticut, on July 1, 1896, aged 85. She was an artist of genius and great moral power, who produced a novel not only of greatness but of decisive usefulness for humanity as it pursues its long and painful trek toward fulfillment. The author of *Uncle Tom's Cabin* came close to demonstrating the ancient Kabbalist dictum that, "One good man [or woman] can change the universe."

# 11

# CAN WE SEE INTO THE FUTURE?

*A Scientist Looks for Evidence of Precognition*

**BY ROBERT M. SCHOCH, PH.D.**

On October 21, 1966, at 9:15 in the morning, a huge pile of coal slag and debris, precariously perched on the side of a mountain and destabilized by underground water and rainfall, came crashing down on the Welsh town of Aberfan. When the tragedy was over and the final death toll computed, 144 lives were lost, most of them children attending the Pantglas Junior School, upon which the main part of the avalanche of black choking slurry descended. The Aberfan disaster was felt throughout Britain, perhaps among some people even before it actually occurred.

Dr. J. C. Barker, a psychiatrist associated with Shelton Hospital in Shrewsbury, was on the scene of Aberfan the next day to help with the aftermath. Dr. Barker was also interested in psychical research, and it occurred to him that, given the violent and shocking nature of the Aberfan disaster, perhaps someone had had a premonition of the event. He made a public appeal for any such information through the media, and as a result received dozens and dozens of responses from people who claimed to have had precognitive experiences that, at least in hindsight, may have related to Aberfan. Dr. Barker carefully researched the best of these through interviews and sought out corroborative evidence, and found nearly two dozen reputed precognitive experiences that could be independently confirmed by witnesses as having occurred before the Aberfan disaster.

As an example of just one such person with apparent precognitive knowledge of the event, we can cite Mrs. Constance Miller who "saw" the disaster about a day or so before it happened. Seven witnesses could testify that Mrs. Miller had related her premonition to them before the event. In her own words (quoted in Archie Roy, *A Sense of Something Strange*, 1990), "First, I 'saw' an old school house nestling in a valley, then a Welsh miner, then an avalanche of coal hurtling down a mountainside. At the bottom of this mountain of hurtling coal was a little boy with a long fringe looking absolutely terrified to death. Then for a while I 'saw' rescue operations taking place. I had an impression that the little boy was left behind and saved. He looked so grief-stricken. I could never forget him, and also with him was one of the rescue workers wearing an unusual peaked cap." Mrs. Miller was not from Aberfan, and the argument that she had a personal interest in, and subconscious worries about, the slag pile as a potential threat does not apply. Very importantly, as we will discuss below, Mrs. Miller reported

How far can we really "see"?

that, after the event, she recognized on a television program covering the Aberfan disaster the little boy and the rescue worker she "saw" so vividly in her premonition.

For thousands of years, going back to the Biblical prophets and the classical oracles of ancient times (and probably much earlier) there has been a belief that at least some gifted people can gain glimpses of the future. The Greeks regularly consulted their oracles, such as the Apollo at Delphi, and all cultures seem to have their methods of divination, whether it be the inspection of animal entrails, gazing into a crystal ball, looking at patterns among tea leaves, or consulting the Tarot or I Ching.

In the book of Genesis it is recorded that Joseph correctly interpreted pharaoh's precognitive dream (seven fat cows eaten by seven lean cows, meaning there would be seven good years of harvest followed by seven years of famine). Daniel, in the book named after him, interpreted King Nebuchadnezzar's dream of a great image or statue and a tree hewn down to indicate that the king and his kingdom would be destroyed, as was ultimately the case. St. John, in what is commonly referred to as the Book of Revelation, or The Apocalypse, relates many prophecies that appear to refer to the End Times. The Four Horsemen of the Apocalypse, found in chapter 6, have household name recognition. Might these events yet unfold?

Closer to our own times, perhaps the greatest (or at least most famous) seer of the last five centuries is Nostradamus (Michel de Nostredame, 1503–1566). Trained as an astrologer and physician (he was very successful at treating outbreaks of the plague in southern France), he was heavily steeped in Jewish mysticism. To this day admirers and detractors argue over the accuracy of his forecasts. It seems clear, however, that in his own lifetime Nostradamus had achieved a reputation of being able to foresee the future and he was in high demand to cast horoscopes for the nobility. Among other stories that are told about him, it is said that while traveling in Italy he met a former swineherd who had become a monk. Nostradamus fell to his knees and addressed the lowly monk as "Your Holiness." Years later, nearly two decades after Nostradamus was dead, the swineherd turned monk was elected the pope, assuming the name Pope Sixtus V.

Nostradamus is now best known for his published predictions in the book *Centuries* (first edition, 1555). Written as quatrains, and in ambiguous language (which, in our time, is often translated quite differently by one modern commentator versus another), the book has been credited with foretelling the French Revolution, the rise of Hitler, the two world wars, and many other momentous events. Detractors, however, have argued that these events are only read into the words of Nostradamus in hindsight, and the prophecies are so vague that they can conveniently be applied to numerous events. I am not an expert on Nostradamus and I will defer judgment; my interest is in whether or not there is evidence that anyone has ever precognized the future. If so, then perhaps there is some validity to the predictions of Nostradamus, St. John, and many other prophets and seers.

Although by no means do I feel I have completed my studies of this rich topic, after studying the subject extensively, I am convinced that there is solid evidence that at least to some extent humans, or at least some people, can receive information from the future. This has profound philosophical and practical implications.

Let's discuss this further.

I find the well-documented evidence of premonitions of the Aberfan disaster, related above, quite thought provoking and even compelling. What is more, evidence of this type is not isolated or even that extraordinarily unusual, but fits a larger pattern of reported precognitive incidents. Many such premonitions appear as "dreams," either in the full dream state while sleeping, during the hypnagogic state (between waking and sleeping), or as daydreams. An early explorer of such phenomena, the aeronautical engineer J. W. Dunne (1875–1949), systematically recorded his own dreams over many years, discovering that among them could be found numerous apparent precognitions of future events. A classic example of a "Dunne phenomenon," from Dunne himself (*An Experiment with Time,* 1927) can be summarized as follows.

While a soldier in South Africa in 1902, Dunne had a dream (or, as he described it, "a most distressing nightmare") about an island threatened by a volcanic eruption. In his dream Dunne was on another island and attempting to convince, without success, the authorities, who happened to be French, to send boats to the threatened island and evacuate the inhabitants or else 4,000 people would be killed. The next batch of mail delivered after his dream to his post in South Africa included a newspaper with headlines and descriptions of the volcanic eruption of Mount Pelée on French Martinique. The city of St. Pierre was destroyed, killing 40,000. The description in the paper matched Dunne's dream, except that Dunne dreamt that 4,000 would be killed when the actual number in the paper was 40,000. However, according to his account, when Dunne first read the paper in haste he misread 40,000 as 4,000 and subsequently in telling people the story of his dream cited the number in the paper incorrectly as 4,000. It was only later, upon rechecking the paper, that he discovered his misreading of 40,000 as 4,000.

Dunne and many others have recorded similar dreams, where the dream seems to reflect something experienced in the real life of the dreamer shortly after the dream occurs. Another interesting example, recorded in the book *Man and Time* (by J. B. Priestly, 1964) is of a fellow who dreamed that a sparrow-hawk was perched on his shoulder and he could feel its claws. About two hours after waking up, he was studying in the lounge where he lived. A colleague snuck up behind him with a stuffed sparrow-hawk that was being discarded and placed it on his shoulder, digging the bird's claws into him.

Here is what may be yet another Dunne-type dream, from my personal experiences. In mid-February of 2008, I had a very vivid, disturbing dream about some kind of large mammals being tortured—something I had never dreamt about before. I did not really think much of the dream, except that it was sort of grotesque and nightmarish. Several days or a

John, the Evangelist, imprisoned on the Isle of Patmos, has a vision of the future (Titian, c. 1547)

week later I was watching ABC News and a story came on about cows being treated inhumanely at a slaughterhouse in California. Immediately I recalled my dream.

Something that these dreams, and others in the same class of dreams, seem to share in common is that they are precognitive of experiences, emotions, and feelings that will actually happen to the dreamer at some short time (usually within the next day to week) after the dream occurs. Note that even where Dunne's dream and my dream are about events that made the news, it seems that the dreams are not really about the events per se, but about the dreamers learning about the events. Dunne dreamt that 4,000 would be killed because in real life, in the future, he misread 40,000 as 4,000. Returning to the precognitive dream of Mrs. Miller concerning the Aberfan disaster, it appears that she did not actually precognize the disaster per se, but rather she precognized that which she saw on a television program about that disaster, the program having moved her emotionally.

Indeed, it seems to me that what appears to be happening in many cases of precognition is that the person experiencing the precognition is somehow picking up on her or his emotions that will be experienced in the future. I believe this concept is supported by a series of experiments on phenomena referred to as presentiments or "prepsonses." These are essentially a form of short-term precognition as measured by physiological parameters (heart rate, electrodermal activity, and so forth). Numerous replicated experiments have demonstrated the physiological responses of individuals to disturbing photographs, for instance, a second or two before they are actually viewed by the person. According to conventional wisdom, it should not be possible for a person to respond to a stimulus that has not yet occurred, even if the response is only a second (or less) before the stimulus. However, modern experiments show that this does happen (see R. Schoch and L. Yonavak, *The Parapsychology Revolution*, 2008, for more details). If we have such "physiological precognition" at a basic, unconscious level, this only reinforces for me the possibility that precognition at a conscious level might also occur.

Note that the prepsonse experiments are recording a form of precognition where there is only a miniscule time interval between the precognition and the subsequent event. These short-time interval precognitions appear to be the most common and thus most readily produced form of precognition in the laboratory. There have been other laboratory studies of precognition, such as precognizing a card or number (the target) that is selected after the "guess" is made. Over dozens of studies, it has been found that the best results occurred when the target is selected less than a second after the guess, and the accuracy of results systematically decreased as the time period was extended over minutes, hours, days, weeks, and months (see discussion by J. Utts, in *The Parapsychology Revolution*). Various studies of collections of spontaneous cases of precognition (including dreams) have found the same pattern of a decline with temporal distance between the precognition and its fulfillment. The most common precognitions are within a day or less of the event.

Does this mean that precognitions into the far future cannot occur at all? Not necessarily. One suggestion is that the temporal duration between the precognition and the event may depend on the "emotional strength" of the event, at least as far as the precognizer is concerned. Thus a highly dramatic, emotionally charged event may be precognized much earlier (all other things being equal, and they rarely are) than a less emotionally charged event. And then there is the issue of "sensitivity" on the part of the precognizer. Perhaps a more sensitive person can pick up more things, and some things earlier than others. Another issue is whether a person can precognize events other than those that he or she will actually "experience" at some level (even if that experience is received vicariously through learning about the event, perhaps even learning about it telepathically). Could Nostradamus or St. John truly precognize events that occurred beyond their lifetimes? Can a person receive information from the future telepathically from both her- or himself as well as from other people? Possibly it is "easier" for most people to receive information from the future from one's future self, but that does not preclude receiving future information from others.

Assuming that we can precognize the future, at least to some extent (as the evidence clearly indicates), what does this say about the future and the nature of time? Is, somehow, the future fully set and predetermined? Or perhaps, only partially predetermined? Can our perception of the future modify and influence our actions in the present, which in turn may change the future? Is time linear, strictly a one-way cause in the present to effect in the future, or can time effectively be reversed in some cases ("cause" in the future leading to "effect" in the present or even past)?

Consider an interesting case collected by parapsychologist Louisa E. Rhine (recounted by E. Douglas Dean in his chapter in the 1974 book *Psychic Exploration*). A mother dreamt that in two hours a violent storm would rock the house, causing a heavy chandelier that hung from the ceiling over her baby's crib to fall on the baby's head, killing the baby. She woke up, and woke her husband to tell him the dream. He dismissed it as nonsense, especially since the weather was calm, and suggested she go back to sleep. Instead, she brought the baby to her own bed. Two hours later a storm did arise and cause the chandelier to come crashing down on the crib, landing where the baby's head would have been. But, the baby was not now there.

What do we make of this precognition? Did the mother's actions change the future, saving the baby? Could she have ignored the dream with the result that it would have been fully fulfilled, and the baby would have died? Is it possible that the baby was always "destined" (some might call it predestined) to be saved? Was the mother's dream a mixture of the future (the chandelier falling on the crib) and her own fears and anxieties (that the baby would be hit on the head and die)? Another way of phrasing the issue is to ask if the mother had free will to decide whether or not to move the baby from the crib. The whole business of precognition raises numerous unsettling questions, questions which for many people defy logic and commonsense. But, if precognition is real, as I believe it is, we must squarely face such issues wherever they may lead.

## 12

# THE PSI IN CSI

*Today's Detectives Are Probing in Other Dimensions*

**BY BARBARA JASON**

Are police departments today more willing to utilize techniques other than the traditional—including the psychic—to solve crime? Do ongoing developments in forensic science and technology obviate the use of the mind in criminal detection? Where does the future lead us?

In truth, the traditional role of the detective is itself a relatively new development in law enforcement. An outgrowth of the recognized need for specialists who could keep some distance from ordinary street policing led to the development of a group of specialists who could apply their entire workday to solving one type of crime. Often dressed in ordinary clothing and carrying badges of a particular color, the "detective" soon created an aura of respect and dedication to which the ordinary uniformed "cop" could only aspire.

The "art" of detection itself has a formal history of little more than a century. Holding strong roots in the fictional epics of such writers as Edgar Allen Poe, Sir Arthur Conan Doyle, and later Agatha Christie, the detective himself is an evolving creation.

The word "detect" implies the use of thought to recognize a crime—what Agatha Christie's Hercule Poirot would have referred to as his "little gray cells"—although the ordinary police detective is usually presented with a crime, and asked to solve it by whatever means he can.

As any fan of the hit TV series *CSI* can tell you, modern advances in biochemistry, DNA, spectroscopic analysis, and even botany are the tools of today's laboratory "detectives." CSI, of course stands for Crime Scene Investigation, and refers to the accelerating science of forensics. Developments in this exciting field have led to such real achievements as the identification of the long-buried corpse of Jesse James, convicted murderers with as little to go on as the torn segment of green plant caught in the bed of a pickup truck, and pulled off many other celebrated triumphs. Wayne Williams, Atlanta's serial killer, for example, was inextricably connected to his victims by a bit of twisted blue-green rug fiber. Indeed, the arsenal of forensic science promises to make any crime, no matter how old or esoteric, solvable.

Psi crime scene investigation

Could developments such as these tend to diminish and render obsolete what was once the detective's best tool—his mind?

No way, cry the traditionalists, pointing with pride to the FBI's Violent Crime Apprehension Program (VICAP), itself a recent development in criminalistics. Through computer analysis, complete projections may be made of the general and sometimes specific physical and physiological characteristics of murderers, especially those known as serial or "repeater" killers.

At the FBI's National Center for the Analysis of Violent Crime (NCAVC), investigative and operational support functions, research, and training are combined in order to provide assistance, without charge, to federal, state, local, and foreign law enforcement agencies investigating unusual or repetitive violent crimes. The NCAVC also provides support through expertise and consultation in non-violent matters such as national security, corruption, and white-collar crime investigations.

Even the creators of the VICAP program, however, will admit that computerized profiling will not by itself solve a crime, no matter how detailed and accurate. There is still the need for the knowledge, talent, and dedication of any one of the specialized unit's "experts." Profiling is a pointing finger, a clue, and a place to begin seeking for the hidden personality behind the profile. Technological advances have not yet and never will replace the trained senses of the human mind.

## DEDUCTIVE VS. INDUCTIVE

Sherlock Holmes was a fictional character given to hallucinogens, acute observation, and pronouncements on obscurities overlooked by bumbling British Police Inspectors and even his amanuensis, Dr. Watson. He, then, was a master of one form of detection, the deductive. Though Sir Arthur Conan Doyle, his creator, was himself a strong proponent of the so-called "supernatural," he never introduced any hint of this into the actions or revelations of his fictional detective. Holmes was careful always to tie up his "clues" by their tails and make them fit naturally into what seemed like brilliant deductive reasoning. And brilliant it would have been, had there really been a Sherlock Holmes. To deduce, then, is defined as the ability to infer from a set of facts or observations, and to reach a conclusion by reasoning.

Induction is reasoning as well, but unlike deductive reasoning (sometimes called "top-down reasoning," or "reductive reasoning"), it relies more on extrapolating or generalizing from a set of facts (known also as "bottom-up reasoning"). In this way, induction brings forth facts and evidence—everything that is known—in order to "lead on, influence or persuade." Induction then is a similar but not quite identical form of thinking. Inductive reasoning allows more room for the bright flash of inspiration, the intuitive "gut" sense of the veteran observer of human criminality, and even the input of that more developed insight often referred to as "psychic." Could the possibilities offered in what is termed the psi arena provide another dimension to the quest of the forensic investigator?

In a 1994 paper in the *Psychological Bulletin*, Daryl J. Bern and Charles Honorton defined psi as denoting anomalous processes of information or energy transfer, processes such as telepathy or other forms of extrasensory perception that are currently unexplained in terms of known physical or biological mechanisms.

In the forensic area, if we accept the hunch of the seasoned police detective, then we may logically take the next step and admit that these flashes of insight into a crime can rarely be backed up by the evidence or fact. These are merely regarded as normal and useful tools of veteran officers. They may later be confirmed by fact, but at the time they occur, they cannot be so explained. Dr. Marcello Truzzi, Ph.D. refers to such occurrences as a "blue sense." It is perhaps odd that some detectives can have such an ephemeral experience upon first sight of a crime scene or the body of a murder victim. There may be no facts to support such a "hunch" until the case is solved by ordinary means.

Such intuitive flashes are as common in police annals as in airplane cockpits where pilots, no matter how advanced the instrumentation, constantly admit to feelings, hunches, and "flying by the seat of their pants." It is precisely to this acceptance of unexplainable intuitive leaps that a decision to use the input of a "police psychic" may be related.

It is often the wiser head of a departmental higher-up or even a Chief of Police who will make the decision to seek or actually deploy such psychic input. The idea is to leave no stone unturned.

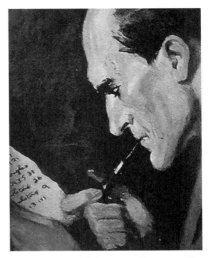
Sherlock Holmes, as illustrated by Frank Wiles, *Strand* Magazine, 1914

Regardless of the purported statistical studies and evaluations so dear to the hearts of professional skeptics, police, both uniformed and plain-clothed, often seek such help. Departments in larger metropolitan areas do so on a regular basis, while smaller police units are often even more likely to seek such help. A quiet but real police "grapevine" exists whereby departments seeking such help may call another whose successful use of psychic help has reached their ears.

According to Truzzi, "studies on the frequency of use (of psychic help) by police departments are incorrect, as one department protested they have not used this resource, although there was good evidence they had." In many cases, says Truzzi, "a smaller department may be more likely to seek this type of help than a larger metropolitan police force." In another study done by Montana Crime Attack Team head Dr. Raymond Worring, it was found that approximately half the departments surveyed had used intuitive help at one time or another. In such cases, the individual responding to the questionnaire may himself be unaware of the usage, or it may have occurred before that person was involved with that department.

## PSYCHIC DETECTIVES

One might, indeed, wonder what inspires a clairvoyant man or woman to offer their services (mostly free of charge) to police. It may be the same urge that leads others to join rescue squads, volunteer fire departments, or search and rescue teams—a simple desire to be of assistance. The motive seems unlikely to be self-serving, since those who psychically assist face hours of work, no pay, and little if any, publicity, unless the case is a "big one," and even then only when the case is over.

Those who volunteer to offer such assistance come from several categories, one of which is the "average Joe" who may be watching TV coverage or reading about a case, and feels suddenly that he knows something about it. Into this category also fall those who may for some unknown reason have nightmares about a crime and later find something similar has occurred. These individuals frequently feel very confident that they know something that can help the investigators.

Police are naturally cautious and skeptical about such unsolicited "tips," and many times the input is rarely recorded or checked out. Yet in a few such cases the information has produced genuine results.

We must exclude from this category the unsolicited calls from the so-called "kook squad" who bombard police with irrational theories, arcane conspiracy details, or those that themselves "confess" to the crimes in question.

Another category is the professional psychic reader, whose clientele may occasionally include a family member of a crime victim, and who may offer information to that person, which then may or may not be passed on to the police. Often the victim's family may introduce their own personal psychic into a case.

The final two categories are different, in that the individual psychic may already be known to the police, and have a track record, good or bad. The well-known Peter Hurkos was one of those psychics who had an undeniable track record, was introduced into cases by a sponsoring individual, and received a fee for his services.

It is in this category that most crime psychics fit. They often do personal readings and criminal work as only a part-time occupation. Success in any given case will naturally enhance their reputations and enlarge their clientele.

The next category includes those who do not do readings for the public, and extend their services free of charge to law enforcement agencies of any kind. This group is much smaller and includes such individuals as Dorothy Allison, and the U.S. Psi Squad, a group which includes working police officers and ex-police, all of whom have been trained to utilize their inherent psi abilities, including what is now known as remote viewing.

Remote viewing is described as the ability to utilize the trained sensitivities of the mind to actually see (in the mind's eye) beyond the perceived barriers of time and space. Both Russian and U.S. authorities have attempted such training, and a third such effort has recently begun in mainland China.

Within this last small group is an even smaller one, composed of those members of former military or SRI Remote-Viewers, some of whom accept criminal case referrals from police. It is these last two groups that most police seek when they feel a need for the psychic detective.

Although portrayed as a "last resort" by skeptics, several members of these groups have been called into cases within hours of the crime itself.

In one case, a police chief from medium-sized Belleville, Illinois, called in the Missouri-based Psi Squad on the day following the disappearance of 14-year-old Elizabeth West. The group's leader, the late Beverly Jaegers, immediately upon handling clothing belonging to the child and a photograph, announced that the child had been kidnapped for sexual assault and murdered, her body discarded in a watery ditch. A description of the assailant was given, including his Elvis-style sideburns, the information that his name began with the letter B, and that he would be caught in the commission of another such crime. These detailed observations were presented to the chief investigator along with a map of the dump-site, marked with a specific X, and a location where the killer himself stayed when in town. Several numbers were included, one of which was a large 5.

Two days later (on the 5th of the month) the girl's body was found in the exact area of the X'ed location, in a small stream flowing along a deep-sided ditch. Another similar kidnap and killing of young woman followed (by the same killer, according to the Psi Squad), and then a third attempt was made on another victim. The killer forced another young woman into his vehicle. She managed to escape, but remembered important details about the kidnapper and his license plate. Sent to jail for attempted kidnap, Bowman was finally confessed to the two killings, and was tried and convicted for the kidnap and murder of Elizabeth West. The narrow-faced murderer not only possessed long Elvis-type sideburns, but resided when in Belleville within the very location pinpointed by Jaegers.

Reams of information had been produced by the psychically trained team and a large proportion of this has proved to be accurate.

There are many such stories in the annals of cooperative efforts between police and psychics or remote viewers dedicated to this type of work, although not all of them reach the pages of the newspaper.

## SHOULD POLICE USE PSYCHICS?

Laughing at a fact or denying its existence will not make it go away. An elephant remains an elephant, though some may call it a giraffe.

Evidential research at institutions of higher learning has proven the ability of the human mind to push the envelope and avoid or surmount the barriers of time as well as distance. Included in the growing field of Psi research is work done at Princeton's Engineering Anomalies Research Laboratory, Stanford Research Institute, and University of Nevada's Consciousness Research Lab headed by Dr. Dean Radin. Many dedicated and forward-looking police have said, "If it works, don't fix it. If it's helpful, use it."

Whether this type of help has always provided specific or evidential information is not the question. What is most important is that they were called upon at all.

Those who are not helpful will be winnowed out in the future processes of criminal investigation.

Where is the future? It lies in the potential of adding this now less unusual method of crime investigation to the training and operations procedures of those uniformed officers and detectives who investigate the crimes.

Research into remote viewing shows not only its probative value, but the fact that this "seeing in the mind's eye" can be done at any distance. A user, then, need not be in the actual place where a crime occurred, and information from months or even years before may be retrieved and put to use. Information exists showing that the ability exists in all minds, and although it cannot be "created" it can be enhanced and developed, like any other innate human potential.

# PART THREE

# SUPER POWERS

Harry Houdini

# 13

# THE CURIOUS DEATH
# OF HARRY HOUDINI

*Did the Great Magician Break His Final Bonds?*
*. . . Or Not?*

## BY JOHN CHAMBERS

Five traits usually characterize the classical tragic hero, according to the experts. He (or she) is born into humble circumstances; from early on he performs great feats of strength; he rapidly rises to the heights of fame; he is abruptly brought down through hubris or excessive pride; and, however briefly, he returns from the dead. Harry Houdini, who lived from 1874 to 1926—and who was arguably the greatest escape artist of all time—seemed in his day to embody all five of these characteristics. Born in Budapest and brought to Appleton, Wisconsin, by Jewish-Hungarian parents when he was 4, he was of poverty-stricken origin. Like King Arthur or Davie Crockett, he early demonstrated great strength, leaving home at 12, taking up the trade of a vaudeville/circus showman in his teens, and becoming famous as an escape artist in Europe in his early twenties. He rose to the pinnacle of fame in his thirties, electrifying the American public with feats like being lowered into the East River in midwinter bolted into a coffin and emerging an hour later, or regularly escaping from straitjackets while suspended upside-down from tall buildings.

The final two classic traits of the tragic hero did not fail to raise their somber faces before this snub-nosed bullet of a man who, at 5 feet 4 inches and 150 pounds, was a wiry mass of exquisitely trained muscle. The first of these was his sudden and unexpected death at the age of 52. To some extent, this death stemmed from Houdini's hubris or overreaching pride—the same flaw that felled Achilles and Oedipus. The great escape artist had challenged anyone in the world to test his claim that his abdominal muscles were so powerfully developed they could take any punch without his being injured. As Houdini sat relaxing in his dressing room on October 22, 1926, after a standing room-only performance at the Princess Theater, in Montreal, Canada, a 22-year-old McGill University student took him up on his challenge, and almost without warning delivered a volley of blows to Houdini's stomach. The showman immediately got up, thanked the student for coming, and walked him to the door. But, as he left his dressing room that night, Houdini was already in pain. The next night, in Detroit, Michigan, it was hubris as much as courage that kept him going through his performance even though his temperature was 104 and he was in excruciating pain. He was rushed to the hospital after the show was over; doctors operated and removed a ruptured appendix and, probably, a ruptured pancreas. They saw that virulent peritonitis was spreading fast. Antibiotics did not exist then; eight days later, on October 31, 1926, after a heroic struggle, the great escape artist had failed to escape the jaws of death.

Yet once more Houdini would seem to show himself a hero in the classical mold. This fierce debunker of mediumship had sworn to his wife, Bess, that he would somehow send her an encoded message from the spirit world

after his death. Bess offered a $10,000 reward to the medium who could deliver Houdini's message. More than two years after Houdini's death—at the end of three months of séances—celebrated psychic Arthur Ford transmitted the decoded words "ROSABELLE BELIEVE" to an exultant Bess. Houdini's wife vowed that this was the agreed-upon message. After all, these were the words inscribed inside her wedding band. All around the world, the media trumpeted the news of the great escape artist's ultimate escape; for one brief moment, Houdini was as famous dead as he had been alive. Then, skepticism set in, even on the part of Bess, who began to doubt; still,

Houdini and his wife Bess

such was the charisma of Houdini—even in death—that there were many who continued to believe.

Even during his lifetime, particularly among his fellow professionals, Houdini was known to be somewhat less than a saint. There were those who claimed he owed his fame to his prodigious powers of self-promotion. His espousal of certain social causes was seen to be merely an expression of his rabid publicity-seeking. Houdini spent much of his time exposing phony mediums, even attending their séances incognito and re-enacting their hoaxes onstage. These activities—which included his testifying before Congress in favor of a bill banning mediumship, fortune telling, and other occult (a bill which sank into oblivion amid derision)—were considered by many stage professionals to be the height of hypocrisy. Houdini had, after all, been a fake medium himself in his early years. He had frequented séances after his mother had died. Bitterness over not receiving a posthumous message from her was thought to be the only other motive—aside from self-promotion—behind his obsessive and vicious medium-bashing.

As the power of Houdini's charisma has faded over the years, more and more of his contemporaries and near-contemporaries have come forward to enumerate the warts on this complex and contradictory figure. William V. Rauscher is a researcher into psychic phenomena who is also a clergyman and a professional magician. He knew many of these witnesses to the dark side of Houdini. In *The Houdini Code Mystery: A Spirit Secret Solved* (2000) a book intended primarily for professional magicians, Rauscher assembles their testimony. A sad conclusion emerges: Houdini, for all his unquestioned courage, persistence, and skills, was not really a hero in the classical mold, but only as much of a hero as our present tawdry modern era can allow—if that. The sometimes harsh glare of Mr. Rauscher's analysis throws light from a new angle on that most mysterious of all the Houdini conundrums: whether or not he really spoke from the afterworld.

Central to Houdini's character, Mr. Rauscher suggests, was a mother fixation so severe that "even as a grown man he liked to sit on her knee, his head resting on her breast, listening to her heart." Receiving in the midst of a Copenhagen press conference the cable informing him of her death, "he crumpled to the floor in a dead faint." In obedience to his written instructions, a bundle of his mother's letters tied with a red ribbon was placed under his head in his coffin and buried with him. Bound up with his mother fixation was the fact of Houdini's being "literally frozen" in the presence of any other woman except for his wife Bess, says Rauscher. This mute terror, along with an absence of acting ability, scuttled his brief career as a film star; he was completely unable to play up to his leading lady. Rauscher concludes that the Great Houdini was at the very least infertile (he and Bess never had children), and most likely impotent.

Out of this brew of impotence and Oedipal rage arose the harsh negative elements which helped drive Harry Houdini to success. Many were his sins, Mr. Rauscher's informants testify: he stole acts from other performers and sometimes sabotaged their performances; he bribed people to swear he had performed feats that he hadn't, such as his alleged escape from a Chicago police station in 1901; his assistants attempted to maim one of his competitors (the German escape artist "Minerva") by putting acid in her water barrel. His detractors assert that Houdini routinely lied about his past and was regularly mean, violent, and brutish—not incapable of generosity, but always unpredictable. The portrait of the great escape artist that emerges from Rauscher's book is one that makes it believable that Houdini could have, well before his death, arranged his triumphal return from the dead.

That is not at all, however, the drift of Rauscher's argument. Rather, the author shifts our attention from the somewhat shabby Houdini to his somewhat shabby contemporaries, notably the celebrated psychic Arthur Ford. Rauscher says that Ford was a close friend of his for 15 years until Ford's death in 1972. He explains that "Ford, an urbane, educated, emotionally up-and-down personality, often reminisced wryly and sometimes wistfully (but never, to me, cynically) about 'the good old days.' Curiously, he would never, except on the rarest exceptions, discuss the Houdini Message episode. However, he could reflect on a vast mass of former 'sitters' (as a medium's clients are called) ranging from movie stars and the intelligentsia to royalty. He had a rare gift (along with less admirable traits, such as episodic alcoholism, a touch of fraud, and a confused sexual identity) of not taking himself seriously—in private at least."

Whatever his reservations about Ford's character, Rauscher also declares, "If you ask me, 'Do you really believe that Ford sometimes—not always, not perhaps regularly, but sometimes—talked with the dead,' the evidence of my own experience compels me to answer: YES!"

The "Houdini Code Message" was allegedly delivered to Ford through his spirit guide, "Fletcher," over the course of nine long and tortuous séances conducted from November 28, 1928, to January 5, 1929. Little more than a word or phrase was produced each session, to finally render up the encoded message: "ROSABELLE... ANSWER... TELL... PRAYANSWER... LOOK-TELL... ANSWER."

Despite Bess's immediate insistence that "Rosabelle believe" was indeed the agreed-upon message, accusations of fraud surfaced within two days. On January 9, Rea Jaure of the *New York Graphic*—one of the reporters who had been present at the final séance—declared that the message was a hoax engineered by Ford and Bess with the connivance of none other than Rea Jaure herself. This cynical claim, advanced to sell newspapers, had to be quashed in the courts, even though not a shred of evidence had been forthcoming from the start, and Ford and Bess had issued stout denials.

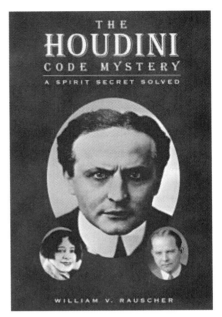

Houdini Book

The world-famous "mentalist" William Dunninger entered the fray almost as quickly, declaring that fraud had been committed by a 28-year-old "fish handler at the Fulton Market" named Joseph Bantano and a curvaceous onetime stage assistant to Houdini named Daisy White. Again, not a shred of evidence was brought forward; when Daisy White threatened to sue for libel, Dunninger dropped the charges.

Arthur Ford had been fairly well known as a medium at the time; with his role in the *Houdini Code Message,* his career took off. This was in no way altered by Bess's changing her mind, at least publicly, in 1938, and declaring that "Rosabelle believe" was not the posthumous message agreed upon by her and Houdini. Those who wished to keep believing could find many good psychological and practical reasons for Bess's denial, and the legend has lived on, with its detractors and supporters, right up to our day.

The new piece of evidence which Rauscher offers comes from one Jay Abbott, a New York Spiritualist and close long-time friend of both Ford and Bess, who spoke to Rauscher in April, 1973—just three months before Abbott's own death in July.

Abbott told Rauscher that Ford and Bess frequently dated before the final Houdini séance, that Bess had been in love with Ford, and that one day while in her apartment with Ford her ring had fallen off as she was washing her hands and Ford had momentarily retrieved it. That was how, asserted Abbott, Ford had become the only other person in the world besides Bess and the dead Houdini to know the words inscribed inside the ring. Ford had used this knowledge in the final séance.

Abbott insisted that Bess had known nothing about this deceit. But, for author William Rauscher, the New York Spiritualist's belated declaration is final proof of something which the author had suspected for many years, namely, that, "Arthur Ford and Bess Houdini were in full cahoots. It was a mutually agreed-upon grand and glorious hoax. Both were full partners. It was like Ragtime and the Roaring Twenties all rolled into one!"

Rauscher's contention has engendered some controversy. A story appearing in *The New York Times* for June 5, 2000, on New York's Parapsychology Foundation, mentioned a talk on *The Houdini Code Message* given by Rauscher at the Foundation a few days earlier. A *Times* reporter asked eminent scientific investigator of the paranormal Hans Holzer, present at the talk, what he thought of Rauscher's lecture. The *Times* quotes Holzer's reply: "It was a waste of time; it had nothing to do with parapsychology. Let me put it this way: I never trust a magician fully. Magicians believe firmly that psychic phenomena are all fake."

Steve Metcalfe, a long-time parapsychologist living in Flagstaff, Arizona, asserts that Rauscher, in assuming a total hoax, finds himself caught up in a fundamental contradiction. "On the one hand, he says Arthur Ford actually did sometimes communicate with the dead. But if he says this, he has to accept that Ford's 'control spirit,' Fletcher—or whatever energies Fletcher represents—had some sort of objective reality bound up with the control spirit's connection to an 'afterworld.'"

What role then, asks Metcalfe, would Fletcher have played in the ten séances which culminated in "Fletcher's" delivering the fake final two-word message to Bess? Was Ford so easily able to persuade Fletcher to go along with the conspiracy? Was he so easily able to put his spirit control aside and make everything up himself?

Metcalfe contends that if Ford was able to do these things so easily, then "he wasn't really psychic, and he never really communicated with the dead." But, says Metcalfe, Rauscher asserts that Ford did sometimes communicate with the dead: "Then, I think, he has to deal with the problem of what role Fletcher played in this conspiracy. I think the presence of a real Fletcher, with all the unpredictability you get in channeling phenomena, would have made it very difficult for Ford to pull off a hoax in any sort of a systematic way."

If the characters of Ford and Bess are slightly questionable, so too is that of Jay Abbott; Rauscher's quotes suggest that Abbott was speaking from a less-than-perfect memory, and/or that he might have had an ax of his own to grind regarding some long-ago, vaguely defined triangular relationship stemming from the confused sexual identity not only of Arthur Ford, but perhaps also of Jay Abbott. The real truth behind the Houdini Code Message séances may be so complex and elusive that they may, to a small but significant extent, exist only in the minds of the various beholders. Rauscher may have clearly stated one part of the truth; the whole truth may also partake of shifting worlds well beyond our own, and impenetrable even to the wily presence of a Harry Houdini.

## 14

# DEFYING GRAVITY

*Could Technology Invented Almost 90 Years Ago*
*Lead to an Antigravity Science? Physicist Paul La Violette*
*Sees Even Greater Possibilities*

**BY LEN KASTEN**

everal books and websites have appeared recently which give reports by insiders about what sort of incredible technology advances have been developed in the so-called black world—the realm of secret military-scientific development. Most of these cite anecdotal evidence and give spare details about the underlying science. However, a recent book by Paul A. LaViolette, *Secrets of Antigravity Propulsion: Tesla, UFOs and Classified Aerospace Technology* (2008) offers complete coverage, including a history of the secret development of antigravity craft, and a comprehensive, detailed discussion of the scientific basis of antigravity technology.

LaViolette is a physicist with a B.A. from Johns Hopkins and a Ph.D from Portland State University; but by reason of his ever-expanding research in astronomy, cosmology, metaphysics, mythology, archaeology, and aeronautics, he has evolved into a multi-disciplinary authority. His efforts to bring these widely diverse studies into a unified view have led to some very surprising hypotheses and discoveries.

*Atlantis Rising* readers may recall our article about his book, *The Talk of the Galaxy* (2000) in which he discussed his theory that pulsars were really beacons put in place by advanced intragalactic civilizations to warn of impending cataclysmic "superwaves" originating in the center of

Paul LaViolette

Defying Gravity

the galaxy and rippling out to the galactic fringes (which is where we are). He is, perhaps, best known for having developed a much more believable alternative to the Big Bang theory. As early as 1986, he showed convincingly that the Big Bang does not fit modern astronomical data; and then in his book *Genesis of the Cosmos* (2004) he made a highly convincing case for a doctrine of "continuous creation" of matter originating in the center of the galaxy out of an all-pervasive etheric flux or "subquantum" matrix, and recycling through Black Holes.

## THE POST NEWTONIAN ERA

*Secrets of Antigravity Propulsion* penetrates the black world of the military-industrial complex by explaining the "Buck Rogers" scientific innovations being developed and utilized in that world. It could only have been written by an iconoclastic physicist like LaViolette who was able to gather up and make sense of the clues that dribbled out of the secret scientific inner-sanctum and put them together brilliantly to present a coherent picture. Maybe it could also have been written by any one of the aeronautical scientists who have been working at a high theoretical level inside the black realm, but since they have all been sworn to inviolable secrecy under threat of "losing their firstborn," that will never happen. A rogue scientist like LaViolette, who has never been involved in that world, is under no such restriction. Prior to putting these clues together, LaViolette first establishes the theoretical foundation of electrogravitics and discusses the discoveries and experiments of T. Townsend Brown, the single greatest, if not the only, pioneer in the field. LaViolette fits it all into Brown's experimental framework. What emerges is a perhaps fuzzy but comprehensible picture of how the military has been utilizing antigravity technology. That picture becomes much clearer though when LaViolette reveals the top-secret, technological details of the B-2 "Spirit" Bomber.

While the scientific explanations given by LaViolette in the book may be, perhaps, somewhat complicated for the lay reader, they deliver a level of technical proof that could never be provided by a journalist, or even by a conventional physicist. As one plows through the science, the conviction grows that LaViolette has, although through somewhat abstruse scientific logic, nevertheless given powerful evidence of these sensational technological developments. At the end, the reader realizes that the world he or she believed in has effectively been demolished, and the "real world" is as different from the old as the Copernican era was from the Ptolemaic. To now learn that we have mastered a means of aircraft propulsion that is based on new post-Newtonian physics—one that requires no fuel and can accomplish superluminal (faster than light) velocities which opens the pathways to the stars—is no less shattering than suddenly discovering that the Earth actually revolves around the Sun after believing for thousands of years that it was stationary.

## Secret Science

LaViolette devotes three chapters to Thomas Townsend Brown's career and his work. Born in 1905 in Zanesville, Ohio, Brown dreamed from childhood of space travel and experimented with devices that displayed exotic propulsion. While in high school, he discovered the electrogravitic effect when he observed that a high-voltage vacuum tube moved slightly whenever the power was turned on. This motivated him to construct something he called a "gravitator." This was a wooden box, two-feet long and four-inches square, containing alternate conductive plates of lead and insulating dialectric sheets. When charged with 150,000 volts of electricity, the gravitator exhibited a thrust in the direction of the positive end. When oriented on end with the positive end up, it lost weight. In 1922, when he was just 17, Brown took out a patent on the gravitator and, it can be argued, initiated the age of antigravity. In later experimentation, it turned out that the greater the insulating capacity of the dialectric, the more electric charge the device could contain, and consequently the greater the thrust. Dialectric capacity is rated in terms of a value referred to as "k." If the k value could be made high enough by using exotic materials, the device could be launched at great acceleration. He then suspended two gravitators from a rotating arm, with both positive poles pointing in the same direction.

When charged with between 75,000 and 300,000 volts, the rotating arm revolved in the direction of the positive poles. Essentially, this was a primitive electrogravitic motor. Brown attended the California Institute of Technology, and then transferred to Dennison University in Granville, Ohio. At Dennison, he worked with Dr. Paul A. Biefeld, a physics professor interested in dialectrics. As a result of this collaboration, the electrogravitic phenomenon became known as the Biefeld-Brown effect.

Of great interest here is the fact that, in 1933, Brown was apparently recruited into a top-secret international intelligence network called the Caroline Group by U.S. businessman Eldridge Johnston and British master spy William S. Stephenson (the man called "Intrepid"). This could explain why so many doors were opened for him to do government sponsored research and development throughout his career; and it is clearly the reason he was chosen to participate in the famous Philadelphia Experiment in October of 1943, along with such distinguished scientists as Albert Einstein, Vannevar Bush, John von Neumann, and Nikola Tesla. Brown joined the Navy as an officer after Pearl Harbor; and in the summer of 1942 he

T. T. Brown and Disk

was assigned to work at the Atlantic Fleet Radar School in Philadelphia, where he remained until the end of 1943, which places him there at the time of the Experiment. The extent of Brown's involvement in the Philadelphia Experiment is not clear. According to William Moore and Charles Berlitz in *The Philadelphia Experiment* (1995), Brown was very much involved. They interpret the fact that he did not contradict their account of his participation when given the opportunity to corroborate. On the other hand, Gerry Vassilatos in his book *Lost Science* (2000) says that Brown bowed out prior to the test on the Eldridge. In any case, Brown had a nervous breakdown two months later, and retired from the navy in December 1943 on the advice of a team of naval physicians. Some see this as indicating that Brown was severely rattled by the well-known tragic results of the experiment, in which sailors were said to have been imbedded into the hull of the ship.

After the war Brown continued his electrogravitic work, financed by his own organization, the Townsend Brown Foundation. He continually improved his results and refined the scientific underpinnings of the effects. Then, in 1953, in an effort to obtain government funding for his experiments, he felt confident enough of to propose that the Navy initiate a 10-year project to develop a manned flying saucer utilizing electrogravitic propulsion with a Mach 3 capability, to be used as an interceptor. He envisioned large discs operating at 5 million volts that could reach a velocity of 1,800 mph in the upper atmosphere. This proposal became known as Project Winterhaven. Perhaps the most revolutionary and important aspect of the Winterhaven document was Brown's proposal for "flame-jet" electrostatic generators. These would be modifications to the jet engines to electrify the exhaust stream turning the engines into powerful electro-hydrodynamic generators to provide the extremely high voltages needed for high-speed electrogravitic thrust. Brown's goal was not military supremacy; he hoped that government funding would hasten the use of electrogravitic propulsion for civilian transportation. The Navy showed no interest, possibly because they already had top-secret development programs under way that were actually technologically more advanced. Apparently, at that point, Brown no longer had access to the top-secret world, probably because of his breakdown and resignation from the Navy. But, it is known that Brown continued to consult to aerospace companies connected to secret military development until his retirement in the 1970s.

## THE ANTIGRAVITY BOMBER

In chapter 5 of LaViolette's book titled "The U.S. Antigravity Squadron," he tells us that an article in the March, 1992, issue of *Aviation Week Magazine* "made the surprising disclosure that the B-2 electrostatically charges its exhaust stream and the leading edges of its winglike body." In other words, the B-2 Bomber uses electrogravitic propulsion. The magazine obtained the information from a group of renegade West Coast scientists and engineers who broke the code of silence, and literally risked their lives by making the disclosure. The B-2 contract was awarded to Northrop Aviation in 1981. Northrop had been experimenting with the electrification of leading wings since 1968 when their scientists reported that their results showed that "when high-voltage DC is applied to a wing-shaped structure subjected to supersonic flow, seemingly new 'electro-aerodynamic' qualities appear." Brown's influence on the Northrop work is evident. From what is known about the B-2's technology and flight characteristics, LaViolette extrapolates the probable principles of its design and makes a very convincing case that the B-2 incorporates much of Brown's research and development. This is most apparent in the four GE-100 jet engines, which seem to incorporate Brown's "flame-jet" principles. He says, "The B-2, then, may be the first military antigravity vehicle to be openly displayed to the public! It may be the final realization of the kind of craft that Brown had proposed in Project Winterhaven and that the 1956 Aviation Studies report had disclosed was beginning to be developed by the military in late 1954. Consequently, the designation 'B-2' might more appropriately stand for Biefeld-Brown effect."

LaViolette says that, in 1997, a three-star general told retired Air Force colonel Donald Ware that "the new Lockheed-Martin space shuttle and the B-2 both have electrogravitic systems on board.... Thus, after taking off conventionally, the B-2 can switch to antigravity mode, and, I have heard, fly around the world without refueling."

## THE NEW CLASSIFIED PHYSICS

While the black aerospace development world has many national security reasons for remaining secret, there is another less obvious, but nevertheless critical reason. It turns out that the phenomena observed and used in antigravity propulsion are not explainable by classical physics, and therefore there are no scientists being graduated from conventional universities who have any idea about how it works! Consequently, all the theoretical work must be taught and contained inside the black world, since it embraces what LaViolette refers to as the new "classified" physics. He claims that one of the informants of the B-2 propulsion system, who he calls Ray, told him that "the physics theories that academics and most laboratory physicists currently understand, teach, and write about are grossly in error." He claimed that the "classical concepts" are "terribly outdated." He told LaViolette that the new physics "postulates the existence of an underlying reality consisting of an...unobservable subtle substance called an ether...which fills all space.... This new physics regards time and space as absolutes and views Einstein's notion of relative time and space as incorrect.... Thus, the ether concept, so long spurned by the academic establishment, turns out to be central to this highly classified new physics."

Ray claimed that ether physics embraces Brown's electrogravitics phenomenon as well as the research that Brown conducted with the Navy (the Philadelphia Experiment?) and much of Tesla's work. LaViolette has evolved a new theoretical framework for the new physics that he calls "subquantum kinetics," which he refers to as an open system that "begins with an ether as its point of departure." He says, "Unlike closed systems, open systems allow the possibility for order to emerge from disorder. Under the proper conditions, the ether is able to spawn subatomic particles that have wavelike characteristics. They form spontaneously from energy fluctuations of sufficiently large magnitude that occasionally emerge from the ether's chaos. Thus, subquantum kinetics espouses a cosmology of continuous matter creation rather than a single big bang creation event." So, subquantum kinetics can be seen as another piece of LaViolette's over-arching cosmological theory as presented in *Genesis of the Cosmos*. It seems to tie in nicely with the now popular Fractal Geometry theory of Benoit Mandelbrot, which takes the position that there is an underlying aesthetic order to seemingly chaotic manifestations.

It seems that we are entering a new era when the old scientific and philosophical bastions are starting to crumble, and the institutions based on those bastions, which have been sacred for so many years, must now also go down. The new physics seems to herald a new age of fantastic achievement, once we get past the pain of the transformation.

# 15

# DID OUR ANCESTORS KNOW HOW TO FLY?

## *There Could Be More than Poetry in the Ancient Scriptures*

### BY DAVID H. CHILDRESS

Throughout history there have been many common myths and legends of flying machines or devices—the familiar flying carpets of ancient Arabia; Biblical figures such as Ezekiel and Solomon flying from place to place; and the "magical chariots," or *vimanas*, of ancient India and China.

There are many Chinese legends of flight, including a legendary flying chariot belonging to an ancient Chinese prince and the more recent Wan Hoo of the 15th century AD or so. He allegedly built a sturdy wooden framework around a comfortable chair and attached 47 skyrockets to the back of the seat. Atop it he fastened two large kites. After strapping himself to the chair, he raised his hand to summon servants carrying blazing torches to advance toward the vehicle and ignite the skyrockets. A moment later there was a mighty blast, followed by an impressive cloud of black smoke. Wan Hoo vanished, leaving nothing behind but a legend.

Among the more famous ancient texts that mention aerial cars (vimanas) are the Ramayana and Mahabharata. Other lesser-known texts include the Samarangana Sutradhara, the Yuktikalpataru of Bhoja (12th century AD) the Mayamatam (attributed to the architect Maya celebrated in the Mahabharata), the Rig Veda, the Yajurveda, and the Ataharvaveda.

According to the Indian historian Ramachandra Dikshitar who wrote the still classic text on ancient Indian warfare, other texts that mention aerial vehicles and travels are the Satapathya Brahmanas; the Rig Veda Samhita; the Harivamsa; the Makandeya Purana; the Visnu Purana; the Vikramaurvasiya; the Uttararamacarita; the Harsacarita; the Tamil text Jivakocintamani; and the Samaranganasutradhara.

In the Manusa, the most elaborate details for building aerial machines are set down. The Samarangana Sutradhara says that they were made of light material, with a strong, well-shaped body. Iron, copper, mercury, and lead were used in their construction. They could fly to great distances and were propelled through air by motors. The Samarangana Sutradhara text devotes 230 stanzas to the building of these machines, and their uses in peace and war:

"Strong and durable must the body be made, like a great flying bird, of light material. Inside it one must place the Mercury engine with its iron heating apparatus beneath. By means of the power latent in the mercury which sets the driving whirlwind in motion, a man sitting inside may travel a great distance in the sky in a most marvelous manner.

Winged deity of Sumer

"Similarly by using the prescribed processes one can build a vimana as large as the temple of the God in motion. Four strong mercury containers must be built into the interior structure. When these have been heated by controlled fire from iron containers, the vimana develops thunderpower through the mercury. And at once it becomes a pearl in the sky.

"Moreover, if this iron engine with properly welded joints be filled with mercury, and the fire be conducted to the upper part, it develops power with the roar of a lion."

The Ramayana describes a vimana as a double-deck, circular (cylindrical) aircraft with portholes and a dome. It flew with the "speed of the wind" and gave forth a "melodious sound" (a humming noise?). Ancient Indian texts on vimanas are so numerous it would take several books to relate what they have to say. The ancient Indians themselves wrote entire flight manuals on the control of various types of vimanas, of which there

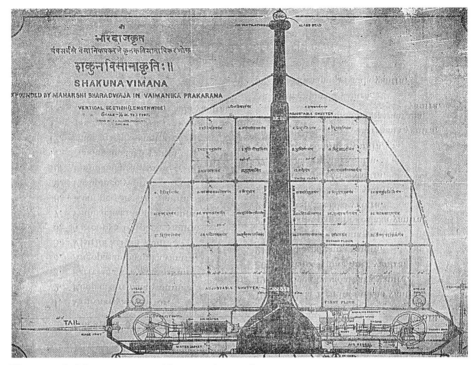

Diagram of a Vimana extracted from ancient scripture

were basically four: the Shakuna Vimana, the Sundara Vimana, the Rukma Vimana, and the Tripura Vimana.

The Vaimanika Sastra is perhaps the most important ancient text on vimanas known to exist. It was first reported to have been found in 1918 in the Baroda Royal Sanskrit Library. Baroda is located north of Bombay and south of Ahmedabad in Gujerat. No earlier copies have been reported, however, Swami Dayananda Saraswati in his comprehensive treatise on the Rig Veda, dated 1875, references the Vaimanaik Sastra in his commentary, as well as other manuscripts on Vimanas.

The Vaimanika Sastra refers to 97 past works and authorities, of which at least 20 works deal with the mechanism of aerial flying machines, but none of these works are now traceable. Says Sanskrit literature professor Dileep Kumar Kanjilal, Ph.D., of the West Bengal Senior Educational Service, "Since the transcripts of the work date from the early 20th century, the authenticity of the Vail Sastra may be pertinently questioned."

On careful analysis it has been found that the work retained some antique features pertaining to an old Sastra. Like the Sutras of Panini the rules have been laid down in an aphoristic style with the explanation couched in Vrittis and Karikas. The Sutra style is to be found in the earliest works on grammar, Smrti, and Philosophy, while the use of Karikas is as old as Batsyayana, Kautilya, and others of the early Christian era. Bharadwaja, the author of a Srauta Satra and Smrti work, is well known and a sage. Bharadwaja as the seer of the 6th mandala of the Rig Veda is also well known. Panini also referred to him in VII. II.63. Kautilya had also shown that Bharadwaja was an ancient author on politics. The Mbh. (Mahabharata, Santiparva Ch. 58.3) refers to Bharadwaja as an author on politics. Authors on politics have very often been found to have written on the technical sciences also. The genuineness, therefore, of any treatise on technical sciences composed by Bharadwaja cannot be ignored.

Says the Vaimanika Sastra about itself: "In this book are described in 8 pregnant and captivating chapters, the arts of manufacturing various types of Aeroplanes of smooth and comfortable travel in the sky, as a unifying force for the Universe, contributive to the wellbeing of mankind.

"That which can go by its own force, like a bird, on earth, or water, or air, is called 'Vimana.'

"That which can travel in the sky, from place to place, land to land, or globe to globe, is called 'Vimana' by scientists in Aeronautics."

The ancient manuscript claims to give "The secret of constructing aeroplanes, which will not break, which cannot be cut, will not catch fire, and cannot be destroyed.

"The secret of making planes motionless.

"The secret of making planes invisible.

"The secret of hearing conversations and other sounds in enemy planes.

"The secret of receiving photographs of the interior of enemy planes.

"The secret of ascertaining the direction of enemy planes' approach.

"The secret of making persons in enemy planes lose consciousness.

"The secret of destroying enemy planes."

The India of 15,000 years ago is sometimes known as the Rama Empire, a land that was contemporary with Atlantis. A huge wealth of texts still extant in India testify to the extremely advanced civilization that is said by these texts to go back over 26,000 years. Terrible wars and subsequent

Leonardo Da Vinci's design for a flying machine

earth changes destroyed these civilizations, leaving only isolated pockets of civilization.

The devastating wars of the Ramayana and particularly of the Mahabharata are said to have been the culmination of the terrible wars of the last Kali Yuga. The dating process is difficult, in that there is no exact way to date the yugas because there are cycles within cycles and yugas within yugas. A greater yuga cycle is said to last 6,000 years, while a smaller yuga cycle is only 360 years, in the theory expounded by Dr. Kunwarlal Jain Vyas. His papers said that Rama belongs to the twenty-fourth small yuga cycle and that there is an interval of 71 cycles between Manu and Mahabharata period, which comes out to be 26,000 years.

The legacy of Atlantis, the ancient Rama Empire, and vimanas reaches up to us today. The mysterious airship wave of the 1890s may well have been a sighting of ancient craft, still in working order, meandering slowly over the preflight world of late 19th century America.

In the latter years of the last century, a number of unusual airship sightings were made, which may well have been of vimana craft. In 1873 at Bonham, Texas, workers in a cotton field suddenly saw a shiny, silver object that came streaking down from the sky at them. Terrified, they ran away, while the "great silvery serpent," as some people described it, swung around and dived at them again. A team of horses ran away, the driver was thrown beneath the wheels of the wagon and killed. A few hours later that same day in Fort Riley, Kansas, a similar "airship" swooped down out of the skies at a cavalry parade and terrorized the horses to such an extent that the cavalry drill ended in a tumult.

The great "Airship Flap of 1897" actually started in November, 1896, in San Francisco, California, when hundreds of residents saw a large, elongated, dark object that used brilliant searchlights and moved against the wind, traveling northwest across Oakland. A few hours later, reports came from other northern California cities—Santa Rosa, Chico, Sacramento, and Red Bluff—all describing what appeared to be the same airship, a cigar-shaped craft. It is quite possible that this craft was heading for Mount Shasta in northern California.

The airship moved very slowly and majestically, flying low at times, and at night, shining its powerful searchlight on the ground. It is worth noting here, as Jacques Vallee did in his book *Dimensions* (2008), that the airship could do exactly as it cared to, because unlike today, it ran no risk of being pursued. There were no jet squadrons to be scrambled after the aerial intruder, no antiaircraft guns or surface-to-air missiles to shoot down this trespassing craft in the sky.

A question sometimes asked by vimana researchers is whether the ancient Indians and Atlanteans ever went to our Moon or to Mars? If mankind had such craft in ancient times, would they have created bases on the Moon and Mars just as we are planning to do today? If they had set up permanent bases, would they still be occupying them today?

This article has been excerpted for *Atlantis Rising* by the author from his book *Vimana Aircraft of Ancient India & Atlantis* (1995). Available from Adventures Unlimited Press.

## 16

# PSYCHOKINESIS

*Did the Cold War Heat Up the PK Research Front?*
*A Scientist Searches for the Reality Behind*
*PK's Representations*

### BY ROBERT M. SCHOCH, PH.D.

During the "cold war" both the U.S. and the Soviet Union worried that the other side had developed the ability to use psychic powers for military purposes. Researchers Lynne Schroeder and Shiela Ostrander in their 1970 ground-breaking book, *Psychic Discoveries Behind the Iron Curtain*, detailed many experiments carried out in the U.S.S.R. and eastern Europe, including psychokinesis (PK). Others who documented the psychic developments behind the iron curtain included authors Henry Gris and William Dick. Many believe that such disclosures were a major impetus behind the U.S. military establishment's development of its own capability and that its widely discussed remote viewing program, which came to be known as Project Scannate, was the result. Whether the military remote viewers could actually influence remote physical objects viewed at a distance is not often discussed, but David Morehouse, a veteran of Project Scannate has hinted that it was possible. Others have suggested that even assassination can be accomplished through such mind-only means.

Thanks to the publicity in the West, several soviet psychics who apparently were able to influence physical objects with mind power alone became internationally famous. Among them was Alla Vingradova, whose husband Victor Adamenko is shown here holding a small electric light bulb which, when placed next to an object which had been influenced by his wife, would spontaneously light. Vingradova is shown moving a metal cigar tube by passing her hand over it. Also pictured is the so-called Russian PK superstar Nina Kulagina in 1977 moving a matchbook by PK. Unlike so-called spoon bender from Israel, Uri Geller, Kulagina complained that her PK efforts for the photography caused her to become physically exhausted.—Editor

In the 1970s, what is perhaps best described as a spoon-bending craze swept across America, and many other regions of the world as well. In large part this was engendered by the Israeli entertainer and "psychic" Uri Geller. Geller was said to be able to bend spoons, keys, and other metal objects by simply stroking them gently with his finger. Among other additional amazing feats, he reputedly could make broken wristwatches and clocks start ticking again, he could "see" inside sealed containers, and he could sometimes read minds. Geller's "mind over matter" abilities were what really excited the crowds. A bent spoon or key, apparently done without applying any substantial force (just a light stroking of the metal so that it would weaken or "melt" to the point that in some cases it would break), appeared to be "objective" evidence of that which was impossible by any normal standards. A bent spoon or key was proof, for many people, of genuine paranormal abilities.

From top:
Alla Vingradova; Nina Kulagina
Victor Adamenko

The concept of matter being influenced by mind or consciousness alone is certainly not new. It encompasses a variety of phenomena, from metal bending to levitation against the laws of gravity and unexplained movements of objects. Sounds heard without any physical source, tables tilting, unexplained temperature changes, breezes, and materializations and dematerializations of objects, are other reputed manifestations of consciousness directly affecting the physical realm. For thousands of years saints have reputedly floated (levitated) free from the normal bonds of gravity while in a state of ecstasy. Victorian era séances, organized around powerful mediums, were attended by all sorts of marvels involving the movement of objects, materializations of objects or even "spirits" taking fully human form, and sounds produced by unknown means. Such

Uri Geller

manifestations were formerly referred to as telekinesis (loosely translated as "distant movement;" that is, movement from a distance without any known physical means). The preferred technical term currently for such phenomena is psychokinesis ("mind or soul movement," that is, movement by the mind), often abbreviated as PK for short.

So, is there anything to PK? Can it possibly be genuine? Many a hardcore, mainstream scientist would emphatically answer with a resounding NO. PK breaks the very laws of physics and thus is, *a priori*, impossible—or so the argument goes. But does it really break the "laws" of physics? Or must we examine the data for PK and then decide whether or not the "laws," at least as currently understood, must be modified? Indeed, such outstanding minds as the Nobel Prize-winning physicist Brian Josephson and the late quantum physicist Evan Harris Walker have suggested just this. According to some interpretations, quantum mechanics and related fields may even predict that in certain instances PK *should* occur.

But just because PK might occur, hypothetically, according to one formulation of what is admittedly a new and complex theory of how the world works at a fundamental level, this does not guarantee that we will ever observe PK at a macroscopic level, whether it be a levitating table or a bending spoon. Furthermore, the typical PK practitioner as known to the public generally does little to engender confidence in the validity of the reputed PK phenomenon, except perhaps among those who are already "believers" or simply overly credulous. Uri Geller, for instance, is primarily an entertainer and has been both suspected, and reputedly caught in the act, of cheating while performing his "paranormal" and "psychic" tricks. The stage conjuror (magician) James Randi has demonstrated that he can duplicate Geller-style spoon- and key-bending using normal means such as sleight of hand (see Randi's 1982 books, *The Truth About Uri Geller* and *Flim-Flam!*). Countering the Randi allegations, Geller supporters have pointed out that his "powers" have been tested and corroborated, at least to some extent, under controlled laboratory conditions, but the Randi camp counter argues that such "controlled conditions" were not adequately controlled and Geller had the opportunity to cheat and bamboozle the poor, naïve scientists.

Here I do not wish to focus on Geller; however, he is representative of the typical psychokinetic "star" who appears to exhibit extraordinary powers under certain (generally somewhat lax, informal, and uncontrolled) situations, but has also been caught cheating or unable to perform at other times. This pattern has been exhibited among "mediums" for over a century and a half, and probably much longer. Does Geller, or a Geller-type, have any true paranormal abilities? It can often be difficult to say. Just because a "psychic" cheats at times, does not mean that all the reputed paranormal phenomena associated with that individual are fraudulent, although cheating in one instance certainly does not encourage one's belief in the veracity of other supposed paranormal occurrences. Indeed, for a century and a half, serious investigators of the paranormal have found that those very individuals who appear at times to manifest authentic paranormal phenomena are also prone to cheat and deceive when the genuine paranormal phenomena fail. One must be careful not to throw the baby out with the bathwater, but one must also realize that in some cases the baby (paranormal phenomena) may be totally absent and very dirty bathwater (egregious cheating) is all there is.

So, to address the question of spoon-bending and the like directly: Do I personally think there is anything to it, as far as the paranormal is concerned? My answer must ultimately be nuanced, but when it comes to stage performances of reputed psychokinetic powers (whether before an audience of thousands, or as entertainment in the privacy of one's own living room), I remain to be convinced that there is anything to them. I can enjoy a good stage conjuror as a diversion, but I don't put any stock in such "paranormal" feats. Indeed, based on my studies of what I will refer to unabashedly as genuine paranormal phenomena, I believe it is highly unlikely (if not virtually impossible) that large-scale psychokinetic phenomena (whether bending a spoon or moving an object) could be consistently elicited "on command" in front of an audience. To put it bluntly, in my opinion the garden-variety spoon bending is nonsense.

So, there is nothing to psychokinesis? Not so fast . . . I never said that. Although I was extremely skeptical at first, after spending years studying the topic, based on literature reviews, theoretical analyses, and first-hand experiences, I do believe that at least some PK is real.

A convenient way to classify certain types of psychokinesis is either as micro-PK or macro-PK. Macro-PK is the old standard PK, basically any PK that can be readily observed with the unaided eye, such as a chair levitating or a jar "jumping" off a shelf. Micro-PK is the manipulation of matter at an atomic and subatomic level, and might include temperature changes of the local air in a room. However, the concept of micro-PK in modern times is applicable primarily to atomic and subatomic changes in sophisticated electronic equipment and the like.

Anecdotally, computers and other electrical-based machines seem to malfunction an inordinate amount of the time when certain persons are present. Could this be the result of micro-PK, even if unintentional on the part of the psychokinetic person (who may not even realize she or he is causing the problem)? For over a quarter of a century the Princeton Engineering Anomalies Research (PEAR) laboratories, located at Princeton University, researched such topics (unfortunately, the facility closed down in 2007). One of the basic techniques of PEAR was to use random event generators (REGs, also known as random number generators, or RNGs) to test for possible micro-PK. A REG uses some random source (such as radioactive decay or electronic "noise") to ultimately produce a binary string of pluses and minuses, or 0's and 1's. Being random, all other things being equal, the number of 0's and the number of 1's produced over a certain interval of time should be equal (odds are 50/50 that any particular number will be either 0 or 1), and this indeed was the pattern observed with the machines when they were left alone.

The PEAR researchers found, however, that in the presence of a person who focused on the machine, the random string of numbers could go non-random. That is, at a significant statistical level, if the "operator" tried to consciously "will" the machine to generate more 1's than 0's, such would occur (or vice versa). And this occurred without any physical contact or conventional means of influence whatsoever (such as holding a magnet to the machine. Furthermore, it was not "psychic superstars" that were causing such influences on the machines but average people. And, one does not even need to be in close physical proximity to the machine, but rather simply focused on it. The effect holds even when the operator and the machine are miles apart. Furthermore, the PEAR researchers found that a

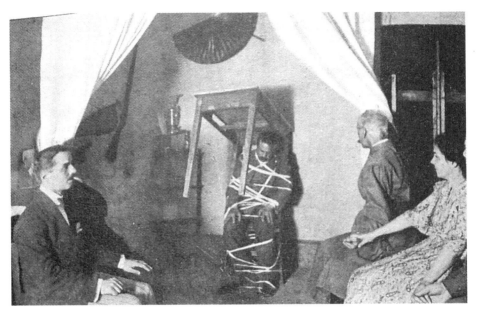

Supposed "levitation" of a table during a séance, late19th/early 20th century

REG placed in the vicinity of a group of people (for example, an audience at a sports event) would apparently detect, by going non-random, times when there was a collective focus of consciousness, such as when a goal was scored during a soccer game. Clearly, to my mind, the PEAR studies (and similar studies in other laboratories) have demonstrated that micro-PK does exist.

What about macro-PK? Could there be any truth to it? I think so, and I believe the best evidence for genuine macro-PK is found not in the laboratory (although there have been plenty of attempts to induce macro-PK on command), but among spontaneous instances in real life. Specifically, in my opinion there is overwhelming evidence that at least some poltergeist manifestations, which involve macro-PK, such as the falling of objects off shelves or objects flying through the air, are genuine and not simply faked by naughty little boys or girls (or naughty adults, for that matter).

What constitutes a poltergeist incident? Here we can quote from the early physicist and psychical researcher Sir William Barrett:

"There was [is] no exact English equivalent for poltergeist, but as the German word *polterer* meant a boisterous fellow, so *poltergeist* was a boisterous ghost. It is a convenient term to express those apparently mean-ingless noises, disturbances, movements of objects and ringings of bells (even when the wires are severed) for which no assignable cause can be found. The phenomena are sporadic, breaking out unexpectedly, lasting a few days or months and terminating as suddenly. They differ from haunt-ings, inasmuch as ghostly forms are not seen, and are associated not so much with a particular locality as with a particular (and usually young) person in a particular room. . . . The phenomena take place equally well in broad daylight, under the searching gaze of investigators, or at night time. Of the genuineness and inexplicable nature of the phenomena there can be no manner of doubt, in spite of occasional attempts at their fraudulent imitation" (Barrett, 1911, *Journal of the Society for Psychical Research*, vol. 15, p. 37).

Poltergeist incidents (dubbed in modern technical language as Recur-rent Spontaneous Psychokinesis, or RSPK) have been noted for thousands of years, and occur among all cultures. In modern times they have been studied extensively by a number of qualified researchers and, after weed-ing out the frauds, it appears undeniable that some such cases are genuine. I will admit that once I personally observed a minor poltergeist incident— a book "jumping" off a shelf when no one was close to it, and there was no shaking or other tampering with the shelf. And this occurred with a woman in the room who has had other poltergeist incidents occur in her presence.

In my opinion, macro-PK as seen in poltergeist incidents is related to the manifestations of micro-PK as documented in the laboratory with REGs. The two, micro-PK and macro-PK, are the ends of a continuous spectrum. However, when it comes to macro-PK, it appears to me that it can seldom, if ever, be elicited "on command." Genuine poltergeist-style macro-PK always appears to be caused by, or emanate from, an agent who is "emotionally charged" and is plagued with anger, hostility, or anxiety, often directed at another person. In the macro-PK case of the book coming off a shelf that I witnessed, the presumed agent was emotionally charged, and the topic of the book was not random but related to the issues at hand.

Psychokinesis is a "physical" manifestation of the paranormal; whereas telepathy, clairvoyance, and the like are "mental" manifestations of the paranormal (see further discussion in *The Parapsychology Revolution*, 2008, compilation and commentary by R. M. Schoch and L. Yonavjak). But what is the function or value, the value to the organism or species, of such paranormal phenomena? If we could determine the value of paranormal phenomena in a natural context, then we might be able to predict, or at least explain, why such phenomena are manifested at some times and not at other times.

In today's age (versus perhaps during humanity's evolutionary origins), paranormal phenomena seem to serve psychological and therapeutic purposes; this is an idea that was expressed long ago. Sigmund Freud (1862–1939), the founder of psychoanalysis, took an interest in psychical research and was a member of the Society for Psychical Research. Though he never took a strong position publicly, from his private writings it is clear that he was favorably impressed by the evidence for telepathy, an important paranormal phenomenon. Below is a telling quotation from Freud's private correspondence:

"I already expressed a favorable bias toward telepathy during our trip to the Harz [a mountain range in Germany]. But there was no need to do so publicly; my conviction was not very strong, and the diplomatic aspect of preventing psychoanalysis from drawing too close to occultism very easily retained the upper hand. Now, the revision of *Traumdeutung* [*Dream Interpretation*] for the collected edition gave me the impetus to reconsider the problem of telepathy. In the meantime, however, my personal experience through tests, which I undertook with Ferenczi [Sándor Ferenczi, one of Freud's colleagues] and my daughter, have attained such convincing power over me that diplomatic considerations had to be relinquished" (Freud quote, circa 1925/1926, posted at *http://www.freud-museum.at/freud/chronolg/1925-e.htm*. Accessed 25 October 2007).

In his 1922 paper titled "Dreams and Telepathy," Freud discusses how telepathic experiences, emotional issues, neuroses, and dreams can be intimately entangled, and ultimately serve psychological needs. Ultimately, Freud's primary point was that telepathy follows the same basic principles of all mental life. There is no sharp demarcation between telepathy and other mental, emotional, and psychological processes.

I believe that the same point Freud makes about telepathy, namely that it serves psychological needs, applies also to spontaneous PK. Genuine macro-PK is a spontaneous phenomenon induced by strong emotions and "psychic energy." Think of an adolescent who is undergoing puberty and all of the confusion surrounding such a life change. She or he lashes out at the world and perhaps at the parents or other close relatives in particular, via normal means and possibly paranormal means (telepathically and psychokinetically). In such a case, PK is on a continuum from mental assaults to verbal violence to physical tantrums of normal mode to, in very rare instances, spontaneous macro-psychokinesis. Note that in most, and perhaps virtually all, cases the agent of the macro-PK poltergeist-type incidents is not even consciously aware that she or he is causing them, and may be just as frightened by the poltergeist activity as anyone else. By this conception, macro-PK by its nature is not something one would expect to be readily manifested on command by an entertainer before an audience. Rather it requires an emotional charging and manifestations will be sporadic.

Besides poltergeist-type activity, could other genuine macro-PK exist? I believe so, but again such incidents are probably highly emotionally and psychologically laden, though in a different way, such as a religious devotee rapt in ecstasy. But such is a topic for another essay.

# 17

# VOICE POWER

*James D'Angelo Believes the Power to Heal and a Great Deal More Could Be in Your Throat*

**BY CYNTHIA LOGAN**

Gguung...ggaang...gginngg: these gargly syllables accompany various groaning, laughing, nonsensical, and utterly silly sounds coming from slack-jawed participants in James D'Angelo's workshop: "Awakening Chakra Energies Through Sound." They're here to "free up" their voices and discover the power of the voice to heal. The circle is composed of professional musicians, singers, orators ,and ordinary people who want to experience what D'Angelo describes in his book, *The Healing Power of the Human Voice* (2005). Readers can join the group by using the accompanying CD, which contains all the exercises described in the book, including Islamic, Native American, and East Indian chanting, breathing and movement techniques, "toning," groaning, sighing, and "keening," a high-frequency sound on the EE vowel ascending or descending like a siren. "The word originated in Ireland and is synonymous with wailing, with grief," reports D'Angelo, who has always had a fascination with language—with "the precision of words" and has found an intuitive process of breaking them into somewhat esoteric meanings. "Person," for example, can be considered *per sonare*, or "through sound." We are at heart, asserts D'Angelo, beings of sound, offspring of the Word that created the worlds. He notes that we use the word "sound" to mean stable and strong when we refer to something as a sound idea, or to someone being in sound health. "In Latin," he continues, "we have OMness—meaning 'all'—and from 'all' we have the sacred sounds of ALLah, ALLeluia and even ALLow."

An American now based in England ("I married a Brit and that's what brought me into the Anglophile world"), D'Angelo is an authority on sound healing therapies and has led therapeutic sound and movement workshops in England, Scotland, Italy, Spain, and the U.S. since 1994. Besides breathwork and overtone singing, participants experience sonic attunement of the nervous system with tuning forks while toning their chakras ("I always come back to the energy centers, because I think they're the key"), as well as the discovery of their unique "fundamental" note for toning, and collective vocal improvisation for freedom of expression. It's a perfect setup for the curious, but self conscious: "No one has to produce vocal sound on their own," reassures D'Angelo in his richly developed timbre. "The quality of your voice is not the issue, only the deep intention behind it."

"Singer with a Black Glove," by Degas

Stressing that he is neither a healer nor a vocal therapist, D'Angelo informs the group that there are many different approaches to voicework, including diaphragmatic breathing for the creation of maximum vocal sound and deep relaxation. "I teach what you would call belly breathing as the preliminary for what we do afterward. I believe the body should be somewhat engaged while making sounds," he announces. D'Angelo brings a longtime practice of sacred Sufi dancing to his work—some of the movements look like T'ai Chi or Ch'i Gung. He also brings a knowledge of self-actualizing psychology and Reiki energetic healing to his students. "I'm completely eclectic and a workshop, for me, is a smorgasbord. Not everything will resonate with everyone," he says, no pun intended.

Workshops also include Taoist healing sounds for each of the body's organs, and therapeutic sound mantras that combine particular consonants and vowels to influence distinct aspects of body, mind, and spirit. "Think of the vowels and consonants as pieces of fruit from which you want to extract as much juice as possible," coaches D'Angelo, who calls vowels "the bowels" of a language. "In all languages the vowels are the carriers, our sentences ride on their wave forms, while the consonants are consorts which, with their brief explosions, propel the vowels along." He expounds on the merits, the sacredness actually, of vowels, citing their universality, purity of sound, and ability to be produced without the use of the tongue, as awesome attributes. He can't resist another etymology lesson: "The very word *language* derives from the Latin *lingua* meaning 'tongue.' Language comes into being when the tongue is used to modify vowel sounds and produce the consonants."

Though he lists Astrosonics, Bioacoustics, Cymatics, Electro-Crystal therapy and other high-tech vocal therapies in his book's resources, his passion and focus is on the human voice and its power to heal. "I considered using the instrument developed by Peter Guy Manners (a researcher with Cymatics pioneer Dr. Hans Jenny)," states D'Angelo, "but I found it uncreative. Working with groups and with the voice is much more interesting than applying electronic frequencies to the body! I want to empower people so they can see the benefits without having to have science back it up."

D'Angelo's approach involves four basic components: natural sounds, toning, chanting, and overtoning. He also believes that the four basic elements express themselves through our vocal cords, with either earth, air, fire, or water predominating in terms of speed, pitch and volume. "Very slow speech is earth, the other end would be air," he explains. D'Angelo likes to think his own voice is very balanced, but when pressed, admits it's probably in the earthy realm. His manner of speaking is hard to place—"people often think I'm Canadian," he says. Surprisingly, it's not proper British elocution he advocates, but the freer, more open voice quality he ascribes to Americans. Minimizing any movement of his lips, he mimics the cliché British speech pattern "the very tight sort of way with very little movement of the mouth—in extreme form it's rather clipped," immediately contrasting it with a lazy Southern drawl. His blue eyes reflect humor and a hint of French ancestry in an otherwise strong Italian heritage. Occasionally afflicted with tinnitus, he considers it "the sound of my nervous system" and doesn't find it particularly annoying. "I actually like listening to it; it's like a signal from someplace out there reminding me to wake up and be!"

Becoming more alive—"waking up and being"—is the inspiration D'Angelo, a pianist who loves both classical and jazz music, takes from Beethoven. "I think Beethoven has Shamanic power in his music," he enthuses. "Mozart says, 'Here's heaven, come on up,' but Beethoven broke open the vaults." On the music faculty at Goldsmiths College since 1987, D'Angelo specializes in improvisation and has introduced therapeutic sound into course offerings. As a composer and pianist, he performs works that he describes as "part of the new consciousness movement in contemporary music." At the same time, he finds most new age music "absolutely irritating" and says he wants music to engage, not relax him. "I want to be drawn in and taken on a journey to that other place, where those sounds came from." His *Portraits of Krishna* was recently released on the EMI Virgin Classics label, and he's just written a mass for the Gloucester Cathedral choir. "I don't know if they're going to perform it, but even better, I'm going to be able to play the Cathedral organ, which is heaven!" D'Angelo notes that though a small country, "England is filled with these wonderful sound chambers." He thinks singing is a wonderful introduction to sound work: "Watch a choir and you'll see how lit up the faces are…years fall off they're so concentrated and the vibrations are so good, it's obvious that a change of state—probably the alpha state in terms of brain waves—is occurring." As enjoyable as this may be, he feels it's not enough to generate therapeutic results. For that, he says, sounds need to be infused with intent, ritual, and thought. And, of course, "the key is to focus on the vowels."

Though D'Angelo attended both the Manhattan School of Music and New York University, where he earned a Ph.D. in 20th century classical music research and music composition, he has always maintained a keen interest in science. He points out that scientists are still discovering evidence of sounds of the Big Bang throughout the universe, and that NASA has decoded the electromagnetic fields of the planets—"they've got the music of the spheres, and it often sounds much like Tibetan bowls and gongs, so the Tibetans knew what they were about. They were encoding in their instruments the music of the spheres." D'Angelo notes that "when you unlock the pulsations lying dormant at the base of your spine through sound-making, you're reconnected to what you could call your personal Big Bang."

A major emphasis in D'Angelo's work is what he refers to as "the DNA of sound." All regularly vibrating sounds (especially the human voice and musical instruments) consist of a fundamental tone that contains numerous higher frequencies, known as "overtones." He considers the overtone patterns to be the genetic blueprint of sound, as they determine its quality, color, or timbre. "Overtones are embedded frequencies within our voices, referred to by musicians as harmonics and by physicists as partials. They're like the aura of sound, like subtle bodies of the voice. They are what make the sound organic, full of vitamins and minerals." He postulates that flat sounds without overtones (think of sine wave signals sent out by TV stations when not broadcasting, or those computerized voices you hear at airports) would strip the voice of its power to heal. He admits he has no scientific basis for this theory, just an intuition. "I would have thought that a mapping of peoples' frequencies would have been a much better project than the human genome. I don't think souls necessarily want perfect bodies…they want to be born into certain limitations so they can work their way through them."

D'Angelo likes the developing new physics cosmology known as "String Theory," which likens the universe to an enormous stringed instrument. It posits that fundamental particles are tiny snips of subatomic "particle strings" 100 billion times shorter than the nucleus of an atom. These strings vibrate in predetermined ways and interact with one another to create the properties of material particles. "From such a theory," writes D'Angelo, "we can sense that the world is a vast chain of overtones of which we are a part, each person vibrating at his or her own particular frequency." He takes this further, stating that "the vibrations of the human voice applied consciously as a therapeutic instrument have the resonating power to stimulate, release, and balance the fine healing energies that create harmony and wholeness of body, mind, and spirit. At every level from the cellular to the surrounding bioenergetic field of the body we are a great network of frequency vibrations which fluctuate, become weakened and literally go out of tune." If this disharmony becomes serious, disease can be the result. D'Angelo thinks that through the focused, resonant use of the voice we have the capacity to alter our vibrations and our state of consciousness, be well-tuned and enjoy true sound health. Of course, the medical community might well scoff at such a theory, though ultrasound is common practice (one which, D'Angelo mentions, sound researchers conclude may not be harmless).

Now in his seventies, D'Angelo still performs Sufi whirling dervish dancing once a week during one-hour ceremonies, something he's done for over 30 years. This, along with "some good walking" comprises his physical regimen, complemented by daily meditation, another discipline he's followed for decades. He's not slowing down. He has conducted numerous workshops in the United Kingdom and U.S. (see *www.soundspirit.co.uk/works.html* for a schedule of upcoming workshops). He likes to quote Sufi leader Hazrat Inayat Khan, who said: "The voice is a light. If the light becomes dim, it has not gone out, it is there. It is the same with the voice. If it does not shine, it only means that it has not been cultivated and you must cultivate it again and it will shine once more."

# 18

# THE SUPERHERO FACTOR

*What is the Meaning of the Superpower Myth?*

**BY LEN KASTEN**

I t's a very persistent myth—this idea that somehow humans can develop super-powers. It seems to be part of the mass subconscious, and various versions of the concept pop up repeatedly in science fiction comic books, television programs, and movies. One has to be careful to differentiate this concept of the super-human, or more familiarly, the "superman" from the man-machine version, more commonly known as a cyborg, which myth has an equal resiliency, especially lately (for example, in the film *Iron Man*). Typically, when such a mythology refuses to go away, it would seem to suggest that subconsciously we are capable of much more than we have been told. Certainly there is an innate intuitive conviction among large segments of the population that such super powers may really be possible—that it is a truth that simply hasn't yet been validated scientifically, yet. It might even be characterized as a yearning—an inexpressible and powerful desire for humanity to be more than it is, allied with the belief that it can be accomplished. A corollary of this is the suspicion that somehow we have been held back from this evolutionary next step by conspiratorial forces that seek to keep us under strict control—the idea that if we knew our real potential, "they" would no longer be able to remain in power.

## SUPER MAGIC

This superhero phenomenon may explain why stage magicians are able to generate so much public excitement. Those who view their amazing feats start to think, in their innermost thoughts, that perhaps the illusions are real because they *want* to believe that humans can develop such powers. For most of the modern era, audiences applauded such tricks in admiration of the magician's abilities, but always went away certain that it was subterfuge and not real magic. Lately, however, audiences are not so sure. With the arrival of David Copperfield in the 1980s, and more recently David Blaine (who, on the *Oprah Winfrey Show*, set the world record for holding his breath—17 minutes and 4 seconds), professional magic took on an entirely different complexion, and a new age of super magic began in which many observers became convinced that paranormal abilities were involved. Copperfield has performed many astounding feats including going through the Great Wall of China, making the Statue of Liberty apparently disappear (mass hypnosis?) and levitating over the Grand Canyon, all live before huge television audiences. The Great Wall illusion was particularly impressive because he did get to the other side of the Wall in minutes.

The latest superstar "illusionist" in the tradition of Copperfield to emerge onto the public stage is Criss Angel. Angel began his career performing in an off-Broadway show called "Criss Angel Mindfreak" in 1998 at the age of 21. It ran for 600 performances. He then moved up to television with a new expanded version of the show, keeping the same name, on the A&E Network, which ran for five seasons, from 2005 to 2010. Angel's stunts on "Mindfreak" were beyond sensational.

Like Copperfield, he apparently has the ability to levitate, but has taken this phenomenon to "new heights." In a scene videotaped from all angles, in broad daylight, while his fans shout and scream from below, Angel effortlessly floats from rooftop to rooftop standing with arms extended, covering a distance of about 200 feet. And then, in what may be the greatest feat ever accomplished by an illusionist, Angel, invoking Jesus and giving guttural shouts, floats high up into the air from the pinnacle of the Luxor Hotel Pyramid in Las Vegas at night, and hangs in mid air for about 10 minutes waving his arms, while floodlights from the hotel apex illuminate the scene, a helicopter hovers nearby, and hundreds of astonished, gaping spectators watch from the street and other hotels. But, in what many believe to be his supreme achievement, perhaps because it emulates a miracle performed by Jesus, Angel walks across a swimming pool in Las Vegas, while swimmers surround him and watch him closely, and a woman swims beneath his feet as he walks. Taking each step carefully, Angel kicks off his shoes in mid-pool and the camera shows them floating to the bottom as he continues his walk barefoot to the other side. Angel is so casual about setting up his feats with random watchers and passersby,

Superhero

that it becomes impossible to believe that they may be confederates, and he apparently uses no props. On an open stretch of road in Pahrump, Nevada, Angel came speeding down the strip in his black Lamborghini toward the crowd. As he passed the spectators, his assistants sprayed $CO_2$ at the car, and it simply vanished into thin air. In a department store, he selected an 8-year-old girl at random, and obtained permission from her mother to work with her. He dressed her up as a 20 year old, and then as they stood on a table facing each other, she actually turned into a 20 year old. She ran off screaming to her mother. The biblical prophecy of "signs and wonders" in the "last days" come to mind, along with the warning about "false prophets."

Both Copperfield and Angel deny that they have super-normal capabilities. And yet, Angel has demonstrated what seem to be yogic powers by walking on knives, remaining submerged for long periods of time, and allowing a steamroller to crush him on a bed of broken glass. It would not be much of a stretch to believe that he has actually also learned to levitate, as the yogis do. At least one super-magician claims that his stunts are based

David Copperfield

on paranormal talents. Legendary performer Uri Geller says that his ability to bend spoons and keys, and to stop and start clocks and watches with his mind, are demonstrations of psychokinetic powers. And he claims that he uses actual telepathy in his mentalism act. Angel, who also includes mentalism in his performances, vehemently repudiates any hint of paranormal capability, and alleges that he has become hyper-skilled at knowing what's in someone's mind by recognizing minute changes in voice inflections. But, there may be a very practical and commercial reason for such repudiation. By keeping everything on an "illusion" basis, he doesn't have to defend or explain anything he does, as Uri Geller is often forced to do.

## GENETIC POWER

In our current age of the Internet, when a piece of information, no matter how strange, can become "viral" within hours and spread all over the world, it is increasingly difficult to keep a lid on secret programs, and stories about covert CIA and military efforts to develop "super-soldiers" are beginning to emerge like leaks sprung from a dam. The most astounding gee-whiz story in this genre is the saga of Andy Pero.

According to the Internet fable, he was born Michael Andrew Pero III on November 25, 1969, at the Fallon Naval Air Station in Fallon, Nevada, the son of a Lieutenant Commander in the Navy. He has fragmented memories of his youth but he recalls being "watched over" by two military men, one army and one air force, who monitored his physical condition and educational progress from the age of 5. The family moved to northern New Jersey, and at the age of 11 his mother enrolled him in a Silva Mind Control course. He excelled in all the mental exercises and could even bend spoons with his mind. He remembers that one of the military men approached him one day in the playground and said to him, "You know you're going to work for me someday." He became an outstanding athlete in grade school, playing baseball, basketball, and soccer. He used the Silva method to visualize all his athletic feats in advance. At the age of 14 in the eighth grade, he set the school high-jump record, and tied the records for the 60-, 100- and 200-yard dash, and could bench press 305 pounds. He played freshman high school football and was one of the best high school running backs in the country, and also threw the shot-put and the discus. Using the Silva technique, he could literally "pump up" his muscles mentally until his coaches thought he was using steroids. And always the two military men he called Mr. Green and Mr. Blue watched him from the sidelines. He frequently caught sight of them in the stands at his major athletic events.

Despite an offer from Penn State for a full ride scholarship, and his strong desire to go there, his father, an Annapolis graduate, insisted that he attend the University of Rochester, threatening never to speak to him again if he refused. He complied, and it was there that his super-soldier training commenced in earnest. Under hypnotic control he reported to "Room 101," a small lab room, every day, where he was shocked and beaten and mentally programmed to obey orders given by "Dr. Green." Thanks to his Silva training, Pero was able to retain one part of his mind as a refuge, a safe place to which he could retreat and avoid the conditioning. In this place his critical faculties remained intact, and his innate impression of "Dr. Green" and his cohorts was that they were Nazis. The shocks and torture were part of trauma-based conditioning designed to insure unquestioned obedience when activated by a code word. He was told never to think, but just "to do." But Pero resisted the robotic transformation by retreating to his inner sanctum whenever he needed to.

## SUPER SOLDIERS

Under hypnotic suggestion, Pero was able to push the boundaries of physical achievement way beyond anything believed possible, as his controllers sought to find the limits. Pero says, "The focus of the initial research, I believe, was to try and unlock the secrets of the mind. How to make the perfect soldier, to make a 'super-human killing machine.' They were finding out how, when under hypnosis, the mind can overcome the physical limitations of the human body.... How can the mind allow the body to do things which would normally be physically impossible?" Since Pero was already a super-athlete—perhaps by genetic design before he was born— his controllers had the perfect raw material to work with. He did push-ups for about an hour, and he was able to squat with 675 pounds for as many repetitions as they asked. He says, "Under hypnosis, they told me I could do it! And I truly believed them!!!" They tried to bury the old "Andy" and to create an entirely new person. Pero says, "They wanted 'Andy' to be totally gone, but I remember they could NEVER destroy or break him. I think that is why I still remember all of these events."

His trainers were especially interested in "the jump." They told him that when he jumped he would be like a cat, and would always land on his feet and always be okay no matter how high he jumped. They told him "When you land, your legs become steel springs and will absorb all impact.... There is no pain, and you have no fear!" They started him off on ladders, and soon he was jumping off buildings. Then he graduated to cliffs and bridges. Eventually they had him jump off a huge microwave tower, which he did easily with only a slight ankle twinge, believing it to be a six-foot ladder! And finally, they pushed him out of a sky-diving plane without a parachute! When he hit the ground, he landed on his feet and bounced about 50 feet into the air. They thought he was dying because he laid on the ground unconscious for hours. Eventually, he got up and walked away.

Ultimately, as the story goes, they did turn Pero into a "super-human killing machine." Even though he suspected what they were preparing him for, he couldn't help but brag, "I could hit ANY target still or moving, at ANY range, with ANY of the guns in the exact center every time." He also became very proficient in lethal hand-to-hand combat techniques. He found that he could actually throw a man across a room with his mind, so he claimed. When the time came to send Andy on his assassination assignments he resisted at first, intrinsically opposed to killing anybody. But they convinced him that his targets were evil, and so he complied. They would fly him out to his jobs in an F-16, and then back to the Rochester Airport. He remembers completing 10 missions, but when they added 15 more, he resisted. Then they tried to kill him, but just like Dr. Frankenstein (or perhaps even a modern-day Jason Bourne), they found that they had suc- ceeded all too well in creating a monster. He estimates that he killed 15 of his "handlers" while trying to escape at various times. Andy Pero survived and eventually found a psychologist who helped him become de-programmed, which allowed him to tell his story as memories came flooding back. Anyway, that is what he says.

Andy Pero

If true, the Andy Pero story opens up new vistas regarding the potential power of both the human mind and the human body. Pero says that they were trying to find out whether the mind, under hypnosis, can "overcome the physical limitations of the human body." But really, he himself doesn't know the extent of those limitations. It seems clear, if his story is actually true, that he has demonstrated the awesome power of the mind. But was he able to actually change the atoms and molecules of his muscles?

It seems likely that the human body has a tremendous built-in reserve power that can be called upon in emergencies, as in the case where a panicky father is able to lift an automobile to save his child. The fact is, we do not know who we really are. We have no idea of our true power. We get glimmers of insight from observing works of genius and watching strong men pull locomotives, and we marvel at David Copperfield and Criss Angel. Is it true, that social forces prevent us from realizing our true capabilities? Or is that just another excuse for failure from the victim society? It's an issue worthy of debate.

# PART FOUR

# LIFE AFTER DEATH

Child and graffiti

# 19

# WAR AND REINCARNATION

## *When Children Struggle with Past-Life Trauma*

### BY JOHN CHAMBERS

The 8-year-old boy had been sobbing into his mother's lap for fifteen minutes. Now he straightened up. He and his mother and father stood on the gently rocking deck of an oceangoing fishing boat that was moored some distance offshore in Chichi-Ima's Futami-Ko harbor. Around them rose up the green mountains of this Pacific island that is close to Iwo Jima and 650 miles from Tokyo, Japan. It was September 4, 2006.

As the crew watched in rapt, awed silence, the boy picked up a bouquet of flowers, walked to the boat's side, and threw it overboard. He returned to his mother and sobbed for a few minutes more.

The bouquet floated in the dark blue choppy waters. Far below, at the bottom of the harbor, lay the rusted hulk of a World War Two FM-2 Corsair fighter plane. Inside rested the bleached bones of 21-year-old ensign James McCready Huston Jr., VC-81, killed in action on March 3, 1945, during a fierce battle with the Japanese.

The 8-year-old boy was James Leininger, of Lafayette, Louisiana. He believed he was the reincarnation of the gallant warrior whose earthly remains lay hundreds of feet below. In tossing him the bouquet, the boy was bidding farewell to his previous self of whose presence he had been aware, as if it were a second personality, since he was 2 years old.

Now James felt bereft but finally freed from a beloved burden.

This heartrending if unparalleled scene is the culminating event in *Soul Survivor: The Reincarnation of a World War II Fighter Pilot* (2009), by James' parents Bruce and Andrea Leininger. It tells how, six years before, James began to have frequent nightmares in which he screamed and from which he awoke with words like, "Airplane crash on fire, little man can't get out." James became obsessively interested in fighter planes, identifying obscure parts like drop tanks. He made crayon drawings of crashing planes,

Child and fighter plane crash (*Atlantis Rising* art)

signing them "James 3" and insisting the pilot was "James 2." His mother and grandmother wondered if a previous reincarnation might be involved. Carol Bowman, a therapist skilled in enabling children to remember and accept their past lives, was consulted and helped James become calmer and more open. He said his fighter plane, a Corsair, had been shot down by the Japanese, crashing in a bay near Iwo Jima. He described features of the Corsair and said it had flown from the ship *Natoma*. He mentioned a name: Jack Larsen.

James' father, Bruce, was as stubbornly skeptical about reincarnation as he was determined to get to the truth. He scoured the Internet, combing through military records. He discovered that an aircraft carrier, *Natoma Bay*, had been stationed near Iwo Jima in March 1945. He tracked down pilots who were on or near *Natoma Bay*. Attending a reunion of the carrier's veterans, he learned that a pilot named James Huston Jr. had gone down on March 3, 1945.

Bruce found and interviewed a real Jack Larsen, who knew where James Huston had gone down. The younger James told him that "Billy, Leon, and Walter" had "met me when I went to heaven"; Bruce discovered that three pilots with these names had known Huston and been killed at Iwo Jima some months before him.

James' mother, Andrea, tracked down James Huston's family. His sister, Anne Barron, was still alive at 84. She was invited to visit with the

Leiningers. She and James shared intimate details of the family that no one else knew. Bruce took his son, then 6 years old, to another veterans' reunion. Without prompting, he identified many of James Huston's friends. He became sad, telling his father this was because "everyone is so old."

The family appeared on nationally-syndicated ABC *Primetime* on April 15, 2004. The program provoked great interest, including phone calls from other vets who were able to give Bruce additional information to further support James' belief that he had once been James Huston. A Japanese network invited the Leiningers to Tokyo to film an interview; the producers would cover all costs and pay a fee. After the filming came the 650 mile sea voyage to Chichi-Ima; and, at its end, James' absolution from his former life as Huston.

Was James Leininger really James Huston? The evidence in favor seems overwhelming, though a determined skeptic can always find much to criticize. But there have been other instances where evidence has emerged, sometimes in a strange and unexpected fashion, that some traumatized children—often they are autistic—are this way because they suffered a violent death, usually in wartime, in a previous life.

James Leininger

Eve Hanf-Enos is an autistic woman now in her 30s and living in the Netherlands. She has rarely spoken; but, at age 16, aided by her mother's hand via the technique of Facilitated Communication, she was able to write passages like, "To mollify the world must one play host to its insane, lost soul-massacring mores, or taste the adverse—the fight to loosen oneself from its welding wrought wretched safety? I am for the desolation of silence at the expense of feasts and friends, taking festive isolation over solitary festivity. I am a different direction from you. I am a didactic early born specimen of some new deeply unknown developmental stage in badly wrong *homo sapiens*."

When Eve Hanf-Enos was one year old, her mother left her for seven weeks to go on a business trip with her husband. When Brigitte Hanf-Enos returned home to Cornwall, Connecticut, her daughter showed signs of being autistic. Eve didn't speak for thirteen years. She didn't dress herself. She seemed unable to learn. When she was 13, a psychiatrist/neurologist urged Brigitte to try "holding therapy" with her daughter. For two years, for close to 24 hours a day, Brigitte held Eve in her arms to recreate the shattered bond between them. Finally, in exasperation and anger, Brigitte grabbed her daughter's hand, thrust a pencil into it, and screamed at her to write something—anything. Eve wrote in huge sprawling letters: "Eve."

This uncorked an avalanche of words. In the days and months to come, with her mother's hand on hers, Eve wrote prodigiously. She wrote in a poetic language all her own, sprinkled with foreign words and some of her own making. She revealed that from before her birth she had lived a rich

Facilitated communication with Eve Hanf-Enos

inner life. She described the fetal monitor that had guided her birth by Caesarian: "A dangerous wondering eager and looking machine sees wooden heart beat but not feelings of child—searing fear—I remember some wiggly movements of eerie…enveloping water. It felt decidedly eerie…I felt so alone." She hadn't wanted to be born because "I didn't do decisive things easily."

From birth on, she had maintained a telepathic connection with her mother. Many of her reactions—seizures, bed-wetting, and so forth—were in response to her mother's unvoiced fears. "I can't help it…I often taste yonder your words afar…wrong I dug in when you hyper doddering thoughts have…ESP droops me." Her mother went on a trip to Germany to visit Eve's dying grandfather. When she returned, Eve described to her, accurately and in poetic prose, what she had experienced telepathically while Brigitte was several thousand miles away: "Again I heard the women's words once more at my grandfather's bedside. I was hearing their wanting to help him to speak final words of wide opening to himself, but the words wouldn't come. I saw his life waning fast, freeing him from his weak body. The women at his bed saw it too. My mother leaned over to feel for his hand and put warm love into the touch. Her words of love drowned in his bogged heart."

There was much more.

Eve, who said she'd taught herself to read at 4 and her favorite authors were Thomas Mann and Dostoevsky, struggled to explain her autism: "When scholarly doctors words describe about autism they are full of dopey garbage. What causes autism is sorrowful soon after birth or during birth despair......I was so mad at the wooly headed sordid simpletons who said I was retarded. Some of them saw through my act....I feel born stuck now." She tied to explain why she was born, referring to reincarnation as if it were a fundamental truth: "I am choosing separate lives wending so I can censor past inequalities. They were segregating you and me ... One life made dead you and I wanted a new chance with you. One life waned before I sensed I was willing to experience it. One life west endured when I wanted east. I was yearning to be words saying wishing to you yell with desire but I was only English and you were Japanese." In what her mother called a "period of intense disturbance fraught with seizures," Eve described her previous lifetime as a child in a concentration camp. She had been caught trying to escape with her starving brother on her back, and thrown into a gas oven onto a heap of burning bodies.

Eve still speaks little, though she writes poetry. She tries to help other autistic children with that poetry.

Tineke Noordegraaf, of Hoeven, near Amsterdam, Netherlands, is a past-life regression therapist who works with children. She believes a horrific death as a child in a former lifetime, such as death by torture in a Nazi concentration camp, can cause a child to be reborn with so much reluctance that he or she can never fully mature in this lifetime. This dynamic may be a factor in the miscarriage or abortion of the fetus carrying the reincarnated soul, she says. Though it's the mother who chooses to abort, the reincarnating soul may be attracted to the vibration of the impending abortion. Such tormented souls seek "mothers who will give them the opportunity to die before they're born," Noordegraaf believes.

Noordegraaf first planned to be a pediatrician. She passed her medical exams but then decided to be a past-life regression therapist specializing in the treatment of children. (Past-life regression therapy assumes that some ailments in this lifetime may be caused by difficulties in a previous lifetime and that bringing the client to a conscious awareness of those difficulties may effect an alleviation of the ailment in this lifetime and even a cure.)

The Dutch therapist employs a smorgasbord of techniques—children can draw their supposed past lives or identify totem animals, mascot, and puppets—to come up with clues about the presence and nature of an interfering past life. In the 1990s, she achieved a high degree of success with these cases:

Nine-year-old Teresa (an assumed name), born in Brazil and adopted by Dutch parents, looked like a 4 year old when she began therapy. She did little more than repeat the words, "I don't want it." After several sessions, it emerged through the girl's comments and drawings that as a child in her previous lifetime, she had been the subject of medical experiments in a Nazi death camp. The doctors wanted to know how much poison it took to kill a child. With Teresa they succeeded on the ninth attempt. Her soul reincarnated in the body of a Brazilian woman who tried several times, unsuccessfully, to abort her. Once she was born, the mother gave her up for adoption. Noordegraaf guided Teresa's adoptive Dutch mother in "re-bonding" with Teresa by constantly telling the child that she was overjoyed to have her. After several sessions, Teresa began to look and act like a 9 year old. For a year after therapy ended, she periodically phoned her former therapist to exclaim: "I'm still breathing! And I'm growing!"

Ludovic was a 12 year old Belgian boy who, it emerged from past-life regression sessions, had been killed when, as a child in his previous life, the atomic bomb exploded over Hiroshima. Noordegraaf writes, "When Ludovic came into my office his legs trembled so much and he was so afraid of falling that he was walking on crutches." Ludovic told her repeatedly there was something terribly wrong with the world and himself; he didn't know what. Slowly, he recalled playing on a street in Hiroshima when, with a blast of thunder and lightning, his world turned black. His final memory, before being incinerated, was that his legs were trembling hysterically. Noordegraaf believed the held-over trembling was a security blanket connecting Ludovic to his previous life. Moreover, he wasn't just Ludovic; Noordegraaf concluded that he was "part of a cluster of people who never realized they had not survived that terrible disaster." Their terror and confusion had prevented them from leaving the earth plane, so that they hadn't been able to move on; they still clung to Ludovic for safety. Noordegraaf writes, "We brought them all to a place where it was quiet and where they could process what had happened to them all. They didn't want to go to the so-called 'Light' because the Light, and light and lightning, meant something terrible to them." She eventually persuaded the terrified entities that the light of God was entirely different from the blinding flash of an atomic explosion. They were able to depart. Eventually, Ludovic gave up his crutches. His legs stopped trembling. He quickly learned how to swim.

Brigit (an assumed name) was severely anorexic. Noordegraaf quickly learned that her father in this lifetime was abusing her, to the extent that she didn't want to look like a female. Noordegraaf resolved this situation. Then it emerged in regression sessions that in a previous lifetime Brigit had been a child chimney sweep in 19th century Italy. One day she got stuck in a chimney and died. This appalling demise set up in her a karmic resistance to being reborn as anything but small. It developed that, in an earlier lifetime, Brigit, then a male child, had worked as a pyramid cleaner in Egypt. This made it possible for him to ferret out buried gold for pyramid robbers. When the child grew up, he used the knowledge he'd acquired to steal gold for himself. One day a in a pyramid corridor jammed shut behind him, and he died after several days. This individual's soul, writes Noordegraaf, "developed [in-between lives] a program: Growing up means I'll be killed. So I have to develop a slim, anorexic body." Through the logic of karma this eventuated, two lifetimes later, in Brigit, a child with anorexia. In large measure through the use of these many insights, Noordegraaf was able to cure Brigit of anorexia.

In *Beyond the Ashes: Cases of Reincarnation from the Holocaust* (1992), Rabbi Yonassan Gershom tells us how, in conducting past-life regression therapy with 250 clients, he determined that child victims of the Holocaust very often reincarnated almost immediately because of their desperate longing for human warmth. He says many clients were still suffering in adulthood from the traumas they'd suffered as children, because, in a previous lifetime, they'd experienced a horrific death as a child in a Nazi concentration camp. In many cases, Gershom was able to help these clients.

## 20

# CIRCLE OF LIGHT

*For Those Who See the Light, There Is*
*Plenty of Evidence for Worlds Beyond*

**BY SUSAN MARTINEZ, PH.D.**

Wielding a camera with infrared film, the postmodern ghost-hunter records a bubble of light—an orb. Going through a near-death experience (NDE), the person sees an effulgent light at the end of a dark tunnel. Even UFOs are lightships—great spinning vortices clothed in the photosphere of its power—woven out of the substance of the finer ethers.

Light—neither wave nor particle, yet both—is our entrée, even here in the sublunary world, to the mystery of life.

Both life and death know Light. Betty Eadie, an NDE author, once related having seen "heavenly beings spinning material out of some bright substance;" whereupon Dr. P. M. H. Atwater replied she believed that "substance to be 'spun light'." Spun—or spinning—that bright substance seems ethereal to us simply because of its higher frequency. Sometimes only the camera can see it. Sometimes only the clairvoyant can see it. Sometimes everyone sees it, like the celebrated psychic light produced at a Welsh revival in 1905 which "resembled a brilliant star."

In the 1950s the science world had been jolted by photographic images of the human aura taken by Russia's Semyon Kirlian. His high-voltage method of photographing human subjects produced—quite by accident—luminous flares or "fountains" streaking out from the surface of the body. A shot in the arm for the budding field

Semyon Kirlian

of parapsychology, Kirlian photography had its instant detractors. True to form, the skeptic squad impeached the brilliant images, supplanting the paranormal explanation with boring, "rational" ones: the so-called aura was nothing more than ionized gas that surrounds living things, or the result of "natural" (read: measurable) variables such as grounding conditions, amperage fluctuations, air pollution, or moisture. Sweat!

But the camera has its own eye, which no amount of "variables" can alter in the capture of the persistent luminous breath

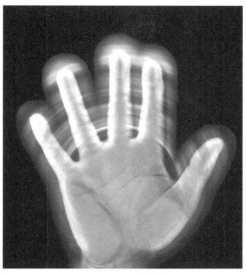

Hand aura, in the manner of Kirlian photography

issuing from living things: leaves, trees, birds, humans. The age of technology, it seemed, had been destined to ferret out the hitherto hidden forces of nature, often accidentally, serendipitously.

"What we see with our physical eyes comprises less than 10 percent of the known universe," says William Tiller, professor emeritus of Materials Science and Engineering at Stanford University.

No sooner had the camera (daguerreotype) been invented in the 1840s than spirit "extras" began appearing spontaneously on the plates, sometimes little more than a blotch of light or misty outline of something. (Today, spirit-extras are still seen to appear "in the middle of the photo [as] a bright light.")

By the turn of the 20th century, radio waves, X-rays, radiation, and so on, came into view as "scientific" evidence of earlier constructs such as "odic force," the animal magnetism of the Mesmerists, or even the halos of saints, like the brilliant light that surrounded St. Ignatius Loyola or the dazzling cloud of gold enveloping St. Colomba.

By 1908, London's Dr. Walter J. Kilner was using specially developed filters that captured on sensitized plates a luminous field embracing the human form. It looked like a blue-tinged haze. Experimenting with different colored screens, Dr. Kilner would pioneer the diagnostic (medical) applications of aura reading. Then, a decade after the *New York Times* applauded Dr. Kilner's rediscovery of "the legendary aura," quartz lens photography came along, enabling cameras to pick up yet other "psychic structures...beyond the range of our optical capacity." Indeed, fluorescing lights and "psychic rods" now appeared on exposed plates of experimenters. The "rods" were now seen as the heavy lifters as well as the knockers and pushers behind assorted levitation and PK events. At the Goligher Circle in Ireland, for instance, it was thought that the table was levitated "by an invisible substance which streamed out of the medium's body and became more or less solidified into psychic rods... [Though] invisible, the ends were sufficiently dense to be palpable."

There have been many times when only the camera, faster than the eye, could see these rods or shafts. At Glastonbury Abbey, England, visitors to the Chalice Well "have been astonished by the photographs they have taken here...show[ing] inexplicable shafts of light." The famous cloister, with its ley lines to Stonehenge, megalithic stones, and "spiritual engineering," has also been the site of automatic scripts, UFO sightings, spectral monks (both seen and heard), and visitors reporting a strange feeling of weightlessness and even teleportation.

Spirit lights, obviously, do not occur in a vacuum. Other "clues" are always there, other signs and prodigies. Frequently, though, only the camera can see what we have missed. Experimenting with infrared film in 1971, friends of Ingo Swann photographed the acclaimed medium during one of his out-of-body journeys. The image showed distinct "balls of light." Similarly, a modern exorcist once decided to film a session; watching his video later, he observed something the naked eye had not seen: "I saw spirit energy, perfectly round, transparent balls." Miniature moons. Orbs.

At a so-called haunted mansion in San Francisco, pictures were taken showing a "lightning flash...[with] two indistinct forms," while other prints revealed "light coming from some unknown source...[and] a woman's ghostly figure."

Nor do the psychic phenomena surrounding autistic children occur in isolation. These clairvoyant youngsters, as their spokesman Bill Stillman has amply demonstrated, are natural conduits between the seen and unseen worlds. Precognitive and "exquisitely sensitive" to invisible forces—their households prone to PK and other paranormal happenings—these clairvoyant kids also attract spectral lights in camera shots. A picture of

Gabriel showed "a cloudy mist" over his head; a group shot with Kyle in it revealed "streaks of light" around the boy.

"Abnormal"—as our case studies pile up—often betrays the paranormal. Multiple personalities, for example, are often psychic; in the case of Kit (a multiple with seven "alters"), all the photographs taken of her "had hazy lights in them." The troubled woman, not coincidentally, could also perform certain feats of PK such as levitating a pen simply by holding her hand above it.

Context is key: Whether we are looking at "hazy lights," "cloudy mists," orbs, or an "aura of lights," the glowing apparition is hardly an isolated event. Taken piecemeal, the unexpected luminosity is swiftly dimmed, if not entirely eclipsed, by the skeptic's battery of prosaic explanations. Taken in context, though, the paranormal is undeniable. Ghost lights, if you care to peruse their documentation, appear always in tandem with other outbreaks. And they are physical.

Sixty miles from London, villagers near Suffolk's Borley Rectory still see the window of Room No. 7 lit up at night, though no one resides there. Rats in the wall? Squirrels in the attic? Overactive imagination? Sweat? I

Unexplained light shaft from chalice well. (Photo by Dr. Eileen Palmer)

don't think so. But human sensitives in the rooms—Yes! The phenomena, it was noted, "are more numerous and more violent when a person possessing some psychic faculty is in the house." This link is actually well known. Spirit communicators have described the psychic or medium as—"for us a lighthouse…kind of little windows." Mrs. Travers Smith's controls once stated "that a bright light attracted them [to her]… a clear white fire," which grows more vivid as the medium gets into better touch with the spirit world. So vivid was the heightened aura of the great physical medium D. D. Home that, even without a camera, on occasion the naked eye could see the top of his head glowing "with lights as if a halo surrounded it." The "tongues or jets of flame" issuing from Home's head would presage the "fountains" of light captured on film 75 years later by the art and science of Kirlian photography.

And why is spirit so drawn to this effluvium of mortal light? More than a window or "lighthouse," it is an energy source! Ghost-hunters will tell you that orbs take on shapes more easily when there is static electricity in the atmosphere. Why do orbs hang around electrical systems, power cables, radar stations? Why is heat loss (ghost cold) such a sure sign of a presence? Why do appliances go on the blink in orb territory, and why do ghost-hunters have to pack so many extra batteries?

Drawing energy from available sources, the apparition is typically attracted to lively human activity, especially children. Observed fact: when the people—that is, the power supply—leave, the orb leaves.

The more clairvoyant or psychic the operator, the more readily can he "host" the disembodied. Exhaustion, headaches, difficulty walking, undiagnosable illnesses—are all occupational hazards suffered by the ghost-seeker or medium. After the great English medium, Stainton Moses, produced glowing globes of light in the séance room, "the drain on Moses' vital strength was too great." The history of mediumship is chock full of trance-mediums prostrated by their sittings. The sitters themselves, if *en rapport*, also contribute some of the "vital energy" essential to manifestations, and may come out of the experience utterly drained.

"Do you make them [tables] move?"—the question was once posed to a spirit. "Yes," came the answer, "but I'm not alone. There have to be people round the table. We're all together."

This subtle rapport between the seen and unseen worlds was recently confirmed by a NASA scientist whose wife, quite by chance, captured "hovering" orbs of light in photos taken at a gathering of healers. Armed with a digital camera, the couple decided to test the mysterious effect, only to find (what ghost-hunters have known all along) that the shimmering circles of light may appear on demand; in other words, "if they asked the apparitions to make themselves visible to the camera. And they found this method worked particularly well when…photographing spiritual gatherings."

In Spanish, orbs are called *canoplas*, cousin to the sky canopy in English. "Tiny pinpoint dots of light" seen where spirits gather can actually be viewed on any clear day. Look up. The myriad of fragile bubbles high in the sky are not spots on your eyes. They are canoplas. And when we ourselves leave our present abode for spirit country, that self-light may also be seen, liberated now for the upward journey.

Tradition portrays Buddha glowing with light just before his death. But you don't have to be Buddha to glow, as John Edward has recently recounted the sudden passing of a friend's father: watching TV in the living room, the father suffered a massive, fatal heart attack. His wife "saw a brilliant glow around [him] and then a light shoot out of him to the ceiling."

It was not coincidence and it was not sweat and it was not imagination when the wife of Bishop Jim Pike watched, in etheric sight, as a "filmy, almost vaporous, cloudlike substance" left her husband's body. Tragically, Bishop Pike, of California, had gotten lost in the Judean desert on a dream trip—no less—to the Holy Land. The vigorous search was in vain. "He's dying," Mrs. Pike, startled awake, now knew. "I can see him beginning to leave his body now…His spirit is very light in color—white…I can see his spirit leaving."

Out from the head of the corporeal body the spirit is born!

The vapor departed through his neck. But wait—now it left behind a trail of the same filmy substance just as it "seemed attached to, somehow, or floating out of, his head." At the same time, the form became a column of light and it connected his spirit to his body.

Then it rose up, drifting to the top of the craggy, deserted canyon.

And even though it has no distinct features, as Diane Kennedy Bishop recalls her most unforgettable vision, still—it is Jim, and "I can tell he is smiling."

## 21

# DEATHBED VISITATIONS

*Can the Dying Communicate with the Other Side?*

**BY MICHAEL E. TYMN**

The night before my 87-year-old mother died, she couldn't stop talking. While asleep, she jabbered away through the night. Because of her slurred speech resulting from several strokes, as well as advanced dementia, I couldn't make out what she was saying. However, she seemed to be desperately pleading with someone.

My wife and I had brought my mother up from her Berkeley, California, rest home several days earlier to spend Thanksgiving 2003 with us at our Oregon home. We moved a spare bed into our bedroom so that we could better care for her. It was on the fourth or fifth night at our house, Thanksgiving night, that she began talking in her sleep.

The next morning, as I was carrying her from the bedroom downstairs to her wheelchair so that I could wheel her out to the car and drive her back to Berkeley, her eyes rolled back in her head and she "gave up the ghost."

In retrospect, I suspect that all the talking the prior night was with deceased loved ones who were trying to convince her that it was time to leave the physical world. Mom seemed very much afraid of dying when she was lucid. Whether that fear remained with her in her demented state, I have no idea, but I have no other explanation for her all-night chatter, other than the possibility that she was pleading with someone to help her disengage her spirit body from her weary physical shell.

Very recently, my mother's sister passed on at age 81. My cousin informed me that her mother, my aunt, had many conversations with deceased loved ones during the last week of her life.

Whether or not my mother and aunt actually communicated with deceased love ones before they died, I have no way of knowing for sure, but I do know that there is considerable evidence to suggest that such deathbed visits are not unusual.

"They're so common I don't think much about them any more," said Ginny Chappelear, senior coordinator of bereavement services at the Tidewell Hospice in Sarasota, Florida, when I asked her if deathbed visions and visitations (DBVs) are common among hospice patients. "We call them the 'Gathering of Spirits'."

Light in the Forest

Chappelear, who has been doing hospice work for more than 20 years, recalled an early experience in which a woman was dying at home. "About five days before her death, she reported seeing a man looking in the window," Chappelear offered. "This was out in the country and we were concerned that it was a peeping tom. But when the man came back, she told us it was her brother who had died many years earlier. 'He's just waiting for me,' she said. 'I'll go with him the next time he comes.' It was very comforting to her."

A more recent case involved a woman who was the sole survivor out of seven siblings. "A day or two before she died, she started calling out the names of all her siblings," Chappelear remembered, "as if she were greeting them and saying, 'Come on, take me.'"

She recalled another case in which a father was dying and told his daughter that there was a loved one standing right there with her hands on his shoulders. "You can't see them," the dying man said, "but some day you'll understand what it is like."

For "people of faith" these visions and visitations make the dying process much easier, Chappelear added.

Skeptics say that the visions of the dying are nothing more than hallucinations. Of course they are if we define a hallucination as something outside of the range of the five ordinary senses. Such a definition does not mean it is not real, whatever "real" means.

Delusions perhaps? However, it is very difficult to discount certain cases. Consider the case of "Jennie" and "Bessie" (both pseudonyms for privacy purposes) as related by Dr. Minot J. Savage, a popular Unitarian clergyman and author, in his 1899 book, *Life Beyond Death.*

Jennie and Bessie, ages 8 and 9, were close friends in a city in Massachusetts, and both were afflicted with diphtheria. Jennie died on Wednesday, but Bessie was not informed of her friend's death as her family felt it might stand in the way of her own recovery.

On Saturday, Bessie apparently realized that she was going to die and began telling her parents which of her brothers, sisters, and playmates should receive her treasured belongings. "Among these she pointed out certain things of which she was very fond, that were to go to Jennie—thus settling all question as to whether or not she had found out that Jennie was not still living," Savage wrote.

A little later, as she approached death, she began seeing deceased grandparents and others gathered around her bed. "And then she turned to her father, with face and voice both expressing the greatest surprise, and exclaimed, 'Why, Papa, why didn't you tell me that Jennie had gone? Why didn't you tell me of it?'" Savage ends the story, commenting that this and similar stories suggest that more than hallucination and imagination are involved.

Savage also reported the case of a small boy who had befriended a judge of some prominence living in the neighborhood. After the boy was put to bed one night, his parents heard him crying. They rushed to him and asked him what was wrong. "Judge says he's dead! He has been here and told me that he is dead!" the boy sobbed. The next morning the parents found out that the judge had died at about that time the night before.

Elisabeth Kübler-Ross

Elisabeth Kübler-Ross, the physician who revolutionized medicine's approach to death and dying during the latter part of the 20th century, wrote that many children with terminal diseases become aware of the ability to leave the physical body and have out-of-body experiences (OBEs). "It is during those out-of-body trips that dying patients become aware of the presence of beings who surround them, who guide them, and help them."

Kübler-Ross, who frequently sat with critically injured children, recalled that many of them were not told which of their family members were killed in the same accident, yet they were invariably aware of who had preceded them in death. "Everything is all right now," one critically injured child told Kübler-Ross. "Mommy and Peter are already waiting for me." Kübler-Ross knew that the child's mother had died at the accident scene, but was unaware that Peter, who had been in the burn unit in a different hospital, had also expired. It was not until she left the child's bedside that she received a phone call from a nurse at the other hospital informing her that Peter had transitioned.

In another case, a 12-year-old girl reported that her brother was there with her and offering great tenderness, love, and compassion. However, the girl was confused because she had, to her knowledge, no brother, living or dead. The father explained that she did have a brother who died about three months before she was born, but the parents had decided not to tell her about him.

"[Such] cases form, perhaps, one of the most cogent arguments for survival after death, as the evidential value of these visions of the dying is greatly enhanced when the fact is undeniably established that the dying person was wholly ignorant of the decease of the person he or she so vividly sees," wrote Sir William Barrett, a renowned British physicist, in his now classic book, *Death-Bed Visions*, first published in 1926, the year after his death.

Barrett reported on a case told to him by his wife, an obstetric surgeon. Lady (Florence) Barrett, who later became dean of the London School of Medicine for Women, was tending to a dying woman ("Mrs. B."), who had just given birth. Mrs. B. commented that it was getting "darker and darker." Her husband and mother were summoned. "Suddenly she looked eagerly toward one part of the room, a radiant smile illuminating her whole countenance," Lady Barrett recalled. "Oh, lovely, lovely," the dying woman said. Lady Barrett asked her to what she was referring. "What I see," the woman replied, "lovely brightness, wonderful beings."

The woman then began to focus her attention on one place in the room and then cried out, "Why, it's Father! Oh, he's so glad I am coming; he is so glad. It would be perfect if only W. (her husband) could come too."

The dying woman's baby was brought to her and she wondered if she should not stay for the baby's sake. She then said, "I can't, I can't stay. If you could see what I do, you would know; if you could see what I do, you would know I can't stay."

The woman's husband entered the room and she requested that the baby not go to anyone who will not love him, after which she asked her husband to step aside so that she could see the "lovely brightness." She died about an hour later.

Scientist that he was, Sir William corroborated his wife's story by talking with a Dr. Phillips, another physician who had been present, as well as with the hospital matron, Miriam Castle, who added to Lady Barrett's story by mentioning that the dying patient also reported seeing her sister, Vida, who had died some two weeks earlier. The news of her sister's death had been kept from her because of her delicate condition.

In an earlier book, *On the Threshold of the Unseen*, Barrett printed a letter sent to him by a Dr. Wilson of New York, who was present at the last moments of James Moore, a well-known American tenor. Wilson told of

Sir William Barrett

being present during the early morning at Moore's bedside. As he examined Moore, he noticed that his face was quite calm and his eyes clear. Moore then took the doctor's hand in both of his and thanked him for being such a good friend. "While he appeared perfectly rational and sane as any man I have ever seen," Wilson related, "the only way I can express it is that he was transported into another world; and although I cannot satisfactorily explain the matter to myself, I am fully convinced that he had entered the golden city— for he said in a stronger voice than he had used since I had attended him: 'There is mother! Why, mother, have you come to see me? No, no, I am coming to see you. Just wait, mother, I am almost over. Wait, mother, wait, mother!'

"On his face there was a look of expressible happiness and the way in which he said the words impressed me as I have never been before, and I am as firmly convinced that he saw and talked with is mother as I am that I am sitting here."

Wilson went on to say that he immediately recorded every word and that it was the most beautiful death he had ever seen.

In his 1900 book, *Man and the Spiritual World*, the Rev. Arthur Chambers, vicar of the Church of England in Brockenhurst, Hampshire, England, reported that a dying man said to him, "You consider, do you not, that my mind is perfectly clear?" Chambers assured him that he did and that he had never known him to be more so. "Very well, then," the dying man continued. "Now I want to tell you what occurred last evening. But first you must understand that I was neither dreaming nor under a delusion. As I lay here, my father, who died some years ago, stood in the place where you are now and spoke to me. He told me I had only a very little longer to remain on Earth, and said that he and other dear ones passed away were waiting to welcome me into the spiritual world. I tried to raise myself in bed in order to attract the attention of the nurse who was at the other end of the ward. I thought you might still be in the building, and I wanted her to send for you, that you, too, might see my father. I supposed the effort to raise myself must have been too much for me, for I slipped back on the pillow and felt I was fainting. When I opened my eyes again, I looked for my father, but he was gone. Don't tell me I was dreaming, because I tell you with my dying breath I was not. My father was as real there as you are now, and I think he will come again."

The man died two days later, after which Chambers spoke to a man in a nearby bed. Without knowing what the dying man had told Chambers, the patient informed Chambers that just before the man died he saw him raise himself into a sitting position, fix his gaze earnestly on the spot where Chambers had so often prayed and conversed with him, smile as if he were recognizing someone, and then fall back on his pillow motionless. A minute or two later, the screen was put around the bed, and he knew the man was gone.

Dr. Charles Richet, the 1913 Nobel Prize winner in medicine for his research on anaphylaxis, the sensitivity of the body to alien protein substance, believed in psychic phenomena, but resisted, at least publicly, a spiritist explanation. He advanced the theory of cryptesthesia, which, in effect, said that there was some sensory organ unknown to science by which certain individuals could see things or beings that others couldn't. Nevertheless, he wrote that deathbed visions "are much more explicable on the spiritist theory than by the hypothesis of mere cryptesthesia."

Charles Richet

More recently, the subject of deathbed visions and visitations has been explored by Carla Wills-Brandon, Ph.D. in her 2000 book, *One Last Hug Before I Go*, and by Dr. Peter Fenwick, an internationally renowned British neuropsychiatrist, and Elizabeth Fenwick in their 2008 book, *The Art of Dying*.

Wills-Brandon looks at the various theories advanced by materialistic scientists to explain away such visions, including mental illness, excessive grief, wishful thinking, hysteria, drug-induced hallucinations of an overactive imagination, and the by-product of random firings of a dying brain, concluding that many DBVs, especially those involving visions of deceased loved ones whose death was unknown to the dying person, go beyond any of these theories. "Sadly, such explanations cannot completely explain the DBV phenomenon and they take away from the spiritual significance of such encounters," Will-Brandon says, referring to caretakers who are unaware that deathbed visions are common, spiritual experiences and who therefore ignore or discount such reports.

The Fenwicks found that drug- and fever-induced hallucinations are quite different from true end-of-life visions and that they have quite a different effect on patients. Drug or fever-induced hallucinations, including such things as seeing animals walking around on the floor, children running in and out of the room, devils or dragons dancing in the light, or insects moving in wallpaper or on the carpet, are rarely, if ever, comforting. "True deathbed hallucinations are quite different," they state. "They are not confusional. Most occur in full consciousness; often, moreover, an unconscious patient will regain consciousness and see the vision in a brief lucid interval before they die."

Like Wills-Brandon, the Fenwicks lament the fact that many caregivers are not trained or prepared to deal with this aspect of the dying process. In fact, many of them do not discuss it as they fear ridicule.

"The evidence points to the fact that we are more than brain function, more than just a speck in creation, and that something, whether we regard it as soul or consciousness, will continue in some form or another, making its journey to 'Elsewhere,'" the Fenwicks conclude their book. "It suggests that when we enter the light, we are coming home, that we do indeed touch the inner reaches of a universe that is composed of universal love. This is the territory of the dying. Until then, perhaps the best we can do is to continue living, prepare for death, and take as guidelines what we have learned about the process of dying."

# 22

# LINCOLN AND THE AFTERLIFE

## Was the Great Civil War President Taking Directions from Another World?

### BY SUSAN MARTINEZ, PH.D.

*"The angels appeared to his mother and predicted that the son whom she would conceive would become the greatest the stars had ever seen—His name was Lincoln and the country in which he lived is called America."*

—A MUSLIM CHIEF IN A REMOTE CORNER OF THE CAUCASUS, AS TOLD TO LEO TOLSTOY

It was one thing researching and writing my book, *The Psychic Life of Abraham Lincoln* (2007), and another thing "explaining" it to the media. Lincoln, having once been a common person, a child of the wilderness, but rising to mythic proportions in American iconography, still captures the public imagination like no other single figure. And because of his almost sainted fame, it has long been thought scandalous to taint that hallowed name with the stigma of what was once called "Spiritualism"—and, for that matter still is by its modern-day adherents. The subject touches a nerve or unnerves what has been a virtual conspiracy of silence orchestrated by historians who would "protect" the Lincoln mystique by inventing cover stories to account for the man's clearly established deep interest in things psychic and the "upper country"— Lincoln's own phrase for the Life Beyond.

Thus it is that the first great hurdle in speaking publicly on the spiritual Lincoln is getting past the whitewash, the taboo, the giggles and sneers, the embarrassment and surprise, the hesitancy and caution that is as predictable as the morning sun. For here is evidence that both the Civil War and the Emancipation Proclamation were placed in the hands of a man in direct contact with the higher powers and that an invisible force guided the destiny of this nation.

Lincoln as "The Mystical Unionist"
[*Atlantis Rising* art]

"He has shown an almost supernatural tact in keeping the ship afloat—The foundation of his character was mystical," said Walt Whitman, a contemporary and great admirer of Mr. Lincoln.

Once the documentation of Lincoln's belief in the spirit world is tendered, many questions spring immediately to mind. Was there political fallout from his White House seances? (Oh, yeah) Why have there been so many Lincoln "sightings" (ghost, the phantom funeral train)? Did he predict his own death? Wasn't it really his crazy wife Mary who dragged him to mediumistic sittings? Did Lincoln shape military strategy around "intelligence" received through spirit communications? Was Lincoln psychic?

Abraham Lincoln, as the bloody War Between the States dragged on, began to perceive that no mortal power could bring it to a conclusion; that he had been chosen, in the sacred sense, to steer the ship of state through this storm, yet that he was merely an instrument of Providence. Just as he was chosen, the country itself was chosen, somehow, to lead the world. And for all this he won the sobriquet, "The Mystical Unionist." Another sobriquet was "The Trimmer," and this meant that he kept his cards close to his waistcoat. And so it was that the Emancipation Proclamation came as a surprise.

What really led up to the signing of that historic document which sounded the death knell to slavery?

Late in December, 1862, the president had one of his dreams—well, more like a vision. He couldn't be sure of what he'd seen and heard. Was it possible, Lincoln asked himself, that, as in the Bible, angels could appear and make their requirements known?

But then, he was given proof.

There was at that moment a reputed seeress living in Washington, and by a strange chain of "coincidences," she was brought before the president and entranced by the same congress of spirits who had promised Lincoln, in the dream-vision, that "we will give thee proof tomorrow." And the young medium, Nettie Colburn Maynard, repeated the words of the inspiring host while, fully entranced, lecturing the president and his small entourage.

Actually, it had been Mrs. Lincoln who, having sat in spirit circles in Georgetown, had been suddenly inspired to ask for a trance-medium. The best person in the District at the time who fit that bill was Miss Colburn. And though she addressed the president for a full hour and a half, it was not her own voice but a booming, sonorous tone that came forth from this tiny and timid young woman. It declared that there was a Spiritual Congress—composed of the men, gone before, who had founded and shaped this republic—that was now supervising the affairs of this nation. "You, sir, have been called to the position you now occupy for a great and mighty purpose. Thou art the man! The world is in universal bondage; it must be set free." Strange to say, those words came forth in the deep bass tones and distinctive English parliamentary manner so typical of the late, great statesman and passionate Unionist, Daniel Webster. All present (including Lincoln) who had known Webster, acknowledged that it was his voice coming through the entranced young woman.

It was "Miss Nettie's" deathbed memoir, written in 1891, that revealed, almost 30 years after the fact, what had been profound state secrets: wartime séances in the President's House (many of them), including sittings that were outright ESPionage—with Nettie, fully entranced, pencil in hand, map spread before her—pinpointing the precise disposition of Confederate forces on the ground. While research has uncovered the names of at least ten psychic-mediums consulted

The brownstone in Georgetown where Lincoln and his wife participated in spiritualist sessions (image courtesy of John Buescher.)

by President Lincoln during the Civil War years, this is no more than the tail end of his lifelong interest in omens, oracles, prophecy, and messages from the invisible world. And although Lincoln biographers are well acquainted with his "death dream" (predicting his own assassination), little if any notice has been paid to his visions, and even less to his altered states of consciousness.

The psychic door had opened early for Lincoln, in pain and loss, through tragedy, accident and abuse (beatings by his father). After losing his mother at age 9, young Abraham, at 10, fell off a horse, sustaining cerebral injury and remaining unconscious for hours—his father thought he was dead. More tragedies followed; gradually the spiritual eye was opening to what he himself variously dubbed "regions unexplored," "Divine interposition," "no earthly power," "the upper country," and most notably—"the new faith." He was a sage in training.

> "I have had so many—instances when I have been controlled by some other power than my own will, that I cannot doubt that this power comes from above."—Abraham Lincoln

Much later, the same philosophy would sustain him through the difficulties of his war presidency and that seething volcano of slavery. In writing and signing the Emancipation Proclamation, he would declare: "I am wholly the agent of a special purpose—a servant." Besieged on every side by conflicting advice and pressures, he would quell the great cacophony of opinions as to tampering with the peculiar institution—or with the Constitution, for that matter—by calmly repeating that "God will direct my hand that holds the pen."

Poet and jokester, mime and orator, humanist and freethinker (the only U.S. president never to join a church), bookworm and seeker, clog-dancer and rail splitter extraordinaire, Abe Lincoln's NDE (near-death experience) at age 10 presaged the "sensitive" life. Today it is a fact that 75 percent of NDErs—regardless of their prior beliefs—become spiritualists as a result of their fleeting but stunning contact with the other world. Is this what happened to Lincoln? It is hardly enlightening to be told time and again by Lincoln scholars that he was "complex" or "elusive." Complex? Nonsense, he was a simple man. And if biographers have called him a mystery or "elusive," this opinion might well be based, as one writer thought, on "their refusal to face and appreciate—his psychic nature." Lincoln's famous mirror vision, in which his double (doppelganger) appeared—ominously—occurred spontaneously: a form of scrying or crystal-gazing which others have gone to great lengths to induce.

Also spontaneous were his very frequent lapses into the alpha state, which everyone who knew him inevitably witnessed—the flatlanders among them supposing that the president had dozed off or gone dopey. Many were baffled by the otherwhereness of his demeanor, in a world by himself, suddenly rejoining his visitors as one awakened from sleep. The long silences, the trancelike behavior, the "peculiar dreaminess of expression," the "extraordinary moods of abstraction" —all convey the timeless, yogi-like, almost disembodied state so typical of the brooding Lincoln. He walked in both worlds. Many tried to wrap a word around those "waves of magnetic force" or that "phantom touch" that defined his persona; at the Laurie Circle in Georgetown he became so influenced by spiritual forces that he admitted seeing his deceased son Willie while in that condition.

Willie. The death of 11-year-old Willie Lincoln in the White House in 1862—right in the middle of the war— was so shattering for Lincoln as to become the turning point in his life. His heart was changed.

It was a metamorphosis, it was an epiphany; for Lincoln, up to that point, was not yet fully convinced of the summerland of the departed. His faith was unfinished. But now, the cloud of doubt lifted and, according to writer Troy Taylor, he "began to look more closely at the spiritual matters which had interested him for so long."

"I feel that he [Willie] is with me."—A.L.

Life-after-death would now become more than a debatable concept, it would become a palpable reality. And as if to affirm or commemorate it, on the first anniversary of Willie's departure Lincoln wrote of the highest interests of this life and of that to come. But confessing the afterlife implied more than personal conviction; with his growing respect for the immortals came his grasp of "the God of Nations" who deals with "national offences": the nightmare war yet had a purpose!

"He will compel us to do right. He means to establish justice."—A.L.

Many, not just the president, had felt the finger of God in the great rebellion, but with Lincoln's "uncanny grasp of the popular mind" (according to Harriet Beecher Stowe), he took on the mantle of Father Abraham,

Lincoln reads the Emancipation Proclamation to his cabinet

man of destiny, and prophet of the people. Yet his own prescience was not always a happy thing.

"I believe I feel trouble in the air before it comes."—A.L.

Many times during the turbulent war did this foreboding kick in. Though far from the front, he could suddenly "see" (his own word) the Confederates crossing federal lines. Though hours away, he "knew" the Dahlgren raid (on Richmond) was a disaster. His young secretary John Hay was astonished that his beloved boss "repeatedly uttered—predictions which have become history." And on the very day of his death, that morning, he could not convince his Cabinet of General Sherman's success in Raleigh, North Carolina, though he felt it of a certainty. (The triumphant news had not yet reached the capital.) And though he did not generally advertise it, Lincoln's informing spirit, it seems, had always been with him: "There never was a time that I did not believe that I would at some day be President."—A.L.

But the grandiose forecast also portended doom, as his dear friend and biographer, Ward Hill Lamon, would recall, that the same omens which assured Lincoln's rise to greatness also convinced him that "he would be suddenly cut off at the height of his career and the fullness of his fame;" for the star under which he was born was "at once brilliant and malignant." The closer the time came, the more explicit was the prognostication: 1864: as told to the *Boston Journal*: "I feel a presentiment that I shall not outlast the rebellion." March, 1865: "I do not think I shall live to see the end of my second term." And then, only hours before his murder, he felt the coming evil, telling his aide, William Crook, of his dream, the past three nights running, of assassination: "I have no doubt they will do it."

Far-seeing, Lincoln reached into the future, bequeathing to posterity his vision of justice to come—men will pass away—die, die—but the principle will live—till the final triumph will come.

Prophet of this new era in the life of man, he gave voice to his innermost conviction—that we are inexorably "giving up the old faith for the new faith." Having come to grips, the hard way, with this new birth of freedom, Lincoln stands today as more than a memorable president or great statesman. He was a sage; and in the history of ideas and its hall of fame, he serves as living proof that mysticism and rationalism are not conflicting isms. Nor can politics and religion be forever held apart. Faith, as Lincoln himself once confided, was the overruling principle that kept "my reason in its seat" in those troublous times.

In the decade prior to his presidency, Lincoln was a "fellow traveler" in the burgeoning movement of modern spiritualism. He shared this interest with many of his illustrious contemporaries—Harriet Beecher Stowe, the Brontë sisters, Elizabeth Barrett Browning, Queen Victoria, Alfred Lord Tennyson, Mrs. Hawthorne, William Lloyd Garrison, William Makepeace Thackery, Louisa May Alcott, Emily Dickinson, James Fenimore Cooper, Mark Twain—to name a few. His favorite poets were also believers in the afterlife: Milton, Burns, Byron, and Shakespeare.

And because his involvement and fascination with the "future state" was known—or at least rumored—he was given the option (by the *Cleveland Plain Dealer*) in 1860 to deny or contradict it. Instead, he declared that the article in the Ohio paper detailing his mediumistic forays "does not begin to tell the wonderful things I have witnessed."

Accused by his enemies of blindly following his "guides" and "spirit-rappers," Lincoln was the dupe of neither man nor angel, but "master in logic," stamped with the "trademark of close reasoning" (Douglas Wilson). Yet it is true that he hearkened to his most trusted "controls" (disembodied mentors) in certain state decisions taken to meet a crisis. Such is the hidden or unwritten history behind both the Freedmen's Bureau and the unprecedented presidential three-day visit to the war front itself—General Hooker's great encampment, in April, 1863.

Called at first the "accidental president" (the insulting phrase disappearing after his re-election in 1864), Abraham Lincoln would collect a colorful array of epithets—The People's President, The Gorilla, The Great Emancipator, Old Ape, widow-maker, Abraham the First. But after his murder—his sacrifice, as some saw it—on Good Friday, the aura of savior and redeemer clung to the 16th president.

"Massa Linkum—walk de earth like de Lord"—a Negro praise-man

Even more persistent were pious comparisons to the prophet Moses who brought his people through the wilderness (read: the chaos and dis-union of war) but lived not to see the Promised Land.

"Alas! Alas! He only saw the dawn."—Rev. Gurley, eulogy

Curious that Vachel Lindsay, the Illinois poet (who, like many, would later sense the spirit of that "bronzed lank man"), also painted Lincoln as a spiritual harbinger: "—He cannot rest until a spirit-dawn—" As conjured by the poet, Lincoln is the mourning figure, cloaked in black, who walks at midnight, unable to rest until the wars and woes of the world melt before the throne of "long peace." Poet Lindsay traces the spiritual footsteps of the immortal Lincoln through Springfield town, near the old courthouse, pacing up and down—

"the prairie lawyer, master of us all—And who will bring white peace, That he may sleep upon his hill again?"

## 23

# SUICIDE DOESN'T WORK

*The Evidence Is Inescapable, Death Is Not the End*

### BY MICHAEL E. TYMN

A s a young boy, I accepted everything the Catholic Church taught as absolute truth. One such "truth" was that all those who committed suicide went to hell for eternity. And so when I was informed that my step-grandfather had hung himself, I struggled with visions of him burning in hell. I wondered why he did not foresee his fate and also pondered on why God isn't more compassionate.

Apparently, the Catholic Church has modified its position on suicide in recent decades. "We should not despair of the eternal salvation of persons who have taken their own lives," one Catholic Internet source states. "By ways known to him alone, God can provide the opportunity for salutary repentance. The Church prays for persons who have taken their own lives."

Although it mentions a number of suicides, including Abimelech, Saul, Ahithophel, Zimri, and Judas, and also tells us that Jesus was tempted by Satan to kill himself while fasting in the desert for 40 days, the Bible does not directly address suicide or the fate of the suicide. However, inferences are made from various passages, including the commandment "thou shall not kill," that it is clearly morally wrong to take one's life. A Protestant Internet source states that it is a serious sin against God, but if the person had accepted Christ beforehand then his sin will be "covered by the blood of Christ" and the sinner will be saved, although he will likely have to "escape through the flames," as set forth in 1 Corinthians 3:15.

Christian orthodoxy has conveniently and self-servingly interpreted the Book of Revelation to be closed—revelation that came through "prophets" and "seers." Such prophets and seers still exist, although the old Hebrew and Greek words today translate to mediums (including clairvoyants) and out-of-body experiencers (including near-death experiencers).

On the brink

By going beyond the self-imposed limits of the priesthood—by studying more recent revelation, properly tested and discerned—we get a better, more sensible and more just idea as to the plight of the suicide in the afterlife environment.

Beyond the evidence that consciousness continues after death, the most important lesson coming to us from sources outside of orthodox Christianity is that we do not face a dichotomous afterlife—the humdrum heaven or horrific hell of orthodoxy. Rather, there are many levels, planes, realms, or conditions on the "other side." This is what Jesus apparently intended to teach when he said, "In my Father's house are many mansions." The Greek word from which "mansion" comes is said to better translate to a "way station," or intermediate stopping place.

A recurring message coming through most Eastern religions and metaphysical teachings, such as theosophy, as well as from many spirit mediums, is that our spiritual consciousness in this world determines our degree of "awakening" and immediate place in the afterlife, and that we continue to evolve from there to realms of higher vibration. In the lower astral planes, where the spiritually challenged initially find themselves, there may be a "fire of the mind," something akin to a nightmare, but it is not a physical or eternal state. Moreover, it is reported that many souls in the lower astrals are "earthbound" and do not realize they are "dead." The idea that one cannot understand he or she is dead is difficult to comprehend until we stop to think how often our earthly consciousness drifts into unreality. For example, when we become absorbed in a good movie or novel, we are not constantly reminding ourselves that it is not "real." We escape into the fiction, identify with the characters, and feel the emotion.

Another important lesson coming to us in alternative revelations is that we are not judged by God or some high tribunal. We judge ourselves. There is no cheating in this respect as our spiritual consciousness manifests in an energy field, which we call the aura, with what might be called a "moral specific gravity." A spiritually-challenged person would have a low vibration rate, one much closer to earth conditions, and would not be able to tolerate a higher vibrational level other than that for which his or her moral specific gravity permits.

In her 1995 book, *Beyond the Darkness*, Angie Fenimore tells of attempting to take her own life when she was unable to deal with her despair, and then having a near-death experience (NDE). After seeing every moment of her 27 years pass before her in an instant, Fenimore awaited the "brilliant white light" and family reunions that she had heard others talk about as part of the initial death experience. "But for me there was no blaze of radiance, no arms waiting to usher me into the Divine presence," she wrote. "There was only blackness, as though I were suspended in outer space, unbroken by a single glimmering star."

Fenimore then found herself among a number of other souls, all of whom seemed to be in a "thoughtless stupor." Through some form of telepathic intuition, she understood that they also had taken their own lives. She then felt a whoosh and landed on the edge of a shadowy plane where the darkness extended to the limits of her sight. "It had life, this darkness, some kind of intelligence that was purely negative, even evil," she continued the story. "It sucked at me, pulling me to react and then swallowing my reaction into fear and dread. In my life I had suffered pain and despair so great that I could barely function, but the twisting anguish of this disconnection was beyond my capacity to conceive."

Fenimore sensed that she was in a state of hell, but the word "purgatory" then came into her mind. She observed people of all ages seemingly wandering aimlessly about while self-absorbed, "every one of them too caught up in his or her own misery to engage in any mental or emotional exchange."

After observing more depressing sites, Fenimore heard a voice of "awesome power" asking, "Is this what you really want?" Needless to say, it is not what she wanted, and she thankfully returned for a second chance at life.

NDE researchers Drs. Craig R. Lundahl and Harold A. Widdison reported on a somewhat similar NDE by a woman named Karen. Going through a divorce, she tried to kill herself by taking a bottle of tranquilizers. Her heart stopped but was revived with the use of a defibrillator. During the period she was thought to be unconscious, she was aware of being enveloped in total darkness. "It was pitch-black all around, yet there was a feeling of movement," she recalled. "My conscious self assured me that I was in the form of a spiritual body." She then heard a male voice tell her that she had a choice to stay or go back.

While many people who have undergone the near-death phenomenon report a positive experience, including seeing a comforting light and being greeted by deceased relatives, NDE researcher Dr. Kenneth Ring reported on a study involving 24 NDErs who had unsuccessfully attempted suicide. Not one of the 24 saw a comforting light or was temporarily reunited with loved ones, and, generally, there was a confused drifting in a dark or murky void.

Communicating through Gladys Osborne Leonard (one of England's most famous mediums) Claude Kelway-Bamber, a British pilot killed during World War I, told his mother that nothing can kill the soul. "You see, therefore, a suicide, far from escaping trouble, only goes from one form of misery to another; he cannot annihilate himself and pass to nothingness," Claude stated.

In her 1964 book, *Post-Mortem Journal*, Jane Sherwood, an automatic writing medium, related information coming to her from a spirit known as "Scott," a pseudonym for a spirit later identified as Colonel T. E. Lawrence, known as "Lawrence of Arabia." Scott told of encountering one of his old friends in the afterlife, one of whom had killed himself. "He was in a kind of stupor and I was told that he might remain in this state for a long time and that nothing could be done about it," he penned through Sherwood's hand. "We watched over him and were loath to leave him in the misty half-region where he was found.... Until he regained consciousness, there he had to remain; had we forcibly removed him, his poor body would not have been able to stand the conditions of our plane."

Now and then, Scott went back to visit his friend, finding him still in the same quiet coma. His astral body was in such bad shape that Scott almost dreaded his awakening. Scott went on to say that such long-lasting comas are common with suicides. "It is really a merciful pause during which some of the damage to their emotional bodies is quietly made good." Scott and others attempted to help their old friend, but his condition was such that progress was slow.

Scott further communicated that there is a belief that suicides remain in a coma until the time when they would have naturally died, but he had no way of verifying that. "This is one of those propositions which are impossible of proof, since no one can say when their hour would have struck had they not anticipated it. It is a fact that this state of coma lasts for varying periods, but there is also a long period of unconsciousness in many who have come by violent deaths. A suicide differs from such a one because his emotional state is usually far worse and takes much longer to clear, but a long period of coma may supervene on death in either case."

Eventually, Scott added, the suicide awakens and takes on the task of fitting himself to enter his own appropriate sphere of being, and this is where others can assist him.

Lillian Bailey, another renowned British medium, also received messages about suicide. One spirit communicated through her that the suicide will have to live through whatever his physical body would have had to endure. "He will see the whole thing happening. He will be consciously living with the same problems, although there will be no one condemning him and there will be beauty all around him."

The spirit added that even though the suicide may feel he was justified in taking his own life, he is still a "gate-crasher" and that things are not ready for him in the spirit world. "It is very difficult to tell you how wrong it is. He can't go very far. He can only reach a certain 'half-way' stage. His dear ones may not be able to get to him—something like Berlin's Wall."

Red Cloud, the spirit guide of Estelle Roberts, still another of England's great mediums, communicated that the person who commits suicide undergoes a premature birth into the spirit world. "He cannot immediately reach the plane of consciousness to which his evolution would entitle him had he fulfilled his allotted span on earth. Instead he remains suspended between the earth and the astral plane, which is the first stage beyond earth. In this state he is deprived, for the time being, of the company of his loved ones in the spirit world, unable to cross the barrier raised by his premature birth. Only when he has advanced in his evolution to the required degree can he rejoin those he knew and loved."

Many similar messages have come through other mediums as well as from people undergoing past-life regressions. "The karmic law points at suicides with a shrug: they merely have to do it all over in the next incarnation," offered Dr. Hans Holzer, a long-time paranormal investigator. "Nobody can cheat or escape earthly commitments."

Clearly, however, a distinction needs to made between suicide (self-destruction) and an act of noble self-sacrifice for a greater good; and if there is any justice in the cosmos it seemingly would not be fair even to treat all who commit suicide alike. The Catholic Encyclopedia defines suicide to include "omitting to do what is necessary to escape death, as

The U.S.S. Bunker Hill hit by two simultaneous kamikaze attacks in WWII

LOST POWERS

in avoiding the obligation incumbent to preserve his life." Since there are indications that Jesus could have avoided crucifixion, either by not incriminating himself or by fleeing from his captors when there was time, should he be classified as a "suicide"? Hardly. What about martyrs who could have avoided execution by repudiating their faith? Is the battlefield soldier who puts himself in harm's way to save his comrades committing suicide and should he be treated like more deliberate suicides? Certainly not.

What of the terminally-ill person who ends his life so that his loved ones will not face further financial or emotional burden? How is he or she different from the battlefield soldier?

And what of suicide bombers? If they truly believe they are doing God's will and see themselves as martyrs to the cause, are they judged harshly, or, if we do judge ourselves, do they judge themselves harshly? Of course, they are also guilty of murdering others, which would certainly outweigh any virtues claimed for their act, though some might argue that they are no different from Samson of the Bible, who knew he and others would die when he unseated the support columns and brought the temple down upon himself and the Philistines. It certainly seems, however, that there can be no moral equivalence between the defiant actions of a tortured prisoner, as in the case of Samson, and unprovoked attacks upon the innocent, as with modern terrorists.

Underneath their supposedly idealistic objectives, most suicide bombers seem to be driven by hatred, anger, envy, pride, fear, frustration, even lust in the case of those who expect to be greeted by 72 virgins. If they see their afterlife as being better than their current condition, it would appear that their reasons are more self-serving than altruistic, although there may very well be some altruistic motives mixed in with the selfish ones.

The case of the Japanese kamikaze pilots of World War II may be somewhat different. History has suggested that they were driven, to the extent they had any choice, by a sense of honor and loyalty to their emperor and country. If the kamikaze pilots and the modern suicide bombers were all victims of "brainwashing," should they be punished severely in the afterlife for having been "simpleminded" and for not having been stronger in resisting more powerful minds?

As with many things, when it comes to suicide, there are no easy answers.

# 24

# THE CASE FOR IMMORTALITY

*Ancient Wisdom Upheld by Cutting Edge Science*

## BY PATRICK MARSOLEK

"When I was fully into the light I realized it was the most incredibly beautiful light that I had ever seen. It seemed to have a personality that was beyond belief—loving. I was happy just being in the light. I remember then that I heard a voice that I thought was the light that surrounded me. Without having a body, somehow I talked to the voice. I was shown that the white light was really made up of all the colors. I was shown the zillions of colors in the light, more than I have seen on earth. They were all beautiful.

"I don't remember the exact words, but I do remember discussing that all things were made of the light. I asked if even mountains and people were, and the voice (which I now think was God) told me even mountains, and a long list of things, everything. He also told me that the people there were in the light. I don't remember much about that except that I was aware that people were about to come to take me into some beautiful place and I wanted to go."

So begins one description of one person's experience at the edge of death. According to a Gallup poll, as many as five percent of the public have had some kind of Near-Death Experience (NDE). This is one description from over 1,300 that have been compiled since 1998 by Dr. Jeffrey Long on the Near-Death Experience Research Foundation website (see *www.nderf.org*). Dr. Long has recently published the book *Evidence of the Afterlife* (2010) documenting the results of research he has conducted using these reports. He concludes that there is reasonable scientific evidence of an afterlife. This is an impressive statement for a nonfiction book that made it as high as number 14 on the *New York Times* bestseller list.

Though the term Near-Death Experience is fairly new, coined and popularized by Raymond Moody in the 1970s, there have been reports of these

kinds of experiences throughout history: in early Greek and
Roman literature, in early Western religious writings, in the
ancient literature of Buddhism,
and in the oral history and folk-
lore of aboriginal societies all
over the world. The typical NDE
experience generally includes
some, but not all, of the following elements: separation from
the physical body; heightened
senses; intense and generally
positive feelings; passing into
or through a tunnel; encountering a mystical or brilliant light;
encountering other beings, often
relatives; a life review; encountering unworldly realms; and
encountering or learning special
knowledge.

Artist's conception of a Near Death Experience

NDE's are a popular topic. There are many books on the subject ranging from scholarly research to personal accounts, all of which have been
scoffed at by mainstream scientific researchers. No doubt Dr. Long's book
will also spark similar criticism since what NDEs offer goes contrary to the
materialistic paradigm that is predominant in our culture. Long is propos-
ing that there is undeniable and verifiable proof that NDEs are real and they
can be studied. I asked him to define what he meant by real. He said, "It
is something that actually happened that is part of reality. Anything that is
consistently observed is real." Materialist scientists have staunchly held that
the content of NDEs are hallucinatory fabrications of the brain and have no
basis in reality.

Dr. Long's research is based on personal reports collected on the web
and does have room for fabrication, exaggeration, and language con-
straints. Thus it will likely be questioned and challenged for validity.
Of course the staunch materialists will ask for physical proof, which is
difficult to come by. Yet, it is the consistency and content of the over

1,300 reports that have been collected that have convinced Dr. long and led him to propose nine lines of evidence proving that they are real. To briefly summarize, they are:

1. It is medically inexplicable to have a highly organized and lucid experience while unconscious or clinically dead.

2. Experiencers may see and hear in the out-of-body state, and their perceptions are nearly always real.

3. NDEs occur during general anesthesia when no form of consciousness should be taking place.

4. NDEs take place among those who are blind, and these NDEs often include visual experiences.

5. There is a life review of real events, many of which had been forgotten by the individual.

6. Experiencers encounter deceased beings and relatives.

7. The consistency of the experiences of young children with adults suggests NDEs are not due to preexisting beliefs.

8. The reports are consistent around the world from different cultures.

9. Experiences are transformed in profound ways by their experience, often for life.

I'll look briefly at a couple of these lines of evidence, starting with Out-of-Body (OBE) experiences. OBEs occur in approximately 50 percent of NDEs. While in the OBE, people perceive things they simply couldn't know by physical means. There are many documented descriptions of events occurring around where the person's body is, such as in an operating room or at an accident scene. In one report a woman saw a tennis shoe on a third-story window ledge of the hospital. She described it as a man's shoe, left footed, dark blue with a wear mark over the left toe. A curious nurse heard the story and looked out through all the windows of the hospital until she did find that shoe exactly as described. In Dr. Long's research, he claims 97 percent of the OBEs that were described were "entirely realistic without any unrealistic content."

It is this lucidity that is also one of the hallmarks of the NDE and Long's first line of evidence. A large percentage of the case reports in his study occurred when the person was clinically dead. In this state, the heart has stopped beating, blood has stopped flowing into the brain, and the electroencephalogram (EEG), which measures brain activity, has gone flat. Though there may still be some lingering electrical activity in the lower parts of the brain, one would expect that if there were *any* conscious experience, it would be fragmentary, delusional, or dreamlike. Yet 80 percent of experiencers described their thinking during the NDE as "clearer than usual" or "as clear as usual." They also often have vivid recollection of these events, continuing for many years after the experience. These experiences contradict the materialist view that consciousness is a product of the brain. If it were so, awareness should be diminished or absent during clinical death. However, this is exactly when many experiencers lucidly report the happenings around their bodies. As the experience progresses, the intensity of their emotions and the clarity of their thinking increases rather than decreases.

As a researcher of other forms of altered states, I find the clarity and consistency of NDEs compelling. In remote viewing, meditation, shamanic journeying, or other forms of altered states, one can have similar experiences: being dislocated from the body, encountering other beings and intelligences, and even having vivid intuitive or clairvoyant perceptions. Yet the content of these altered states tends to be quite varied and contain elements colored by a person's belief system and cultural beliefs. These kinds of experiences rarely can be recalled with the clarity of NDEs months and years later, or have the same long-term impact on a person's life. It makes me wonder if it is the complete separation from the physical body and brain that gives rise to the profound clarity and impact of NDEs.

When I asked Dr. Long what he thought about the quality of consciousness in NDE, he said, "We're saying that consciousness can exist apart from the body, and it does this fairly regularly. Now during our everyday, waking state, I don't think we're aware of that. Perhaps you can be during meditation or other alert, conscious experiences. However, when you're unconscious or clinically dead, you have that ability to be aware of what another person is thinking or feeling. This is clearly a shared consciousness."

"Visione Dell'Aldila Ascesa All'Empireo," Hieronymous Bosch

This assertion of separation of consciousness from the body in NDEs seems to support the philosophical thesis of dualism: that mind and matter are independent substances, neither of which can be reduced to the other. Some of the strongest critics of the validity of NDEs are scientists who are also materialists who believe that consciousness is simply an epiphenomenon of the brain. For some materialists, there is no possible evidence that could convince them of something that is false to begin with; hence, there is no point in arguing the matter. The philosopher and NDE research Neal Grossman has suggested that for people whose belief in materialism is more an ideology than a working hypothesis, we could use the term "fundamaterialist."

The verdict of materialistic science is usually that, although the reported NDEs are most certainly real and powerful, they can be explained more easily in terms of the brain and its altered states of consciousness than in terms of consciousness being separate from the brain and interacting with it. This case is often made regardless of the quality and quantity of evidence that it may not be a mechanistic phenomenon. This view is perhaps most strongly argued by neuroscientists, biologists, and even psychologists who spend their whole lives in the realm of the physical brain.

A recent proposed explanation for NDEs was published in the *Journal of Neurology*, suggesting that Rapid Eye Movement (REM) intrusions may cause NDEs. Common examples of REM intrusion occur in phenomena such as sleep paralysis and hypnagogia. This research suggested that over 60 percent of the people who had near-death experiences also commonly experience REM intrusion during wakefulness; or more clearly stated, people who have near-death experiences are more likely to find REM-related phenomena intruding on reality. These researchers stated that "even the most complex psychological process is dependent on brain function," indicating the belief in the primacy of the physical brain over consciousness.

Other physical theories that have been proposed to explain NDEs range from oxygen starvation, hypoxia, hypercarbia, ischemia, hypoglycemia, temporal lobe epilepsy, and the presence of naturally occurring ketamine in the brain. Some of the mental processes that are offered for explanation are a reactivation of birth memories, regression to a pre-verbal level as a result of confronting death, and depersonalization.

Dr. Long suggests that the difficulty with all of these explanations, including the REM intrusion hypothesis, is that none of them can explain all of the phenomena of NDEs. These materialist explanations can give no account of how a person acquires accurate information about events remote from his or her body while the person is clinically dead and experiencing no brain activity. Nor can they account for the long-term effects of the experience on people's lives which is generally not the case from hallucinations, oxygen starvation, and other brain aberrations.

The philosopher Neal Grossman has said that the materialist approach to explaining the NDE is "fundamentally misguided." He says, "It is only with respect to our deeply entrenched materialist paradigm that the NDE needs to be explained, or more accurately, explained away." He contends that the NDE is "at a minimum, the direct experience of consciousness—or minds, or selves, or personal identity—existing independently of the physical body."

Not all neuroscientists have such a strong materialist view, though. Mario Beauregard, who authored the book *The Spiritual Brain—a Neuroscientist's Case for the Existence of the Soul* (2008) with Denyse O'Leary claims "that materialism is out of step with modern physics." Beauregard and O'Leary propose "The reason that consciousness is a problem for materialist neuroscience is that it does not appear to have a mechanism. Modern quantum physics conceives of the universe as superimposed states. These states do not exist apart from each other, so their interaction is not governed by a mechanism." Quantum physics may be shedding light on the possible relationship between the brain and consciousness.

The philosopher B. Alan Wallace goes farther to suggest that mainstream neuroscience's conviction that consciousness is a phenomenon of the brain and must vanish at death is unfounded. He says, "Given its ignorance of the origins and nature of consciousness and its inability to detect the presence or absence of consciousness in any organism, living or dead, neuroscience does not seem to be in a position to back up that conviction with empirical scientific evidence."

The mounting evidence for the validity of NDEs is not only stirring up the neuroscientists. Philosophers and theologians also are resisting acceptance of them. Philosophers who are atheists and materialists are doing their best to ignore the evidence of the validity of NDEs. Not only is any hint of dualism suspect, but any research that seems to confirm the presence of a larger loving being or God immediately relegates NDEs to the pseudoscience category. What is equally profound is that many theologians refuse to accept the data. Though NDEs seem to confirm that there is a God, the research also means that science is treading too closely into their domain. Also, the reports of experiencers suggests that God is not vengeful, does not judge us or condemn us, and is not angry at us for our "sins," which is in direct conflict with some religious beliefs.

Regardless of the quality or quantity of research, a staunch materialist would conclude that the experience was false, simply because it can't possibly exist. I asked Dr. Long what he thought it would take to convince a materialist of the truth of NDE. "A near-death experience cures disbelief in NDEs," he replied. "About 99 percent of people who have them are convinced that they are real. Scores of people with doctorate level degrees have had them." For most experiencers of NDE, the explanation is a non-issue. Dr. Grossman writes, "No one who has had an NDE feels any need for an explanation in the reductionist sense that researchers are seeking. For the experiencer... it is exactly what it purports to be."

In *Evidence of the Afterlife*, Dr. Long describes how NDEs can be very transformative. Whether a person is an atheist or a believer, a materialist or a dualist, people who've had them tend to become much more interested in spiritual matters, loving relationships, and develop a sense of compassion. The effect that a NDE can have on a person's life is profound. Sometimes, he says, it takes up to seven years to see the full effects, but experiencers may report less materialistic interests, an increased appreciation of life, a belief in sacredness, a sense of God's presence, becoming more spiritual or religious, an awareness of deeper meaning or purpose, a belief in the afterlife, no fear of death, increased love of self, others and nature, an increased sense of compassion and empathy, and even physical and emotional healing.

I asked Dr. Long if he thought there was an overarching intention or a purpose to NDEs. He replied, "As far as I can tell, an NDE is a natural expression of what happens when we all die, of that reality that we are all going to be encountering. NDE is a much more clear expression of who we are as conscious beings, apart from the pain of earthly experience, worries, and frets. The ego is pretty much set aside during the experience. One thing you get over and over is that there's an overwhelmingly compassionate and intelligent God that is about choice and creation. I doubt the intent is an endpoint of an expected shift, but to help people understand a certain aspect of reality and then have the potential to make that shift."

Researcher P. M. H. Atwater has had NDEs and has written several books on the subject. When I asked her the same question, she felt there was more intention in connection to a person's life. "NDEs always," she says, "on some level, meet or address or challenge the needs of the individual at that point in his or her life, even with children." She went on to say, "The first phrase given by the vast majority of experiencers after their episode is, 'Always there is life.' Those four words tell us that there is no afterlife or before life; there is only life, eternal and forever."

NDEs and the message they bring have risen up again in popular consciousness like the phoenix rising from the ashes. They are powerfully spiritual experiences that show us we may be transformed at death into something much larger. Also, like the phoenix, the acceptance of a higher power by new paradigm science may be on the rise. "The strongest line of evidence is the tenth line, the overwhelming consistency of the spiritual content." Dr. Long said, "It was so powerful and so far reaching, I didn't feel that it would be appropriate to put in the first book. I didn't think the world was ready for it, or maybe I wasn't. But I am now."

If you want to know that spiritual message, you can go online yourself and access all 1,300 reports or better yet, talk to someone who has had an NDE and hear how it has affected them.

# PART FIVE

# META-DIMENSIONS

Art by Randy Haragan, for *Atlantis Rising*

# 25

# PLACES THAT NEVER WERE

*For Some People, Contact with Other Dimensions Is a Vivid Reality*

**BY FRANK JOSEPH**

An episode from the old *Twilight Zone* television series concerns an airliner on an otherwise ordinary cross-country flight, until the plane inexplicably accelerates into a cloudy void. Eventually emerging from the overcast, everyone on board is dismayed to behold a Jurassic jungle populated by hungry dinosaurs instead of the New York skyline. Reluctantly taking his microphone in hand, the captain dourly proclaims the obvious by informing passengers, "We have apparently flown back in time." He guns the throttles and climbs the lumbering Boeing 707 back through the cloud cover in an effort to find 1960 again. As a discernibly 20th century Manhattan begins to roll into view a few thousand feet below, he appears to have succeeded. That is, until he tries to make radio contact with the airport. Its ground-controller informs him that the jetliner is just in time for the 1930s World's Fair, but still too early for the Kennedy Era. The *Twilight Zone* episode ends with the captain flying his bewildered charges back into the overcast sky, still searching for their lost place in time.

While this well-known teleplay was a piece of fiction written by Rod Serling, it nonetheless dramatizes similar events reported by credible eyewitnesses who claim they have similarly visited the past or alternate realities. Sometimes, these encounters with an otherworld are confined entirely to sound. The phenomenon is then known as clairaudience. A case in point is illustrated by Thomas Janes, a classical history student at the University of Wisconsin, who traveled alone to Turkey during the early 1990s. The chief goal of his visit lay outside the Dardanelles city of Çanakkale, an archaeological park featuring the ruins of Ilios, the fabled capital of Troy. He spent two days at the site, relishing the personal fulfillment of a dream nurtured since childhood: to actually walk the battlements depicted in Homer's *Iliad*.

The area today has changed much since the Bronze Age events portrayed in that epic. The bay where invading Greeks beached their ships silted up many centuries ago, and the Trojan pastoral realm has been replaced by modern farms. But as Janes sat on one of the ancient walls, he tried to envision their mid-13th century BC milieu, with its glistening city of heroes surrounded by rich peasant lands. In the midst of this reverie, the light tone of a shepherd's flute came floating on breezes from the Mediterranean Sea, about three miles away, in the west. The simple tune seemed to accompany his thoughts, until he realized with a start that shepherding was a no less extinct form of employment in modern Turkey than it is in the U.S. He made a thorough search of the archaeological park. Perhaps someone was playing the replica of a Bronze Age pipe, as part of some reenactment, as occasionally takes place in archaeological precincts open to the public. But no one else was visiting that early week-day morning. He had the entire site to himself. Or did he?

The plaintive, unfamiliar strain continued to come from everywhere and nowhere. The farmer's fields below were deserted. Scrambling to the top of the ruined acropolis, he could see clearly in every direction for miles. Not another soul was around. The persistent, haunting refrain began to make him feel uncomfortable. But just as it had come, the reedy sound drifted away on the wind. He ran to the tourist building at the far end of the park, near its entrance. No, the lone attendant on duty informed him, no one else was visiting today. And there were certainly no musicians about! Janes never forgot that memorable, disembodied performance.

"The sound was so ghostly and sad," he remembered, "and so appropriate for such a place. I know in my heart that the music I heard was not of this world or time."

More like the *Twilight Zone* episode, a father and his 6-year-old son attended a Civil War reenactment at Gettysburg, Pennsylvania, during the summer of 2001. Frederick Catalano and Fred, Jr. were thrilled to see hundreds of men and women dressed in authentic period costume and regalia at the very location of a great event in American history. There was a re-creation of the famous battle with military bands, booming cannons, charging horse-soldiers, volleys of smoking muskets, and troops in blue and gray marching under colorful banners.

After the commemorative confrontation, Frederick and Junior joined thousands of other onlookers in visiting numerous stalls set up to display Civil War era memorabilia adjacent to a rather primitive but large grandstand draped with red, white, and blue bunting. At the center of this structure the day's reenactment continued with a tall actor obviously portraying Abraham Lincoln delivering the Gettysburg Address to a sizable crowd of soldiers and civilians attired in mid-19th century dress. Fred and son stopped to hear the well-known words recited in a Midwestern twang by the lanky "President," and then applauded with the other listeners.

Afterward, some gathered around "Mr. Lincoln" to congratulate him, as he sat wearily at an outdoor table. Carrying Junior in his arms, Fred made his way through the well-wishers: "See? That's the man who led the Union during the Civil War."

"Lincoln" looked up at the father and son with a suddenly bright smile. "What's your name, little man?"

"Fweddie," the boy piped up, and the tall, gaunt man laughed.

Getting into the spirit of the occasion, the elder Catalano asked, "Well, Mr. President, how's the war going?"

The actor fell back into character. "I fear it will never end," he sighed authentically.

Before he could explain, he was hustled off by a "general," and the crowd melted away. Fred took his son to visit a few other booths before the grounds were closed.

As they were leaving, they were approached by an organizer of the event who was also an old friend. "How'd you like the presentation, Fred?"

"Oh, it was great! Everybody played their roles so realistically, except that guy reading the Gettysburg Address. He just didn't look very much like any of the photos I've ever seen of Abe Lincoln. He was tall, but seemed too old for the part."

The organizer stopped in his tracks. "What are you talking about? We didn't have anybody reading the Gettysburg Address or portraying Lincoln at the reenactment." Fred described in detail the large, apparently improvised grandstand with its patriotic bunting, and crowd of listeners in blue uniforms, top hats, and gingham dresses.

"Nope," the organizer insisted, "nothing even remotely close to that was staged this year. I know everything that goes on here. It's my job. Look at your program. It lists all the events and facilities. No mention of Lincoln making the Gettysburg Address at a grandstand or anyplace else. What you saw must have been a ghost!"

But Fred's experience seemed more than that. He and Junior had unknowingly stepped back in time through an event aimed at recreating the same, long-gone era.

Some trips to the Otherworld are less clearly identified or as pleasant, however. In early spring, 1983, Larry Miller and his wife Claire were driving from Alsip, a Chicago suburb, to visit relatives in New Mexico. While traveling through a southwestern section of Missouri, Interstate 44 was closed for repairs, so Larry exited an off-ramp and followed signs to a detour. The mid-afternoon was clear and perfectly gorgeous, as the Millers enjoyed their unhurried trip over rolling countryside and broad pasture lands.

Perhaps half an hour after leaving the highway, they arrived at a small, charming town of little shops and a friendly-looking diner, like the one in Edward Hopper's famous painting, "Nighthawks," with its big glass windows and invitingly casual atmosphere. The main square was dominated by an attractive, well-preserved city hall building with a tall, brick clock tower. It was obviously constructed sometime in the late 1800s and was now surrounded by its own park.

Claire observed that the big clock-face with Roman numerals was wrong. Its Victorian hands had apparently stopped at 1:30; she had 3:00. Traffic was light, the sidewalks uncrowded. A young, red-haired woman was pushing a stroller around the park, and some kids were playing hopscotch, but that was about all. After a few stoplights, the Millers drove out of town and were back on the road, speeding over the indistinguishably repetitive landscape of endless farmlands. Again, the speed limit dropped, as they approached another town. It seemed remarkably similar to the one they just left behind.

"All these places look alike," Larry said, a trace of boredom in his voice.

But as they arrived at the town center, they passed on the left what seemed to be the very same diner with its big glass windows. Still more surprising, the old town square with its high clock tower appeared, as before, on their right. "How about that," Larry exclaimed, "they made an exact duplicate of that other place we came through!"

"Yeah," Claire agreed, "but the clock is different here. In the other town, it said 1:30. Here it's 1:00." Before her husband could respond, she exclaimed, "This IS the same town! We must have driven around in a circle. Look! There's that same lady pushing the baby buggy and those kids playing in the park we saw last time."

Larry was confused. "But how can that be? We drove in a straight line."

"It just SEEMED that way. Pay more attention to the road next time," she lightly scolded, but did not mention the altered clock tower.

As before, they followed the main street out of town, this time in silence. Larry was careful, never missed a sign. He avoided all turns, and closely followed the indicated detour that must eventually bring them back to the highway. About thirty minutes later, the speed limit dropped at the approach to another town.

"It's not possible!," Larry exclaimed, as he pulled over to a curb in the same town they passed through twice. Claire crouched in grim silence, gazing out her window at the all-too-familiar street, while her husband furiously studied a road map. "Maybe we should ask somebody," he suggested.

"No!," she demanded. "Let's just get out of here!"

Larry pulled out into the light traffic on Main Street. In a few minutes, the classic diner reappeared on their left, followed shortly thereafter by the main square with its old public building. The red-haired woman was still walking around the park with her stroller, and the children's hopscotch continued unabated. But when Claire looked up at the clock tower, she screamed. It read 12:30.

"Let's get out of here!," she pleaded on the verge of tears. "I'm scared! I'm real scared! Go, go, just go!"

Unnerved, Larry put the pedal to the metal. Their car raced through the last few stoplights, luckily avoiding any collisions.

Once out of town and on the open road again, Larry did not let up on the accelerator. While endeavoring to control his speeding car, he tried to console Claire. She was shuddering and tearful and on the verge of panic, but he soon ran out of words. His chest seemed to tighten with fear. Breathing came hard and fast. But his anxiety eventually began to subside with the expanding distance being swiftly covered.

"Claire, we've been driving about eighty miles per hour for more than twenty minutes. We should have arrived back at that town by now, but we're still on the road!"

She stopped weeping long enough to look uncertainly at the uniformly similar farmlands blurring past her window. Maybe he was right. But no. There were the same signs, the same town!

Larry slowed down only enough to maneuver through the two-lane streets and avoid an accident. He was still doing 50 in 35 mile-per-hour zones. In moments, the glassy diner was on their left. The park with its red-haired mother and stroller, together with the hop-scotching kids had not changed. Only the clock tower was different. Its immense, black hands pointed straight up at noon. As the careening car sped by the park, the brazen lungs of the old clock rang out striking the hour, a doomsday tolling that seemed directed at Larry and Claire. It followed after them, as they lurched at top speed out of town. Man and woman were filling the inside of their car with screams. Larry did not care what or who he might crash into. A collision would at least put an end to this endless horror.

The speedometer needle went passed 100, and the echoes of the big clock faded rapidly in the distance. Larry was determined to fly through the town at full speed this time. Terror and hatred for whatever it was that so frightened him had somewhat unhinged his mind.

But soon the environment seemed different. The countryside was not the same as before. Unfamiliar farmhouses appeared on either side of the road. Larry slowed down to the 55 mile-per-hour limit. Suddenly, there was a sign announcing the end of the detour. Another one pointed toward Interstate 44. He pulled over to the side of the road, and turned off the engine, then took Claire in his arms.

"I don't know what happened," he said, "but its over."

While their powerful experience was something they would never forget, neither could later remember the name of the strange town, even after consulting a detailed road map of their travels through southwestern Missouri. Not surprisingly, they took an alternate route on their return trip to Illinois.

# 26

# THE VERY STRANGE WORLD
# OF MARY SHELLEY

*The Writer of* Frankenstein *Left the World
More than a Little to Worry About*

**BY JOHN CHAMBERS**

At the end of August 2006, a helicopter was scheduled to hover above the red bluffs near Tucson, Arizona, and film scores of National Guardsmen dumping corpses from garbage trucks into a pit of fire.

It would mark an initial production stage in A.I.A. Film Productions's screen adaptation of *The Last Man*, a novel by Mary Wollstonecraft Shelley, that, published in 1826 and not reprinted until 1965 (University of Nebraska Press), has attracted little attention compared to the author's first and still wildly popular novel, *Frankenstein or The Modern Prometheus*, published in 1818.

Though *The Last Man* was panned by critics when it first appeared, it is a brilliant and complex account, written in the grand romantic manner, of the annihilation of humanity in the years 2073–2100 by a devastating worldwide plague. One man alone, Lionel Verney, survives the plague (which originated on "the shores of the Nile") to tell the story. As the novel ends, he sets sail for India in hopes of finding survivors on the other side of the world. Verney's last words are, "Thus around the shores of deserted Earth, while the sun is high and the moon waxes or wanes, angels, the spirits of the dead and the ever-open eye of the Supreme, will behold the tiny bark, freighted with Verney—the LAST MAN."

The A.I.A. Productions film version, released in 2008, has been radically altered from the Mary Shelley story. In the movie, the plague victims have metamorphosed into blind or semi-blind mutants who resort to cannibalism for food. As the action moves from Siberia to Arizona, the eponymous hero, untouched by the plague, tries to wipe out the mutants

Mary Shelley

one by one with an automatic rifle. Despite the differences, the producers insist their film is based on Shelley's *The Last Man*, even arguing that the "last man on earth" genre, ostensibly launched by the 1954 Richard Matheson science-fiction novel *I Am Legend* (which spawned three film adaptations: 1964's *The Last Man on Earth*, 1971's *The Omega Man*, and finally *I Am Legend*, in 2007) was actually inspired by Mary Shelley's novel.

In both the book and the movie versions of *The Last Man*, God does not intervene to save mankind. The life of Mary Wollstonecraft Shelley (1797–1851) was so crowded with remarkable achievements, in an age when women were not allowed to express themselves as freely as men, that she must have sometimes wondered if she herself were the recipient of divine guidance. But there were other, powerful, reasons why Mary was able to accomplish all she did. The first was heredity. She was the daughter of two geniuses, William Godwin (1756–1836), a radical philosopher who believed man should live by reason alone, and Mary Wollstonecraft (1759–1797), an educator and the author of the first great feminist tract, *A Vindication of the Rights of Women* (1792). Though Godwin's books had an impact on his times, his greatest influence came through the works of his devoted disciples, who included Robert Southey, William Hazlitt, Thomas De Quincey, Samuel Taylor Coleridge, and others. William Wordsworth said of Mary Wollstonecraft that she was the most influential of Enlightenment radicals, with the possible exception of William Blake.

Mary Wollstonecraft Godwin died ten days after giving birth to Mary. William Godwin, remote, unemotional, and preoccupied with his work, would be forced to raise a daughter on his own. Not quite four years later, he eased the burden on himself by taking a second wife. But he insisted Mary be schooled at home. He increasingly allowed his intellectually precocious daughter to take part in the almost nightly meetings with his disciples at his home. This was the second source of Mary's future strength: She was educated and very quickly treated almost as an equal by some of the greatest Romantic poets and artists of the time.

A number of these atheists, agnostics, and pantheists of genius nonetheless took an interest in spiritualism. From age 8 to 12, Mary listened in on brilliant discussions about ghosts and unexplained physical manifestations of spirits from other worlds. She developed a keen interest in the occult, devouring the part of her father's library devoted to the subject. Though discouraged from doing so by her father and stepmother, she began visiting her mother's grave in the cemetery behind Saint Pancras Church; there, lying on the grass, she talked to her mother's spirit.

Percy Bysshe. Shelley

When Mary was 17, a third, enormous, and unorthodox influence entered her life. This was Percy Bysshe Shelley (1792–1822), aged 21, soon to become one of England's great Romantic poets, who began appearing regularly at her father's house as his newest disciple. Shelley soon fell desperately in love with the very brilliant and very attractive Mary. Soon, Mary reciprocated his feelings, even taking him to her mother's grave and telling him her dead mother's spirit actually answered the questions she asked. Totally sympathetic, smitten forever, Shelley begged Mary to run away to Italy with him.

But there was a problem. Shelley was already married, with two children. The high-minded Mary refused his advances again and again—but, every bit as smitten as he was and a person whose totally unconventional upbringing made her open to unorthodox behavior, she finally yielded to Shelley's advances and the two of them (along with Mary's half-sister Jane Claremont) set off together for Venice.

Soon the trio was out of money and had to return to London. They had sparked an enormous scandal and now faced near-total ostracism. Mary became pregnant and had a baby girl who, born prematurely, died two weeks later. Mary became pregnant again and her second child, William, was born in January 1816. The couple fled once more to Europe— again with Jane (now Claire) Claremont, who was pregnant by the now world-famous Romantic poet George Gordon, Lord Byron (1788–1824).

It was late spring 1816. The three rented a villa close to Byron's on the shores of Lake Léman near Geneva in Switzerland. Mary was not yet

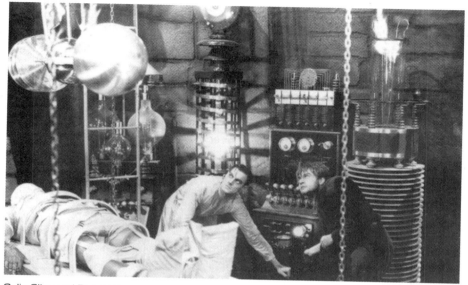
Colin Clive and Dwight Frye prepare to animate the monster in the 1931 Hollywood production of Frankenstein

19. Several weeks of blossoming creativity—sprinkled with soupçons and actual expressions of sex—got underway. Just one element remained to be set in place for Mary Godwin to begin her first novel, *Frankenstein*. Nature itself supplied that final element. Across much of the northern hemisphere, the year 1816 was the coldest ever recorded. Severe climate anomalies destroyed crops in northern Europe, the American northeast, and eastern Canada. It's now believed that these aberrations occurred because of the April, 1815, volcanic eruptions of Mount Tambora on the island of Sumbawa in the Dutch East Indies (in today's Indonesia), which spewed immense amounts of volcanic dust into the upper atmosphere. As is common when such eruptions take place, temperatures fell worldwide owing to less sunlight passing through the atmosphere.

The eruption caused constant rainfall in Switzerland in the late spring and summer of 1816, far beyond the annual norm. The rain caused Mary Godwin, Percy Shelley, Lord Byron, Claire, and Byron's friend John Polidori, to be closeted together in one house or another day after day. On a certain night, the enforced confinement caused the hothouse atmosphere, stoked by at least three persons of genius, to reach a kind of literary critical mass. The five invoked the spirit world and transcribed messages from the beyond (unfortunately, the transcripts are lost). They told ghost stories. Byron suggested they each try to write a ghost story. Mary seemed lost at first, but was obsessed by the project. All talked heatedly about the latest developments in science. Mary would write (referring to herself in the third person) in the 1831 edition of *Frankenstein*, "It was after one such conversation that Mary Shelley received the *donnée*, the gift every artist prays for that seems to come from beyond the self. Lying in bed, her eyes tightly shut, she saw 'the pale student of unhallowed arts kneeling beside the thing he had put together. I saw the hideous phantasm of a man stretched out and then, on the working of some powerful engine, show signs of life and stir with an uneasy, half vital motion.' "

Mary completed the book the year after, in London. She and Shelley had returned to an even greater scandal: Shelley's wife Harriet had committed suicide. Happily if guiltily, Mary and Percy Shelley married. *Frankenstein, or The New Prometheus* was published to acclaim in 1818 (anonymously; and for years people thought it had been written by Percy Shelley, or at least heavily edited by him). Mary was 21 at the time the book appeared and the couple had returned to Italy.

*Frankenstein* has been popularized in numerous movies and everyone knows the story. A scientist, Victor Frankenstein, creates an eight-foot-tall monster out of bits of flesh acquired from butchers' shops. With blasts of electricity the scientist brings the monster to life. From then on it makes Frankenstein's life a misery, causing the death of all his dearest friends and even of his wife. Mary Shelley wrote *Frankenstein* at the dawning of an era when science would come to threaten the rule of theology. Her book seems to ask: Will man someday be able to create man, just as God created man? And should man try? Given the torment the monster himself endures and inflicts on others, Mary Shelley's answer is at the least ambiguous.

Back in Italy, Mary wrote, studied and had five pregnancies in all, with only one son, Percy Florence Shelley, surviving to become an adult. But, in July, 1822, an unspeakable tragedy struck: Mary's husband, on the path to becoming an acclaimed poet, was caught in a storm while sailing near Livorno and drowned at sea on July 8, 1822. He was 29 years old.

Mary now showed the incredible strength that had matured in her over the years. She returned to London with her young son and over the next three decades came close to supporting herself with her writings while editing and promoting the works of Percy Shelley. She wrote five novels in all after Frankenstein: *Valperga: The Life and Adventures of Castruccio, Prince of Lucca*; *The Fortunes of Perkin Warbeck*; *Lodore*; *Falkner*; and *The Last Man*. Many of her works feature a single, absolutely unique (sometimes disastrously so, as in Frankenstein's monster) individual who is set apart by his strange, almost occult, uniqueness. Often, the uniqueness is self-inflicted. In the short story "The Mortal Immortal," an alchemist—in fact, the renowned Paracelsus—creates an "Elixir of Immortality," which is consumed by his student Winzy, the narrator of the story. At the beginning Winzy, who is 323 years old, says, "I have lived on for many a year—alone and weary of myself—desirous of death, yet never dying—a mortal immortal." At the end, he wonders, wistfully, hopefully, if he will ever die; he is not pleased with the change that the medieval "technology" of the Elixir of Immortality has wrought within him. Some of Mary Shelley's other tales deal with life and animation. The stories "Roger Dodsworth" and "Valerius" are about reanimation, a theme from *Frankenstein*. Her story "Transformation" deals with a doppelgänger, also used by E. T. A. Hoffmann and Robert Louis Stevenson in *Die Doppelgänger* and *The Strange Case of Dr. Jekyll and Mr. Hyde* respectively. Mary Shelley plays continually in her works with the theme of the dangers of (purposefully or inadvertently) imposing technologies upon mankind.

If *The Last Man* is—quite literally!—the omega of Mary Shelley's writings, *Frankenstein, or the New Prometheus* is certainly the alpha. For Shelley, the creation of a human being by human hands comes to be the ultimate usurpation of God's power; it is the supremely heretical act. This is the problem of the modern world, where the constant making and remaking of nature by technology is a kind of idolatry. So, at least, the torment of Frankenstein's monster suggests. The annihilation of mankind in almost biblical fashion by God in *The Last Man* is God's revenge, for there is nothing easier for the deity, who has created man, than to eliminate him. Perhaps we'd do well to take *The Last Man*—and Mary's earlier, electrifying *Frankenstein*—as two cautionary tales to be pondered on carefully.

# 27

## TIME TRAVEL EVIDENCE

*Does a 16th-Century Painting Show Technology
from the Future?*

### BY JOSEPH ROBERT JOCHMANS

Our world is filled with many anomalies, most of them well documented and incontrovertible, which demonstrate that space and time are not what we think they are. One of the strangest of these is an enigmatic object which appears in a painting in the little church of Montalcino in Italy, dating over four hundred years old. The object can be classified as a genuine "out-of-place" artifact, because it incorporates several apparently advanced aspects within its design.

But the context in which it was placed in the painting and portrayed in detail opens up a whole different level of technological inquiry and potential achievement. The item's existence raises not only the question of where it came from, but more importantly, *when* did it come from? For here we are faced with something that is more than out of place, it also appears to have come from a totally different time.

In essence, what we may be looking at could be the first real evidence for time travel.

At this point, we cannot be sure if the item in question manifested from our future or if it represents some kind of ancient time-traveling technology, the product of the unknown past, built and sent forward to our period from some prehistoric civilization now lost to us. Let the readers judge for themselves.

In 1595, Italian artist Bonaventura Salimbeni (1567–1613) was commissioned to produce a painting for the right-hand altar of the Church of St. Peter at Montalcino, located within a few miles of Florence. He was a member of a prominent family of artists from nearby Siena, and the goal of his commission was that his work be completed for the Christian Jubilee Year of 1600. According to the message accompanying his signature, Salimbeni's painting was finished right on schedule.

"The Glorification of the Eucharist," Bonaventura Salimbeni (1567–1613), right-hand altar of the Church of St. Peter at Montalcino

The Montalcino art masterpiece is entitled "The Glorification of the Eucharist," and features a vertical work divided into three segments. The lower third depicts a number of worshipping figures seated before the altar, including priests, cardinals and one individual wearing a papal crown believed to represent Pope Clement VII.

The middle third shows the altar itself, and prominently displayed in its center is the Cup of the Eucharist emblazoned in glowing light.

The upper third of the painting symbolizes heaven, dominated by the three Beings of the Holy Trinity who are looking down on the earthly scene below and giving their blessings—God the Father depicted as a Moses-like bearded old man, God the Son as Jesus Christ, and the Holy Spirit portrayed as a Dove hovering above the center.

What immediately catches the viewer's attention, however, is something pictured among the Trinity that to modern eyes seems very familiar, but not from the right time period. The first impression is that it looks exactly like a spheroid satellite with two antennae, something akin to the old Russian sputniks or American vanguard orbiters of the late 1950s. But what is it actually supposed to be?

Renaissance art experts interpret the strange sphere as representing the universe, showing the faint lines of celestial longitude and latitude, plus the images of an obscure sun and an exaggerated crescent moon shining from inside. The two "antennae"—one held by God the Father and the other by God the Son—are said to be "scepters" symbolizing divine rulership.

But the closer one examines the object, the more inconsistencies arise with this somewhat limited interpretation. If the "sphere" is supposed to be the universe, why are there no stars or constellations depicted shining from inside it? In fact, there is nothing transparent about it—the sphere on the contrary appears to be solid, with what looks like a metallic sheen reflected off its exterior. The so-called celestial "lines" more realistically suggest the seams of metal plating covering the outer circumference, made of a strange blue-black material.

The "sun" is too indistinct to represent the solar body, and in a technological context more likely is an electrical light source designed to illuminate the sphere's immediate surroundings.

As for the "moon," its unnatural double crescent with touching ends was not meant to depict a flat circle in two dimensions, but forms the

Close-up of time traveling technology?

edge of a three-dimensional narrow-width cylinder seen from an angle—what we today would identify as a camera lens protruding off the sphere's surface.

Without a doubt the most outlandish features are the two "antennae." They bear no resemblance whatsoever to any type of "scepter" or staff of power used by Renaissance officials, political or religious. Usually a scepter is pointed at the bottom end and has some symbol or figure prominently displayed at its apex. In contrast, the two objects held by the Trinity members are slightly wider at their bases than their tops.

In fact, on much closer inspection, it can be clearly seen that both objects have an inherent "telescoping" design. They are segmented into distinct sections which could be collapsed into a smaller size, and when pulled apart would extend to greater lengths.

The problem is, "telescoping" was a mechanical innovation that was not invented until the early 18th century. What is it doing portrayed in a painting over a hundred years too soon?

Even stranger, it can be observed that the two antennae are fastened to the sphere with gold or brass-colored grommet-rings, and certain lengths of the antennae also have grommet-rings. A grommet-ring is a threaded eyelet that is used to tighten and hold metal segments in place. Once again, we are dealing with something from another time, for such an innovation did not appear in industrial machinery design until the mid-19th century.

And then there is the anomaly of the antennae themselves. We today of course are very familiar with their utilization as "rabbit ears," used for television, radio and other signal receivers and transmitters. Even the recognizable wide-angle dispersion configuration is faithfully pictured in the Renaissance painting. Yet the existence of antennae for the earliest radio transmissions did not appear until the first part of the 20th century.

Going a step beyond, it can also be noticed that the sphere is clearly depicted as not resting on the background cloud it is pictured with, nor is it sitting on any surface whatsoever; rather it is hovering in place, held up by the "invisible powers" of the Trinity. Also, the sphere casts no well-defined shadow, which means that it did not appear in the physical but was more likely seen as a projected image. Here we are now dealing with possible anti-gravitational or electrostatic levitation, as well as sophisticated holography, which are beyond our present abilities.

Looking at all these various anomalies and their technical implications incorporated together into one object, the upshot is that we are apparently being confronted with the presence of an artificial mechanism specifically designed to illuminate and photograph scenes with a camera, and then broadcast the images to somewhere else. It could project itself to a specific location, levitate in place, perform its remote viewing task perhaps for only a few seconds, then disappear and return to its original point. But where would that "origin point" have been?

UFOlogists and "ancient astronaut" theorists have been quick to seize upon this out-of-place object as being proof of an extraterrestrial visitation, possibly a spaceship seen by the artist. The problem is, there is nothing especially "alien" about this device. In fact, every one of its aspects is recognizable as the product of a purely earth-bound technology.

The real mystery is not one of place but one of time. The sudden appearance of something displaying elements of a futuristic technology in the 16th century strongly suggests that this is ultimately where it must have come from—the future. Either that, or it was a projection far forward from a lost advanced civilization, long disappeared, that developed along technological lines not much different from our own today.

The questions remain, what exactly did the artist see, and why did he portray it in the manner shown in his painting?

Undoubtedly, Salimbeni regarded his encounter as a God-given vision, and through his artistry sought to comprehend it in that context. The device could have suddenly and unexpectedly appeared before him as if out of thin air, then quickly vanished after only a few seconds. But having an artistic eye sensitive to details, he very likely immediately made sketches of what he saw so he could later better remember it and portray it in the larger and more permanent masterpiece work we see today.

Steeped in a church-oriented upbringing and education, Salimbeni could only interpret his experience as heaven-sent. This may be why, in his painting, he placed the object among the Trinity, because in his time period they were the only acceptable source of truly miraculous events.

Being a good Catholic, and having been responsible for numerous other art pieces of a religious theme, there would have been no question in Salimbeni's mind of the true origins of the apparition. The fact that the object had hovered before him with no earthly supports could only mean that it had been held aloft by the hands of Divine Providence, and he deliberately pictured it that way.

The artist may very well have thought that the sphere in his vision symbolized the universe, and purposely reinterpreted the two exterior items he saw on its surface—the light and the camera lens—as being the "greater illumination" and "lesser illumination" of the sky, namely the sun and moon.

Luckily, Salimbeni's excellent memory overcame his desire to reduce everything he saw to a religious context. He preserved enough details in his painting that he could not fully understand in his day, but which we, in our time, seeing through our modern technological eyes, can better recognize.

Rather than being "heaven-sent," the evidence instead points to the mysterious device having been "time-sent." As to just when in history, either past or future, it was sent from remains the real unanswered enigma.

LOST POWERS

# 28

# RELIGION AND THE PARANORMAL

*What is the Interaction Between Them?*

## BY ROBERT M. SCHOCH, PH.D.

The paranormal can conjure up thoughts of flying books and dishes associated with poltergeist activity, séances where mediums supposedly communicate with the deceased, fortune tellers gazing into crystal balls, ghosts, haunted houses, and any number of other bizarre phenomena that seem better left to midnight musings safely forgotten with the break of dawn. Many people dismiss the paranormal out of hand or will only discuss this topic in hushed tones while making excuses for their passing curiosity concerning such an embarrassing subject. Yet virtually every major religion of today is based, to some extent, on paranormal phenomena. The Hebrew Moses, who could talk to the Lord in the form of a burning bush, strike a rock and produce water, and part the Red Sea, was not alone among Old Testament characters to apparently manifest paranormal abilities (besides run-of-the-mill prophecy, clairvoyance, and healing). Consider, for instance, the story of Elijah and the miracle of a widow's meager oil and food supply which was inexplicably replenished for many days. The Prophet of Islam, Mohammed, is reported to have healed the sick and summoned rain. Buddha reputedly had well-developed psychic abilities, including the ability to read minds and levitate. Jesus performed numerous miracles, from walking on water to raising the dead, supposed proof to the faithful of his divinity. Some Christian saints, following in their master's footsteps, have carried the miraculous to extreme heights; one example is St. Joseph of Cupertino.

## THE CASE OF THE FLYING SAINT, JOSEPH OF CUPERTINO

According to well-documented contemporary reports, the 17th-century Italian friar St. Joseph of Cupertino (Giuseppe da Copertino, 1603–1663) experienced numerous miraculous levitations during which he would

"Joseph of Cupertino," by Ludovico Mazzanti

literally travel short distances through the air, later giving him the appellation of the "Flying Saint." In one instance, during the Feast of the Nativity, Joseph is alleged to have suddenly flown from the middle of the church to the high altar, a distance of about forty feet. Prominent persons of the time testified to Joseph's odd flights. The Spanish Ambassador to the Papal Court observed him fly over the heads of bystanders to a statue of the Immaculate Conception (the Ambassador's wife also witnessed the event; fainting, she had to be revived with smelling salts). John Frederick, Duke of Brunswick, watched through a chapel door as Joseph floated above the floor during mass. Formerly a Lutheran, John Frederick converted to Catholicism after witnessing this miracle. When attending a papal audience at the Vatican, Joseph was so overwhelmed upon meeting Pope Urban VIII (pope from 1623–1644) that he rose into the air and only descended again when so ordered by a superior. (As a curious side note, it was Pope Urban VIII who summoned Galileo to Rome in 1633 to recant his heretical notions that the Earth travels around the Sun.)

Levitations were not the only phenomenon in Joseph's miraculous repertoire. It is said that he could read other's thoughts at times, so he knew when people were holding back a full accounting of their sins during confession. He is also credited with gifts of healing, even producing rain during a drought.

Despite his miracles and the incredible attention they attracted (Joseph was very popular with the masses during his lifetime; the church had to relocate him several times, sometimes to secret locations, attempting to forestall the crowds that would often gather to see him), Joseph was far from "perfect." Intellectually challenged (or, to put it crudely, dim-witted), in modern parlance, he probably suffered from some major learning disabilities. Apparently he could barely read or write, and at times he would blankly stare off into space or wander in a confused daze.

The veracity of the supposed miraculous, or in modern terms paranormal, events centered on Joseph of Cupertino is not at the moment our concern, but rather how such events were interpreted by religious authorities and believers. In the case study of Joseph we have a microcosm of the larger, often strained, relationship between the paranormal and what we might term conventional or mainstream religion. Paranormal phenomena and religion have a long, convoluted, intertwined relationship, sometimes antagonistic (such as when paranormal feats are attributed to devils or witches) and sometimes mutually reinforcing (such as miracles that are interpreted to confirm true divinity or sanctity). Far from universally embracing Joseph's miracles, church authorities often found them somewhat of an embarrassment.

Joseph's flights were unannounced and apparently uncontrollable for him, at least at a thoroughly conscious level. Unexpectedly Joseph might go into a trance-like ecstatic state during a moving mass or festivity, or even at the slightest provocation (for instance, a chance thought about the beauty of God). His flights were often disruptive; at times Joseph was banned from participating in masses and processions. At one point in his life Joseph was accused of unduly attracting attention to himself with his "miracles," and as a result he was investigated by the Inquisition, but not found guilty of any crime. Joseph is said to have been apologetic for his odd behaviors, though they continued. Indeed, the primary and best documented miraculous (that is, paranormal) phenomena attributed to Joseph may have been rather dramatic and visually exciting, but when it comes right down to it, also rather trivial and hardly worthy "evidence" of an omnipotent, omniscient, omnipresent God. Rather, Joseph's literal "flights of fantasy" might say more about Joseph as a person, perhaps a rather unstable person at that, characterized by strong emotions (it has been asserted that he had a violent temper at times) and the release of pent-up "psychic energy" directed at his own body, resulting in the famous relatively uncontrolled levitations.

## PARANORMAL PHENOMENA IN A RELIGIOUS CONTEXT

One common view is that on the path to enlightenment, salvation, or union with the gods (or God, if you prefer), paranormal phenomena may become manifest, but such paranormal phenomena are not an end goal unto themselves, and may become a distraction that one must move beyond. Arguably, without impugning his deep faith or piety, St. Joseph's levitations were just such a distraction. I have known individuals who possessed moderately developed paranormal abilities and, based on their "powers," deluded themselves into thinking that they were exceptionally "spiritual," when indeed any modest gains toward true spirituality they may have once accomplished were, in my opinion, lost as they sank into self-adulation and delusions of grandeur. We must distinguish between *thaumaturgy*, or simple "wonder working" (such as being able to predict a future event, read a mind, or heal a sick person using apparent paranormal powers), and *theurgy*, the harnessing of "wonders" or "miracles" (that is, in modern terms, manifestations of the paranormal) for higher inspirational purposes, perhaps ultimately resulting in salvation or enlightenment. For instance, assuming a modicum of reality and historicity concerning the Jesus of the Christian Bible, was he merely a thaumaturgist, or was he a true theurgist? This was a fundamental question that plagued the members of the incipient Christian community nearly two thousand years ago. Pondering such issues brings us to questions of both the origin of specific religious beliefs and practices (many a religion traces its beginnings to a pivotal individual to whom miracles are attributed), and more generally the issue of the origin, the basis, and the continuing inspiration of religion more generally.

The concept of religion is as old as civilization (and most likely much older) and has been a driving force behind human actions and development from earliest antiquity through the present day. Classically, anthropologists and sociologists have attempted to account for and explain the origin of religion through theories of primitive humans trying to make sense of the physical and biological world—lightning in the sky, the movements of celestial objects, the seasons, the growth of plants, dreaming versus waking states, and so on. Presumably, some have argued, primitive man populated the world with spirits and invisible beings (ultimately to become gods and then a supreme God), helping to explain that which could not be understood otherwise, and at some point came to conclude that humans too had spirits or souls, and later came to believe that such souls might survive physical death. Some evolutionary biologists have suggested that religiosity in humankind makes good sense evolutionarily, both as a bonding mechanism and constraint on individual behaviors that might be detrimental to the population as a whole. Thus religiosity would be favored by natural selection (independent of any objective truth or veracity that might be found in particular religious beliefs).

Without necessarily refuting the above factors, in the earliest years of psychical studies as a distinct and serious scientific discipline, it was suggested by some researchers that the foundations of religion might lie in paranormal phenomena (often referred to as supernormal or supranormal phenomena by psychical researchers of the late 19th century). Indeed, to this day, it is generally acknowledged by the faithful that much of the foundation for many of the world's dominant religions lies in reputed prophecies, revelations, and miracles—in short, phenomena that might be explained in terms of the paranormal. The question for many is whether there is any truth to such phenomena. Traditionally the adherents of one religion typically accept the truth of the phenomena upon which their own religion is based, and further interpret such phenomena as authenticating their particular religious beliefs, while dismissing the phenomena upon which other rival religions are based; or, if not outright dismissing such rival religious phenomena, perhaps attributing them to demons or other malevolent spirits, or accusing the practitioners of a rival religion of misinterpreting the signs. Agnostics, atheists, and modern rationalists and materialists have often either not allowed religious phenomena to come under their purview, or have simply dismissed such phenomena outright as superstitious nonsense. But there is another way to approach religion and its characteristic phenomena: We can consider the possibility that some (though not necessarily all) of the foundational phenomena of religions are genuine and of a paranormal nature.

Before the end of the 19th century the psychical researchers Andrew Lang (1898, *The Making of Religion*) in Britain, and Cesar de Vesme on the European continent (Italy and France; see the two-volume 1931 edition of his *A History of Experimental Spiritualism*, where he cites his 1896 work on the subject) suggested that paranormal phenomena "are practically the only ones which could have engendered the first religious beliefs of mankind" (de Vesme, vol. 1, p. 75). Lang, an active member of the newly formed Society for Psychical Research in London, took an anthropological approach to the origin of religion. "We may . . . collect savage *beliefs* about visions, hallucinations, 'clairvoyance,' and the acquisition of knowledge apparently not attainable through the normal channels of sense. We may then compare these savage beliefs with attested records of similar *experiences* among living and educated civilized men. . . . Out of that region [that which Lang refers to as the "X region of our nature", i.e., the paranormal], out of miracle, prophecy, vision, have certainly come forth the great religions, Christianity and Islam . . ." (Lang, p. 3, italics in the original).

## TELEPATHIC COMMUNICATION WITH GOD AND THE SEPARATION OF MIND FROM MATTER

Though it seems to be rarely acknowledged (particularly by certain contemporary rationalists who, somewhat inexplicably to my mind, continue to hold traditional beliefs in a God and an afterlife yet dismiss the paranormal in general), one form of the paranormal is widely held by practitioners of most major religions today: telepathy. Say a silent prayer to your God and you are practicing telepathy. As the early psychical researcher Frederic W. H. Myers (1843–1901) wrote in his classic work *Human Personality and Its Survival of Bodily Death* (two volumes, 1903):

"Now as to telepathy, there is in the first place this to be said, that such a faculty must absolutely exist somewhere in the universe, if the universe contains any unembodied intelligences at all. . . . Men have in most ages believed, and do still widely believe, in the reality of prayer; that is, in the possibility of telepathic communication between our human minds and minds above our own, which are supposed not only to understand our wish or aspiration, but to impress or influence us inwardly in return. So widely spread has been this belief in prayer that it is somewhat strange that men should not have more commonly made what seems the natural deduction—namely, that if our spirits can communicate with higher spirits in a way transcending sense, they may also perhaps be able in like manner to communicate with each other. The idea, indeed, has been thrown out at intervals by leading thinkers—from Augustine to Bacon, from Bacon to Goethe, from Goethe to Tennyson" (Myers, vol. 1, pp. 241–242).

Here Myers has highlighted an important aspect of most religions: the concept of "unembodied [that is, nonmaterial] intelligences," or to put it another way, the concept of gods (in the sense of being non-corporeal [incorporeal] beings), souls, and so forth—the concept of something other than, or beyond, the material world. Andrew Lang wrote in 1894:

"At present, of course, the theistic hypothesis, and the hypothesis of a soul, do not admit of scientific verification. The difficulty is to demonstrate that 'mind' may exist, and work, apart from 'matter'. But it may conceivably become verifiable that the relations of 'mind' and 'matter' are, at all events, less obviously and immediately interdependent, that will and judgment are less closely and exclusively attached to physical organisms than modern science has believed." (Andrew Lang, *Cock Lane and Common-Sense*, 1894, pp. 337–338)

Furthermore, how do god-like entities manifest their presence in the material world? How do they turn thoughts into actions? One can argue by the direct effect of mind acting on matter, or in technical jargon, by psychokinesis (PK for short, also referred to as telekinesis). It should be pointed out, however, that the very concepts of telepathy, clairvoyance, precognition, retrocognition, psychokinesis, and related phenomena allow the possibility that a God could take on a corporeal, a physical bodily form. For instance, an all-knowing, all-powerful God could obtain his/her/its knowledge through telepathy and clairvoyance, and exert his/her/its power through psychokinesis, even if such a God is physically embodied in virtually any material trapping (perhaps God is physically a particular insect in the Amazonian jungle, or a remote asteroid in a galaxy in a universe other than our own; the possibilities are infinite, and in some cases quite distasteful to certain human minds!).

This separation of mind and matter, and the influence of mind directly on matter (psychokinesis), which makes certain notions of a God or gods, souls, spirits, and so forth possible, is at the core of much parapsychological research. Arguing that parapsychology supports religious beliefs, the Methodist minister Alson J. Smith stated in 1949: "E.S.P. [extrasensory perception; that is telepathy, clairvoyance, and related phenomena] affirms the reality of that spiritual world which is the true homeland of all religion—that world beyond the cabined world of space and time which Dante said is 'so strong to fight against all that is false and low and mean in life.' It brings to bear on the terrible problems of our day the tremendous and inexhaustible resources of that world which is just beyond our fingertips. It opens the way for a healing of the lesions torn in the world and in the church by the impact of a material science, a healing which may have come just in time to enable mankind to transform its knowledge of the atom from curse to blessing. It opens the way for . . . a new priesthood trained in the technique of using the resources of the spiritual world for the healing of the heart-sick, mind-sick, and body-sick men and women. . . . If nuclear physics has brought us 'the good news of damnation,' parapsychology is now bringing us the infinitely better news of salvation, the news of new horizons, new frontiers, new resources . . . " (quoted by Allan Angoff, 1970, "The Psychic Force: Essays in Modern Psychical Research" from the International *Journal of Parapsychology*, p. 219)

The separation of mind from matter allows and even confirms, in the opinion of many persons, the reality and discreteness of the soul—and the soul may not only be separate from the material body, but may "outlive" the dissolution of the physical organism. However, to hypothesize or believe in the existence of a soul is one thing, to suggest that it might survive the death of the body, either temporarily or permanently, is another matter. The latter assertion does not necessarily follow from the former. Arguably, for instance, at least some sects of the early Hebrews believed that humans have souls, but did not accept that such souls survived, at least for any significant amount of time, the death of the physical body. Personal immortality, or even some more limited survival beyond the grave, is not a necessary component of religion *per se*, but it is certainly of great interest and bears on the fundamental tenets of many religions.

Paranormal phenomena and studies, such as materials collected through mediums interpreted as channeling discarnate entities (in some cases, supposedly once living persons now deceased), ghosts and apparitions, or apparent memories of past lives held by now living persons that are interpreted as evidence for reincarnation, have been cited as evidence for the survival of the soul. With a little extrapolation, such data has been used to support the concept of personal immortality. Perhaps this is correct, but there are other ways to interpret the data as well. For instance, is an apparent "apparition" the manifestation of telepathically acquired information on the part of the "viewer"? Does a

Is healing in response to prayer a paranormal phenomenon?

child who appears to remember a past life actually access this information and various trait characteristics by paranormally gaining information from the past directly, rather than actually being the incarnation of the previous person? Or might the child in question pick up the information telepathically from still living persons who knew, or at least know about, a deceased person? Might a medium do likewise? Such are thorny questions, in my opinion as yet unresolved, but certainly worthy of our attention as serious research of the paranormal continues.

## 29

# THE PARANORMAL TRAVELS OF MARK TWAIN

*The Great Humorist Could Think Outside the Box
in More Ways than One*

**BY JOHN CHAMBERS**

In late May, 1858, about to disembark with his younger brother Henry as a cub pilot on board the steamboat *Pennsylvania*, Samuel Clemens, then 22, one day to call himself Mark Twain, had a terrifying precognitive dream.

The future author of *The Adventures of Huckleberry Finn* (1884, 1885) later wrote that, in this dream, he "had seen Henry's corpse. He lay in a metallic burial case. He was dressed in a suit of my clothing, and on his breast lay a great bouquet of flowers, mainly white roses, with a red rose in the center. The casket stood upon a couple of chairs."

Sam wrenched himself out of sleep. His heart was filled with grief. He was sure Henry's coffin lay in the next room. He got up, dressed, and went toward the door. But then, he says, "I changed my mind. I thought I could not bear to meet my mother. I thought I would wait awhile and make some preparation for that ordeal." Clemens actually left the house and walked a block "before it suddenly flashed upon me that there was nothing real about this—it was only a dream." He ran back, charged up the staircase to the second-floor sitting room, "and was made glad again, because there was no casket there."

The *Pennsylvania* cast off for New Orleans later that day, with Sam and Henry on board. On June 3, Sam had a fight with the steamboat's pilot; he was put off the boat when it arrived at New Orleans. The *Pennsylvania* continued on its way on June 9, with Henry, aged 19, still on board.

Sam obtained a new berth, on the steamboat *Lacey*. He was back on the Mississippi River by June 11. Two days later, the *Lacey's* crew and passengers heard a chilling shout from the shore: "The *Pennsylvania* is blown up at Ship Island, and a hundred and fifty lives lost!" A boiler had exploded, destroying the steamboat; passengers had been blown into the river, boiled alive, decapitated, impaled. A first report indicated that Henry was among the uninjured. A second stated that he was "hurt beyond help."

When the *Lacey* arrived at Memphis, Sam Clemens rushed to the makeshift hospital where his injured brother lay on a mattress among the burned and scalded. Henry had been sleeping above the boilers; he was blown into the air, dropped back on the heated boilers, and bombarded by falling debris.

A local newspaper reported that "on approaching the bedside of the wounded man his [Sam Clemens'] feelings so much overcame him, at the scalded and emaciated form before him, that he sank to the floor over-powered." Henry lingered for three days. Then an accidental overdose of morphine—this is one version of his final days—brought on his death.

At the time, the coffins provided for the dead were made of unpainted white pine. A few Memphis ladies collected sixty dollars and brought Henry a metal casket. When Sam arrived to view the body, he found Henry lying in the open coffin dressed in a suit of his older brother's own cloth-ing. He immediately remembered his dream. Just then, an elderly lady brought a bouquet of white roses with one red rose in the center. She placed it on Henry's chest.

When several men took the casket to his brother-in-law's house in St. Louis and were carrying it upstairs, Sam stopped them, as he did not want his mother to see Henry's face; one side had been distorted by the effects of the drug. When Sam went upstairs, there stood the two chairs he had seen in his dream. Had he come two or three minutes later, the casket would have been resting on those chairs, just as they had in his dream. Thus, by stopping the men, Sam had changed the predictive details of the dream.

Sam Clemens—better known as Mark Twain—had many brushes with the supernatural during his life, but none as spectacular as this, and none so horrible in its outcome. The Missouri-born writer, who would become known as "the American Voltaire," got used to rubbing shoulders with the beyond. He even developed a theory to explain the mechanics of these psychic encounters: he had a second, "spiritualized," or "dream," self.

Twain wrote in 1897 that we have "a spiritualized self which can detach itself and go off upon affairs of its own . . . it and I are one, because we have common memories." Though in real life Twain was happily married to Olivia "Livy" Langdon, this other self frequently gamboled in dreams and visions with Twain's platonic sweetheart, an actual woman named Laura Wright whom Twain had known briefly in 1858, and loved, before she disappeared. The author claimed to make daring excursions in the guise of his spiritualized self (we might call it the astral self), including even a highly sexually-charged tryst with an alluring black woman. It would be some years before Mark Twain would accept this other self as a reality, and he almost never mentions it in connection with his precognitive dreams and visions.

Samuel Langhorne Clemens was born two months premature, on November 30, 1835, in what he called the "almost invisible village" of Florida, Missouri. He just barely survived birth and was frail and sickly and mostly bedridden until he was 4. It seemed to his mother that he existed in some kind of dream state that blurred the boundaries between sleeping and wakefulness; for one thing, he constantly sleepwalked. His mother was sure he had the gift of "second sight;" she was all the more sure when Sam's 9-year-old sister Margaret became seriously ill and the 4-year-old boy drifted into Margaret's bedroom, fiddled with her blanket, then drifted out. This was a gesture of second sight known as "plucking the coverlet" of somebody who is about to die; a few days later, Margaret died. Mark Twain might have said himself, in later years, that this was a first, brief excursion of his spiritualizing self into the future.

In 1839, Sam's father, in search of better opportunities, relocated his family to the tiny town of Hannibal, Missouri, on the banks of the Mississippi. Here Sam lived through many of the fears, pleasures, pranks, and trials with which he would fructify the lives of his two greatest fictional heroes, Tom Sawyer and Huckleberry Finn. In 1848, Sam's father died; now 13, and not only psychic but moody, volatile, and given to rages, he was forced to leave school and become a printer's apprentice in Hannibal. He went on from this to become a typesetter in Philadelphia, an editor in Virginia City, and a reporter for the San Francisco *Examiner.* On and off between 1857 and 1861, he was a cub pilot and pilot on Mississippi steamboats (from whence he derived his pseudonym, Mark Twain, from the pilot's cry of "Mark twain!," or "Measure out two fathoms!"). In 1866, while he was on a visit to Hawaii, the *Examiner* asked Sam to interview survivors from a nearby shipwreck; he returned to California with such a fund of vivid detail that it formed the core of his later book, *Roughing It* (1872). Mark Twain had caused a stir in 1865 with his short story "The Celebrated Jumping Frog of Calaveras County"; the publication of *The Innocents Abroad* in 1869 brought him national acclamation. His career as a writer and world-class humorist progressed in leaps and bounds. It would attain its zenith with the publication, in 1889, of the novel *A Connecticut Yankee in King Arthur's Court*.

One of the ways our spiritualized self expresses itself is by making telepathy possible. Twain took a fierce interest in this process, which he called mental telegraphy. His friend and biographer Alfred Bigelow Paine wrote that, "In thought transference, especially, he had a frank interest— an interest awakened and kept alive by certain phenomena—psychic manifestations we call them now. In his association with Mrs. Clemens, it not infrequently happened that one spoke the other's thought; or perhaps a long procrastinated letter to a friend would bring an answer as quickly as mailed, but these are things familiar to us all."

In an article in the December, 1891, issue of *Harper's*, Twain endorsed the Society for Psychical Research and described some of his own telepathy-related experiences. One took place during a personal visit to Washington, D.C., when he arrived very late. Deborah Blum summarizes the experience in *Ghost Hunters* (2006): "He knew that a good friend was also planning to be in the Capitol; but 'I did not propose to hunt for him at midnight, especially since I did not know where he was stopping.' Although it was late, Twain found himself restless. He went out for a walk, drifted into a cigar shop, and stayed for a while, 'listening to some bummers discussing national politics.' Suddenly his friend came back into his mind, with startling specificity. If he left the shop turned left, and walked ten feet, his friend would be standing there. Twain immediately walked out the door and turned left. There was his friend, standing on the edge of a street corner, chatting with another man, delighted to see Twain stepping up to join the conversation. 'In itself the thing was nothing,' Twain commented. 'But to know it would happen so beforehand, wasn't that really curious?'"

Was it also his astral self, peering forward into the future, that delivered the details of all Twain's futuristic insights and inventions? Critic Shirley Anne Williams notes that in the novel *The Tragedy of Pudd'nhead Wilson*, "Twain's argument about the power of environment in shaping character" ran directly counter to "prevailing sentiment where the Negro was

Mississippi River Boat and Mark Twain (*Atlantis Rising* artwork)

concerned." Bobbie Ann Mason shows us that in the novel *The American Claimant,* Twain predicted DNA cloning, fax machines, and photocopiers. Cynthia Ozick points out that the "telelectrophonoscope" we meet in the short story "From the London Times of 1904" greatly resembles a television set. And Malcolm Bradbury suggests that, with the "phrenophones" of Mark Twain's article "Mental Telegraphy," we are at the beginning of the Internet era.

Twain did not depend solely on his spiritualized self. He periodically attended séances, often trying to contact his brother Henry. The great Scottish psychic and levitator Daniel Dunglas Home, though largely retired in 1878, agreed to see Twain despite the latter's publicly aired criticisms of

Home. Something—we don't know what—happened at that first séance to convince Twain of Home's authenticity. He attended several other séances with the medium in the U.S. and, in 1879, a number in Paris. A strong bond grew up between the two men, severed only by Home's death in 1886.

His spiritualized travels notwithstanding, Mark Twain, from his twenties on, took an increasingly cynical view of mankind's religions and mankind itself. "If Christ were here now," he wrote in a notebook, "there is one thing he would not be—a Christian." In his essay "Concerning the Jews," he declared, "I have no race prejudices. All I care to know is that a man is a human being—that is enough for me, he can't be any worse."

In Twain's short story "Captain Stormfield's Visit to Heaven," the deceased Stormfield chases a comet while on his way to heaven, loses his way, and ends up on the threshold of the heaven of a different planetary species. The gatekeepers have never heard of Earth. To help Stormfield, they get in a balloon, fly across the surface of a gigantic vertical map of the universe, and, after two days of hard work, find our solar system. It's a mere smudge, only fly specks; it's called the Wart. With the help of the gatekeepers, Stormfield finally makes it to our heaven—but Twain has already made his point that our planet and our species are utterly unimportant in the cosmic scheme of things.

A series of personal catastrophes late in life would destroy Mark Twain's peace of mind and very nearly his soul. They would confirm his belief that man is worthless. They would not ingratiate him to God. Critic Bernard DeVoto explains:

"He had expanded it [the publishing company he founded himself] to publish the memoirs of General Grant, and the over-extended business required better management than Mark could give it. . . The firm faltered, the going got worse, and finally, as a result of the freezing of credit in the panic of 1893, it had to go into receivership. It could have been saved—except that a greater loss had drained Mark's fortune and his wife's as well. Always a speculator, . . . he had poured nearly a quarter of a million dollars into the development of an invention that was going to make him many times a millionaire, the Paige typesetting machine. . . .[But it] failed altogether and carried Mark Twain down with it, just at the time when his publishing firm went bankrupt. Furthermore, these same years saw a mysterious alteration in the personality of his youngest daughter,

Jean; and finally the terrible mystery was cleared up by the discovery of the still more terrible truth, that she was an epileptic. During these years also his capricious but usually excellent health failed."

Racked by bronchitis and rheumatism, Twain set out with his wife and middle daughter on a heroic one-year, round-the-world lecturing tour. His goal was to earn enough money to pay off all his creditors dollar for dollar. He almost—not quite—succeeded. But, as he arrived in London at the end of the tour, the greatest horror of all awaited him: his eldest daughter, Suzy, had died of meningitis at the age of 24 after two weeks of terrible suffering.

Twain, in his deepest nature an artist, sought desperately over the next several years for metaphors to contain the appalling pain that all this caused him. But his creative faculties were broken—even his spiritualized self seemed to have fled—and he could scarcely complete a story. Repetitiously, he ground out fragments portraying all humanity as icebound passengers on a frozen ship, lost in an endless Arctic sea, at the mercy of monstrous, capricious, unseen forces—in a state that would go on for all eternity. Finally, Twain's bleakness lifted slightly, and he completed *The Mysterious Stranger,* in which we discover that Satan is responsible for everything because, though a malign and criminal being, he is the true face of God. But even this is not true, Satan finally tells the narrator: the universe— including Satan himself—is nothing but a dream that all of us dream separately.

Mark Twain died in his seventy-fifth year, on April 21, 1910, at Stormfield, near Redding, Connecticut. We should not mourn the near-madness and despair of his final years. Rather, we should rejoice at the life of this great man whose magnificent sense of humor brightened the lives—made the day, made the month, made the year—of millions of people, and still does. The tragedy is that he too well exemplified the ancient maxim that behind the laughter of the clown lie tears. But Twain himself might have told us, at least in his younger days, that if our imaginations can create so much more than what seems to be the world, then finally we are masters of the world.

# 30

# ALEXANDER SOLZHENITSYN AND THE FORGOTTEN SENSES

### Was the Great Russian Writer Aided by Supernatural Powers?

**BY JOHN CHAMBERS**

On his first night at Lubyanka Prison in Moscow, the lean, frightened army captain was subjected to subtle cruelties he never knew existed. And this despite the fact that he had been battling the Nazi invaders across the steppes of Russia for four years, first as a soldier, then as an officer, in the Soviet Union's Red Army.

Alexander Solzhenitsyn, 26, had been arrested at the battlefront on February 9, 1945, for making derogatory remarks about Soviet leader Joseph Stalin in letters to a friend. He had been stripped of his rank and quickly transported from East Prussia to the Russian capital by train.

On that first, sleepless, night in prison, he was taken to one cell after another and made to strip three times. The first time was to search his body cavities and rip his shoes and clothes apart to see if he was hiding a weapon. The second time was to make him shower, then clip off all his body hair. The third time was to subject him to a rigorous medical examination. He was forced to give his name and birthplace over and over again. Solzhenitsyn ended up in a cell without a bed, a cell so small he could rest on the floor only perpendicularly, a cell continuously lit by a 200-watt bulb. He wasn't allowed to sleep.

Then came three days of interrogation. Sometimes he was beaten. He passed this time in solitary confinement.

Late on the fourth night, he was transferred to a cell containing three other prisoners. This made him happy. Other human beings were here, in the same predicament as himself, with whom he could talk.

Solzhenitsyn didn't meet these fellow prisoners until everyone woke up the next morning. He liked and trusted two of them. He completely mistrusted the third.

Twenty-nine years later, he wrote in *The Gulag Archipelago* (Vol. I, 1973), "I sensed something alien in this front-line soldier who was my contemporary, and, as far as he was concerned, I clammed up immediately and forever.

"I had not yet even heard the word *nasedka*—'stool pigeon'—nor learned that there had to be one such 'stool pigeon' in each cell. And I had not yet had time to think things over and conclude that I did not like this fellow, Georgi Kramarenko. But a spiritual relay, a sensor relay, had clicked inside me, and it had closed him off from me for good and all. I would not bother to recall this event if it had been the only one of its kind. But soon, with astonishment, and alarm, I became aware of the work of this internal sensor relay as a constant, inborn trait. The years passed and I lay on the same bunks, marched in the same formations, and worked in the same work brigades with hundreds of others. And always that secret sensor relay, for whose creation I deserved not the least bit of credit, worked even before I remembered it was there, worked at the first sight of a human face and eyes, at the first sound of a voice—so that I opened my heart to that person either fully or just the width of a crack, or else shut myself off from him completely . . . On the other hand, the sensor relay helped me distinguish those to whom I could from the very beginning of our acquaintance completely disclose my most precious depths and secrets—secrets for which heads roll . . . During all those seventeen years [of imprisonment, exile, and underground authorship] I recklessly revealed myself to dozens of people—and didn't make a misstep even once. (I have never read about this trait anywhere, and I mention it here for those interested in psychology. It seems to me that such spiritual sensors exist in many of us, but because we live in too technological and rational an age, we neglect this miracle and don't allow it to develop.)"

For Solzhenitsyn, who had excelled in physics and mathematics at school and university and distinguished himself in combat, this stay at Lubyanka prison—it would be almost four months—was to pale into insignificance beside the frightful seventeen-year-long ordeal that now awaited him. Those seventeen years—during which he abandoned the Marxism he had fervently believed in—included eight years of imprisonment, principally in a scientific research center and then, for a longer length of time, in a gulag in Ekibastuz, Kazakhstan; a bout with cancer that almost killed him; release from prison into political exile, during which he taught high school; and a period when, though now free, he had to labor clandestinely, under much harassment by the government, to put into words the experiences he had brought back on bits of paper, in his heart, and in his memory, from the dark places he had known.

The inhuman conditions of Stalin's slave labor camps killed off most prisoners. For the few possessing a great potentiality for the expression of inner power, these conditions sometimes goaded supernormal coping mechanisms into re-emergence—mechanisms that seem to have lain dormant in mankind for several millennia. The "hidden sensor relay" that clicked into play for Solzhenitsyn in the cell in Lubyanka was the first of a number of suppressed inner senses that would be galvanized into resurrection in the author. He describes this in his books, and he describes it in other prisoners. These hidden faculties included a tapping into, and an obedience to, one's "conscience"—though perhaps "discernment" is a better word, as we'll see—in every instant of one's life.

These supernormal faculties, slowly birthing, enabled Solzhenitsyn to survive and prosper: In 1970 he received the Nobel Prize for Literature.

In novels like *One Day in the Life of Ivan Denisovich* (1962) and *The First Circle* (1968), in the non-fiction work *The Gulag Archipelago* (1973-1978), the author was almost the first to lay bare the brutalities of Stalin's slave labor camps ("gulag" means "labor camp," and "archipelago" means "group of islands;" Solzhenitsyn himself coined the term "Gulag Archipelago"). This "archipelago," writes historian Paul Johnson, constituted "a vast series of substantial territorial islands within the Soviet Union, covering many thousands of square miles." Mass executions often took place in the gulags; in the Kolyma camps alone, in 1938, 40,000 men, women, and children were machine-gunned to death. Johnson quotes historian Roy Medvedev as asserting that "the total number of victims in the years 1936–39 was about 4.5 million; the total of deaths caused by Stalin's policy was in the region of 10 million." Almost all the prisoners toiled for sixteen hours a day. A strong man's health could be broken in a month. The arrests were completely arbitrary; Stalin's aim was to terrorize and cow the populace through these abrupt arrests of innocent people. His cruelty extended even to sending thousands of Russian soldiers, newly returned from imprisonment in German prisoner-of-war camps, back to prison, this time a gulag, as "traitors to the U.S.S.R." Solzhenitsyn was arrested just as this monstrous policy was beginning to take shape.

There's another example in literary history of mystical expansion, similar to that experienced by Solzhenitsyn in the camps. The extreme privation that awakened his hidden senses had also awakened those of Italian Renaissance goldsmith Benvenuto Cellini (1500–1571) in the dungeons of Rome's Castle of Sant' Angelo. Incarcerated in one of the deepest and dankest cells, Cellini attempted suicide; this provoked his "guardian angel"

Solzhenitsyn in the Gulag in the late 1940s

(or so he tells us in his autobiography) into taking action. Even as his prisoner days and nights continued to be harrowing, this ever-more-explosive manifestation of his personal power continued to bear Cellini up in impossible circumstances until, at last, he was freed.

But what exactly are these hidden senses?

That's a hard question to answer, since we've forgotten about their existence, and almost forgotten that we've forgotten. The myths of antiquity seem to bear witness to the presence of expanded senses in earlier stages of humanity. The Book of Genesis tells us that "there were giants on the earth in those days." The Book of Joshua alludes to Og, King of Basan, who ruled a race of giants; some feel this race, perhaps helped by extraterrestrials, was superior to our own. Colin Wilson and Rand Flem-Ath are two among many journalist-scholars to speculate (in *The Atlantis Blueprint*, 2001) about ancient, long-vanished civilizations, such as Atlantis, that were likely superior to ours.

Solzhenitsyn was certain that modern technology played a crucial role in the continuing atrophy of mankind's supernormal senses. In the novel *Cancer Ward* (1968), the brilliant, old-school, semi-retired oncologist says to his much younger colleague, "You know, I worked for twenty years before X-rays were invented. And, my dear, you should have seen the diagnoses I made! It's like when you have an exposure meter or a watch, you completely lose the knack of estimating exposure by eye or judging time by instinct. When you don't have them, you soon acquire the trick."

Perhaps the faculty he describes—can we call it orientation?—is vanishing from the everyday world; but Solzhenitsyn observed in abundance in the camps the presence of what perhaps can be called the faculty of discernment. He writes in *The Gulag Archipelago* (Vol. II):

"Survive! A powerful charge is introduced into the chest cavity, and the heart is surrounded by an electrical cloud so as not to stop beating. They [the camp guards] lead thirty emaciated but wiry zeks [camp prisoners] three miles across the Arctic ice to a bathhouse. The bath is not worth even a warm word. Six men at a time wash themselves in five shifts, and the door opens straight into the subzero temperature, and four shifts are obliged to stand there before or after bathing—because they cannot be left without convoy. And not only does none of them get pneumonia. They don't even catch cold. (And for ten years one old man had his bath just like that, serving out his term from age fifty to sixty. But then he was released, he was at home. Warm and cared for, he burned up in one month's time. That order—"Survive!"—was not there. . . .)

Solzhenitsyn adds: "Simply to survive does not mean 'at any price.' 'At any price' means: at the price of someone else." One of the highest expressions of the rebirth of the hidden senses of mankind, which ultimately demands tapping into a moral dimension—and which, in the following example, may perhaps be called the faculty of Judgment— can be seen in the character of Grigory Ivanovich Grigoryev, the soil scientist/prisoner, as Solzhenitsyn describes him in the same volume:

"{He} was subjected on all sides to the camp philosophy, to the camp corruption of soul, but he was incapable of adopting it. On the Kemerova camps (Antibess) the security chief kept trying to recruit him as a stoolie. Grigoryev replied to him quite honestly and candidly: 'I find it quite repulsive to talk to you. You will find many willing without me.' 'You bastard, you'll crawl on all fours.' 'I would be better off hanging myself on the first branch.' And so he was sent off to a penalty situation. He stood it for half a year. And he made mistakes which were even more unforgiveable: When he was sent on an agricultural work party, he refused (as a soil scientist)

Prisoners brought to Lubyanka prison in 1928

to accept the post of brigadier offered him. He hoed and scythed with enthusiasm. And even more stupidly: in Ekibastuz at the stone quarry he refused to be a work checker—only because he would have had to pad the work sheets for the sloggers, for which, later on, when they caught up with it, the eternally drunk free foreman would have to pay the penalty. (Or would he?) And so he went to break rocks! His honesty was so monstrously unnatural that when he went out to process potatoes with the vegetable storeroom brigade, he did not steal any, though everyone else did. When he was in a good post, in the privileged repair-shop brigade at the pumping-station equipment, he left simply because he refused to wash the socks of the free bachelor construction supervisor, Treivish. (His fellow brigade members tried to persuade him: Come on now, isn't it all the same, the kind of work you do? But no, it turned out it was not at all the same to

LOST POWERS

him!) How many times did he select the worst and hardest lot, just so as not to have to offend against conscience—and he didn't, not in the least, and I am a witness. And even more: because of the astounding influence on his body of his bright and spotless human spirit (though no one today believes in any such influence, no one understands it) the organism of Grigory Ivanovich, who was no longer young (close to fifty), grew stronger in camp; his earlier rheumatism of the joints disappeared completely, and he became particularly healthy after the typhus from which he recovered: in winter he went out in cotton sacks, making holes in them for his head and his arms—and he did not catch cold."

Only with the death of Stalin in 1953, and in particular with the emergence after 1956 of Nikita Khrushchev, did Stalin's gulags begin to be dismantled. Not until 1970 did the publication of Solzhenitsyn's works really get underway in the Soviet Union. The ruling elite couldn't bear the subsequent elated public reaction to his revelations, and banished him from the U.S.S.R. He spent two years in Switzerland, then eighteen in Cavendish, Vermont. In 1992, Boris Yeltsin forgave him, and in 1994 he returned to Russia. Solzhenitsyn died in 2008, almost 90, and revered, however nervously, by his fellow countrymen.

# ENTANGLED MINDS AND THE QUANTUM FACTOR

*Putting Orthodox Thinking to the Test*

## BY PATRICK MARSOLEK

D o you believe in psychic phenomena or are you skeptical? Have you had an experience not explainable by materialistic science? If you have and you're curious about your experiences, you may have already delved into the realm of parapsychology. This field of anomalous leftovers is what the early psychologist and philosopher William James called the "unclassified residuum," a field which has been labeled pseudoscience by many mainstream scientists.

If you explore with an open mind, you will find a large amount of scientifically valid research showing that phenomena like telepathy, remote viewing, distant intention, and gut feelings are real. In terms of science, the evidence is important but not sufficient. An explanatory framework is required to account for the data and bridge to our existing scientific understanding of reality.

That's what Dean Radin, the author of the book, *Entangled Minds* (2006) has attempted to provide. He has demonstrated how the concept of quantum-entangled minds can be compatible with the concept of quantum-entangled particles, an already established scientific fact. His theory suggests that your mind may be linked with other minds and perhaps other things as well. Information from that connection comes into your conscious awareness through intuitions, gut feelings, or other subtle perceptions. This information is not transmitted by normal means. You are interconnected at a place where consciousness and matter intersect.

Physicist Erwin Schrödinger first coined the term *Verschrankung* in German. Verschrankung is translated into English as "entanglement." Some argue that this translation is misleading. It might be better to talk about this concept as a "folding of arms" or an "orderly folding." Entanglement refs to how pairs of subatomic particles behave as if they are connected even when separated by a large physical distance. A change in one particle is instantaneously reflected in the other. The change is too fast to be the result of any kind of cause-and-effect connection that we know.

Entanglement is one phenomenon from the realm of quantum physics that New Age thinkers take as confirmation that there is a spiritual or energetic connection between everything. If subatomic particles can become entangled, why not larger bits of matter? Why not people? Maybe entanglement is what causes a person to feel anxiety in his gut and to think of his brother at the exact moment that his brother has an automobile accident.

Let's take a brief look at some of the trends in quantum physics and parapsychological research and see how these two fields may be pointing toward a partnership and a new theory of reality. Physics has come a long way since Max Planck dubbed packets of light "quanta" around the turn of the last century. Since its inception, quantum physics has moved further out from mainstream science into the realm of extraordinary possibilities, consciousness, and belief. There are now scientific conferences that combine quantum mechanics, consciousness, and quantum computing.

Yet skeptics and many scientists argue that quantum entanglement can't be an explanation for things like intuition and telepathy because these quantum events only occur in simple forms between pairs of subatomic particles in the very small, cold, and fast quantum world. They believe there is no evidence of any quantum effect in our every day lives and that there isn't even any proof that there is a psychic connection between people.

With the push to develop quantum computing, current research is revealing how there might be much more quantum phenomena in our daily world. It seems that almost every week there is a new study, showing that quantum effects have been observed in much more "sexy" environments that are hot, wet, lasting, and much larger. In a 2004 article in *New Scientist*, Michael Brooks says: "Physicists now believe that entanglement between particles exists everywhere, all the time, and have recently found shocking evidence that it affects the wider, 'macroscopic' world that we inhabit." Quantum entanglement has been shown in paired neurons, in physical particles that are large—the current record is now up to 108 atoms—and even in super conducting chips. Quantum gravity has even been shown to affect things on a much larger scale.

As quantum physics makes its way more into the mainstream, the assumptions about the nature of reality are being challenged. Consider the five basic assumptions of classical physics:

- Reality—The world is objectively real.

- Locality—Objects can only be influenced through direct contact.

- Causality—The arrow of time flows one direction and cause and effect is a fixed sequence.

- Continuity—The fabric of space and time is smooth.

- Determinism—Things progress in an orderly, predictable way so we can predict everything if we know all the pieces.

The quantum world shows us that these assumptions no longer hold true. The reality of the world we observe may not be absolute. With entanglement, we have nonlocality; things can be affected at a distance without any physical or energetic connection. Causality isn't reliable then either, since the "when" of events may be changeable and may be affected by the observation of it. Continuity isn't reliable; at quantum levels, space and time don't appear to be smooth or contiguous. Determinism doesn't work any more because it relies on the other assumptions. It's understandable why there is so much resistance to the idea that the reality of the quantum world may be as true of the properties of the physical world we all know. Everything we know to be true may be challenged. Even the physicists don't know and don't understand what it all means.

The anomalies of the quantum world are leading us to different understandings. What if our everyday, objective reality were entangled? We might be able to experience a connection to others. We might know things without sensing them (that is, with our traditional five senses). Our intentions might interact with matter or with other people. All of these ideas lie within the field of parapsychological research.

Eighty percent of people, skeptics and believers alike, have had some type of gut feeling experience. Yet because of the bias of science toward what is physical and objectively verifiable, these experiences are not considered real, and much of mainstream science is not interested in them. Of the approximately 17,500 higher learning institutions worldwide, only

30 have faculty who are interested in extended human capacities. Only a handful of these learning institutions are in the United States (Stanford and Duke among them).

There is a whole range of phenomena that is part of human experience that materialistic science cannot account for. Dean Radin has described this as the Noetic Spectrum of human experience. Noetic refers to a form of direct knowing that hasn't been valued in our materialistic culture.

In this Noetic Spectrum, experiences are graphed from bottom left to upper right in terms of frequency and impact. Almost everyone has had a gut feeling, but very few of us experience mystical union or epiphany. Yet all of these experiences can be transformative and meaningful to people. There is a wealth of scientific research showing that people do feel a connection with others, do know things without sensing them, and are even connected to each other without knowing it. Telepathy, for example, has long been studied using the Ganzfeld experiment.

In a typical Ganzfeld experiment, ping-pong balls are placed over the eyes and white noise is played through the head phones of the person who is the receiver. A receptive state is created in which the conscious mind can relax and receive information. A second person in a different room then attempts to send the receiver information by focusing on him and trying to

Entangled minds concept (*Atlantis Rising* artwork)

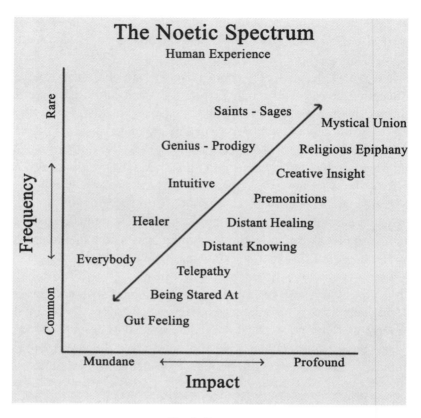

Noetic Spectrum

"send" him images. The receiver describes his perceptions. Afterward, the receiver chooses one of four targets, based on his perceptions. Cumulative results from over 3,000 sessions in 25 labs has resulted in a 34 percent success rate, with an expected random chance of success at 25 percent. The probability of this happening randomly is 29 million trillion to 1.

More recently, researchers have developed studies that focus on unconscious physiological systems to test for telepathy and distant intention. Many body responses have been studied including heart rate variability, sweating, digestion and elimination, emotional arousal, eye dilation, blood pressure, and skin resistance. For example, one study looked at EEG correlations from visually evoked responses. One person is in a room watching a television while connected to EEG equipment. The TV flashes on and off randomly, showing an image of the receiver, another person who is in a different room and is also wired up to EEG equipment. The only instructions for the sender are to focus on the receiver when they see his image on the screen.

In repeated trials in different laboratories, it has been shown that there is a statistically significant correlation between the two brains at the moment of stimulation. When the sender sees the image of the receiver on the TV screen, the receiver's brain responds. In this experiment, both the sender's and the receiver's brain activity peaks at about 200 milliseconds after the image flashed on the TV screen. Similar studies using functional magnetic resonance imaging also showed similar results and showed that the same parts of the brain were active. This research confirms some kind of connections between the two people's brains, although there is no known physical means for this. Interestingly, if one of the subjects falls asleep, the two brains do not show correlation. Sleeping serves as a control showing that intention and attention do play a role.

One element of these experiments that boggles the mind and hints at quantum phenomena is how the receiver's brain consistently shows a surge in activity and stimulation at around 100 milliseconds before the sender's brain is stimulated. That's *before* the sender sees anything on the TV and has any response in their brain. Somehow, the receiver registers the stimulus before it even happens. This slippage in time has shown up in many of the other studies working with other unconscious body responses. As these experiments show, the continuity and causality that we have come to rely on may not as reliable as we think.

Similarly with gut feelings and other intuitive experiences, we may perceive something in our physical body shortly before an event actually occurs. Have you ever been driving down a road, had an image of a deer come into your mind, then slowed down just before you actually saw a deer in front of you?

Skeptics of parapsychology often called these kinds of experiences, and all the experiences in the Noetic spectrum, nonsense or impossible. In a way they are right, they seem to be non-*sense* based. There is no physical way the receiver in these experiments could sense anything that would stimulate his unconscious. Perceiving something before it happens can't happen through the senses.

Dean Radin has proposed that this kind of communication is explainable by quantum entanglement. Psychic phenomena may be the human experience of our entangled universe. We know there is quantum entanglement and have even shown bioentanglement in neurons. We can see that there is sentient bioentanglement in living systems through telepathy and intuition. Could there be a social, worldwide entanglement?

The Global Consciousness Project (GCP) has been studying randomness on a global scale since 1998, using random number generators (RNGs). The idea is to look at randomness, something that is thought to be a constant, unchangeable part of physical reality, and see if it fluctuates in correlation to worldwide events. The GCP has established 65 sites around the world where computers are recording the randomness of electronic noise in resistors and diodes. Every five minutes the data is collected and sent to a central computer in Princeton, NJ.

By 2005, a total of 185 events of global interest had been correlated to changes in the measured randomness. Somehow, random noise in our physical reality becomes less random when significant human events, natural disasters, celebrations, outbreaks of war, and tragic deaths occur. Some events that did have effects were the deaths of Pope John Paul II and Lady Diana, the change over of the century (Y2K), the Asian tsunami in 2004, and the 9/11 terrorist attacks in the US. Natural events that do not effect humanity, don't affect the entropy being measured. An earthquake that occurs in a remote region or under the ocean, without causing a tsunami, doesn't have an effect; but an earthquake that causes disaster and human suffering, does.

Similar to the EEG study mentioned above, the randomness of the data is affected before the event occurs, sometimes several hours before. In the case of the 9/11 terrorist attacks, the change in data peaked around two hours before the first jet crashed and returned to normal some eight hours later. Dean Radin was conducting online intuitive experiments at this time. (These are still running at www.gotpsi.org) Around the time of 9/11, the success of participants' intuitive trials dropped significantly for some time before and during the attacks. People seemed to be unconsciously avoiding or suppressing their intuitive impressions around the time of the attacks. Field-consciousness experiments like these suggest that mind-matter interactions are happening on a larger world-wide scale.

Radin proposes that we may be living in a gigantic entangled mind. Of course, believing in this kind of reality is not accepted in many scientific circles because it stands much research on its head. Not only can your intention affect other people or things, but your consciousness may be connected to the physical world. Information may flow both directions through that connection. Read Radin's book if you would like a more thorough exploration of our entanglement.

To explore this theory we must stretch our beliefs. If you want to stay current with the progress of quantum physics and parapsychological research, you have to practice believing what you thought to be impossible. Take a moment and think about the time shifting that shows up in these experiments. How is it possible? There may not be an explanation for it. To explain means there is a cause and effect. The quantum reality of these effects may not be causal.

The tools of science have shown us that some of these phenomena and theories are real, yet the tools of science and even the language we use are not inadequate. If your mind feels a bit entangled trying to understand or explain this quantum world, you may be on the right track. Like the scientists at the leading edge of quantum physics, you may want to practice thinking about impossibility. You may want to shift from the "I'll believe it when I see it" stance to "I'll see it when I believe it." On a lighter note, you could listen to the advice of the Red Queen and practice believing these fascinating impossibilities of an entangled world:

"I can't believe that!" said Alice.

"Can't you?" the Queen said in a pitying tone. "Try again: draw a long breath, and shut your eyes."

Alice laughed. "There's no use trying," she said: "one can't believe impossible things."

"I dare say you haven't had much practice," said the Queen. "When I was your age, I always did it for a half-an hour a day. Why, sometimes I've believed as many as six impossible things before breakfast."

—Lewis Carroll, *Through the Looking-Glass*

# 32

## GETTING THE DREAM THING RIGHT

*Ken Eagle Feather Thinks We Can Do a Lot Better*

### BY CYNTHIA LOGAN

Right off the bat, Ken Eagle Feather tells me he's not Native American, but is "white as wonder bread." The name was given to him by don Juan Matus, the same don Juan encountered by Carlos Castaneda, author of *The Teachings of Don Juan, A Separate Reality,* and *Journey to Ixtlan*. He had it legally changed in the 1970s, during the time he was actively engaged with the controversial figure. "The argument as to whether don Juan is or was a real person has spilled over into academia big time," states Eagle Feather. Claims that Castaneda himself was a fraud and that his Ph.D. in anthropology from UCLA had been revoked were put to rest when Eagle Feather telephoned the university, which assured him the bestowal is still intact. His own opinion is that Castaneda may well have been "the Copernicus of our time."

Self-described as "a silver-haired rascal," Eagle Feather asserts that he met and was apprenticed to don Juan, and that he was given the instruction to study Castaneda's books ("they contain a sophisticated worldview to focus energy, as well as disciplines and techniques to harness energy") and present the Toltec teachings within them from a different perspective. He spent 16 years poring daily over the material, adding another two years of intermittent study that included other esoteric writings and the world's sacred texts. Eagle Feather's first book, *Traveling with Power* (1992), explained his encounter with don Juan and basics about the path revealed. His second, *A Toltec Path* (1995) describes the overall structure of don Juan's teachings. He then wrote *Tracking Freedom* (1998) "for good measure, to consolidate and synthesize Toltec teachings with other systems of learning."

Since Eagle Feather feels he has moved beyond that identity ("Ken Eagle Feather has flown away") and is now writing under his given name, Ken Smith, let's call this 50-something author 'Smith' from here on. It's easy, and reflects the man's focus on conveying his understanding to the ordinary person. "And how ordinary can you get?" he asks, chuckling at the simplicity of his "new" name. In an upcoming title, he'll do away with the somewhat cumbersome terminology in his most recent book, *Toltec Dreaming* (2007), which illuminates don Juan's teachings on the energy body. A hefty topic, admits Smith, who says the energy body includes not only the physical body but all the various "bodies" thought to exist in other traditions. "While the Taoists gave us the meridian system and yogis developed the chakra model, this concept and the mapping out of

its anatomy is the unique contribution of the Toltecs." (The Toltecs are thought to have ruled central Mexico between 3,000–7,000 years ago. Though masterful in the control of energy, the old order grossly misused such abilities.) According to Smith, Castaneda built a bridge between the old and modern (circa mid-1700s) lineages. "Don Juan is part of a specific line dating to 1723 and is dedicated to using extraordinary capabilities only for positive purposes. He also thinks drugs warp personal energy and should be used rarely, with caution and reverence, and only if meditative exercises fail."

Ken Eagle Feather (a.k.a. Kenneth Smith)

The whole gig of being human, according to don Juan, is that we are luminous creatures. As such, our natural function is that of being aware, of perceiving. "The metaphysical philosophy known as the Toltec Way deals with the nature of reality, including how reality is perceived, formulated and experienced," writes Smith. "Its philosophy of action and behavior superimposes on the waking world the subtle physics of the dream world in order to create a conscious dreaming body that, when fully realized, can act as a vehicle to higher consciousness."

The energy (dreaming) body has eight cornerstones of perception which, when diagrammed, look somewhat like the Kabbalist Tree of Life. Realities are created and congealed as patterns (termed "cohesions" by Smith) within this body. Often culturally constructed, a particular reality determines what you think about, which in turn determines how you feel; how you feel determines what you think about, as well as your behavior, and how you behave determines what you think about (is that a Catch-22?). This Uber-Body, the energy body—E-B for short—has, of course, a left and a right side, just like our physical body does. And we supposedly access only 7 to 12 percent of E-B, just as we only use about 10 percent of our brain's capacity. For most of us, E-B is lopsided; the right side, which holds what we're conscious of, is markedly smaller than the left, and relates to what Smith calls "the first field of awareness." The larger side holds all that is unconscious, and relates to the "second field of awareness."

The goal, similar to Jung's process of individuation, is to unite the two and move into a third field of infinitely larger possibilities (chaos theory's combo of opposites spiraling into a "third thing" comes to mind). In this reality, we would "Be Here Now" and directly perceive our world, leaving behind the tendency to create "mirror bubbles" that reflect back to us our interpretations and judgments of that world. By expanding what we're conscious of, we can experience alternate realities. (Great with analogies, Smith likens this to attending college; for most, the experience opens doors to new thoughts, feelings, and behaviors that create new worldviews). But it's when we enter the third field (which contains everything outside E-B) that we encounter truly transforming energies.

No stranger to transformative experiences, Smith grew up in a military family and, as a child, almost drowned in Lake Michigan. He remembers a vague form approaching him as he stopped struggling underwater, enveloping him in a sense of peace. Pulled to safety, he recalls seeing his father standing next to his mother after he was brought home. Later, he learned his father had not been there. After the accident, his life felt "lackluster"; psychic comic books provided a few bright spots. When he was in high school, his family moved to Virginia Beach, where the Edgar Cayce Foundation is located. In the metaphysical library of the Association for Research and Enlightenment (A.R.E., the Cayce organization), he researched a term paper on the lost continent of Atlantis, giving his fertile young mind exotic food for thought. His path took him, at 17, into the U.S. Navy. While serving in Vietnam, Smith found himself merely thinking of where he wanted to be transferred, only to be given a set of orders directing him to just that place, a phenomenon that occurred numerous times. Back in the U.S., he experienced emotional malaise as well as internal bleeding that sometimes left him hospitalized. Facing invasive surgery, he practiced the exercises in Castaneda's books and experienced respite. "Don Juan's Toltec world has given me physical, mental, and spiritual renewal," says Smith. "His teachings literally saved my life." While apprenticing with don Juan, Smith earned degrees in education and journalism, pursued graduate work in religious studies, and served on the A.R.E. staff and then at the Monroe Institute (where sound technology is used to facilitate the exploration of consciousness).

Currently the Communications Director for the Institute for Therapeutic Discovery in Virginia, Smith considers himself a very ordinary guy, holding down a serious job, leading a completely normal life. But he may "knock out 20 hours of meditation on the weekend," which for him means "dreaming," occasionally visiting alternate realities (he's been to the moon and has experienced himself as a tornado and as a lizard, among other things). The tall, slim Smith says he has "dazzling crys-

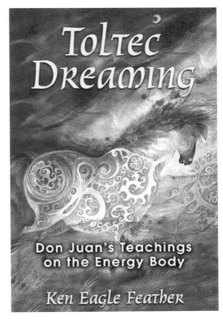

talline eyes that are completely blood-shot." He's a tech-geek who sneaks in a Southern accent now and then, along with the truly '70s expression, "far out." But he's not, really. For all his dreaming and traveling, Smith is extremely down to earth—grounded, he would say. He isn't out to have psychedelic experiences, but focuses on connecting with what you might call the Will of God. "I have a problem with 'creating your own reality'— take the energy of desire and use it to get more in touch with how God created you, nurture that and let it grow." He doesn't drink alcohol, and says he tries to eat well, but moderately. "I'm going out to Burger King as soon as we get off the phone," he informs me. "Come on, a Junior Whopper?" No worries; he'll walk or swim it off. He loves living in Virginia with both the mountains and the ocean nearby, and enjoys experiencing the four seasons. His daughter is "the best part of the joy in my life."

While *Toltec Dreaming* requires some serious mental processing, it is clearly written, and alternates conceptual material with personal anecdotes and comments on don Juan's transmissions, as well as many practical exercises for "controlling your internal cohesions," thereby shaping your external world. The work is influenced by more than Smith's experiences with the Toltec seer; including talks with people who have had Dreaming Body Experiences (DBEs), the perusal of the Edgar Cayce psychic readings, and his own explorations. As a result, he has come up with a three-step process for inducing a dreaming state. "This '3E' method focuses on expectation (opening perception), excitation (balancing perception), and exploration (focusing perception). "A major theme in the Cayce readings is that as you develop spiritually, you shed the binding and restrictive forces isolating you in a three-dimensional, physical reality," notes Smith, who offers another set of procedures "to exercise the dreaming body" and prepare for a conscious DBE. One of these—Too Tired?—grabbed my attention right away. Try this:

1.  Allow your fatigue to saturate your physical body. This facilitates relaxation and the notion that it is OK to be fatigued.

2.  Perceive a hollow core at the center of your physical body.

3.  From that core push or expand the fatigue energy outward in all directions. As you do so, the core of the energy also expands.

4.  Contract that energy. The core of the energy will contract as well. Exhale as you expand the energy away from you; inhale as you retract the energy.

5.  As you fall asleep (attention, insomniacs!), expand and contract your fatigue energy at your own pace. As you expand and contract the energy, know within yourself that you are doing so in order to build dreaming intent.

Many of the exercises are designed to help access cues from the physical body. Smith thinks that if significant numbers of people could access their body-wisdom and achieve deep relaxation, humanity might be able to mitigate a point of no return, known to military pilots as QNR. "We may be there," he says, immediately mitigating his own statement: "But, if humans made it, they can temper it with actions like those Al Gore recommends. We need to develop a natural balance with nature; right now we're taking and pooping, not taking and giving back."

Ken Smith advocates developing and harnessing personal power for the purpose of unity with the God-Self, the Field, the Eagle of the Toltec world, and for creating a full, balanced life that is an inspiration to others and a boon to the planet. With both feet on the Earth, dare to soar beyond its bounds. Live in the world well, but be not tethered. "Dreaming is a land of potential, a no-money-down virtual reality technology," he promises. "Anything can happen, and often does! Ordinary reality is but one dream, as is non-ordinary reality." Shakespeare said it through Prospero in *The Tempest*: "We are such stuff as dreams are made of, and our little life is rounded with a sleep." And of course, Hamlet's famous soliloquy, "To sleep, perchance to dream…" conjures a sobering reality indeed. As Smith repeatedly advises, clarity and intent are prerequisites for healthy altered states. Before embarking, take a reality check. But do row merrily, for Life, after all, is but a Dream.

# Contributing Authors

**JOHN CHAMBERS** is the critically acclaimed author of *Conversations with Eternity: The Forgotten Masterpiece of Victor Hugo* and *The Secret Life of Genius: How 24 Great Men and Women Were Touched by Spiritual Worlds.* He lives in Redding, California. (*newpara.com/johnchambers.htm*)

**DAVID HATCHER CHILDRESS**, known to his many fans as the real-life Indiana Jones, is author or coauthor of over 20 books. He has appeared on Fox-TV's *Sightings and Encounters*, two NBC-TV specials, *The Conspiracy Zone*, and segments for the Discovery Channel, A&E, The Sci-Fi Channel, The Travel Channel and others. (*adventuresunlimitedpress.com*)

**JOSEPH ROBERT JOCHMANS** (deceased 2013) was an American resarcher with a special interest in ancient mysteries. Jochmans is credited as the researcher for Rene Noorbergen's 1977 book *Secrets of the Lost Races*, as well as a number of other books by Noorbergen. Jochmans was a frequent contributor to *Atlantis Rising Maginine,* with a particular interest and focus on the subject of Atlantis.

**FRANK JOSEPH** is a leading scholar on ancient mysteries, and the editor-in-chief of *Ancient American* magazine. He is the author of many books, including *Atlantis and 2012*, *The Destruction of Atlantis*, *The Lost Civilization of Lemuria*, *Survivors of Atlantis*, and *The Lost Treasure of King Juba*. He lives in Minnesota. (*ancientamerican.com*)

**LEN KASTEN** has written numerous articles for *Atlantis Rising*. While in the Air Force, Kasten experienced a UFO encounter that transformed his life. Since then, he has been deeply involved in UFO research, life after death, sacred geometry, Atlantis, and related subjects. He brings his extensive metaphysical background to he writing of *The Secret History of Extraterrestrials*, which provides the reader with a depth of understanding of UFO phenomena not otherwise readily available. (*et-secrethistory.com*)

**CYNTHIA LOGAN** has been a freelance writer and editor for over 20 years. Her articles have appeared in *Atlantis Rising* magazine, as well as numerous regional, national, and international publications.

**PATRICK MARSOLEK** is an author, teacher, facilitator, and director of Inner Workings Resources. He leads groups and teaches classes in consciousness exploration and personal development, and also has a private hypnotherapy practice in Helena and Great Falls Montana. He is the author of *A Joyful Intuition, Transform Yourself: A Self-Hypnosis Manual,* as well as several articles on spirituality and consciousness. (*www.AJoyfulIntuition.com*)

**SUSAN B. MARTINEZ**, is a writer, linguist, teacher, paranormal researcher, and recognized authority on the Oahspe Bible with a doctorate in anthropology from Columbia University. The author of *The Psychic Life of Abraham Lincoln* and *The Mysterious Origins of Hybrid Man*, she is the book review editor at the *Journal of Spirituality and Paranormal Studies.* (*earthvortex.com*)

**ROBERT M. SCHOCH**, a full-time faculty member at Boston University, earned his Ph.D. in geology and geophysics at Yale University. He is best known for his re-dating of the Great Sphinx of Egypt featured in the Emmy Award-winning NBC production *The Mystery of the Sphinx*. He is a frequent guest on many top-rated talk shows. His latest book is *The Parapsychology Revolution*. (*robertschoch.com*)

**MICHAEL E. TYMN**, a resident of Hawaii, is vice-president of the Academy of Spirituality and Paranormal Studies, Inc., and is editor of the Academy's quarterly magazine, *The Searchlight*. His articles on paranormal subjects have appeared in many publications and he is widely read and referenced on these topics. He is the author of *The Afterlife Revealed, The Articulate Dead*, and *Running on Third Wind*. (*whitecrowbooks.com/michaeltymn*)

**JOHN WHITE** is an internationally known writer and educator in the fields of consciousness research and higher human development. He was formerly Director of Education for The Institute of Noetic Sciences founded by Apollo 14 astronaut Edgar Mitchell. His fifteen books include *The Meeting of Science and Spirit*, *Pole Shift*, *What Is Enlightenment?*, *Kundalini, Evolution and Enlightenment*, and *A Practical Guide to Death and Dying*. His writing has appeared in *The New York Times*, *Reader's Digest*, *Omni*, *Esquire* ,and *Woman's Day*. His books have been translated into several languages.

## About the Editor

**J. DOUGLAS KENYON** is the editor and publisher of *Atlantis Rising* magazine. He is also the editor of *Paradigm Busters*, *Missing Connections*, *Forgotten Origins*, *Forbidden History*, *Forbidden Science*, and *Forbidden Religion*. (*atlantisrising.com*)